THE SECOND BATTLE OF THE MARNE

1918

For Hilary & Peter
with much
affection —

Paul Greenwood.

on the 80th Anniversary
of the battle.
July. 1998.

THE SECOND BATTLE OF THE MARNE
1918

PAUL GREENWOOD

Airlife
England

Copyright © 1998 Paul Greenwood

First published in the UK in 1998
by Airlife Publishing Ltd

British Library Cataloguing-in-Publication Data
  A catalogue record for this book
  is available from the British Library

ISBN 1 84037 008 4

Typeset by Phoenix Typesetting Ilkley, West Yorkshire.

Printed in England by Biddles Ltd., Guildford and King's Lynn.

Airlife Publishing Ltd
101 Longden Road, Shrewsbury, SY3 9EB, England.

To all those who died there, and in particular memory of my father who fought, and received a 'blighty'.

PREFACE

Now, several decades later, though more and more people are again starting to use 11 November to hold their personal two minutes' silence, the pace of life has changed so much it seems hardly possible traffic will ever again come to a respectful halt at the eleventh hour of the eleventh day of the eleventh month. 'Armistice Day' has for many years been amalgamated with 'Remembrance Sunday', rightly commemorating the sacrifices of later wars; the captured German field gun in the local park has long been melted down to fuel a later conflict, and the First World War tends to be remembered by place names such as Passchendaele, Thiépval and Verdun rather than Marfaux, Grimpettes Woods and Villemontoire.

But Marfaux, Grimpettes and Villemontoire not only saw the German Army's last advance of the War – they also saw the start of its final retreat in a battle that formed the hinge on which the door of defeat began to swing, finally to slam in the faces of the Kaiser, General Ludendorff and the German High Command –

- The Second Battle of the Marne.

CONTENTS

CONTENTS

CHAPTER 1

THE SITUATION

– The events that led to Ludendorff's meeting to plan for victory in 1918 – the Allies' 1917 offensives – the struggle between 'Easterners' and 'Westerners' to control policy – a strategic German retreat –

> *"Where shall I begin, please, your Majesty?" he asked.*
> *"Begin at the beginning," the King said, gravely,*
> *"and go on till you come to the end: then stop."*
>
> *(Lewis Carroll)*

On Martinmas day – 11 November, 1917, – exactly a year before the Armistice was to bring the War to an end – members of the German High Command, in a coincidence of place as well as date, had made their various ways to Mons. The British Expeditionary Force had been blooded there in 1914 and eventually, as the wheel came full circle, when the Allies retook the town four years later, the last Canadian casualty was to fall to a sniper's bullet two minutes before that Armistice came into effect.

The meeting had been called by the German Quartermaster General, Erich von Ludendorff. By now he, rather than his superior, Field Marshal Paul von Hindenburg, was dictating military policy and so, instead of von Hindenburg, the German Crown Prince, and possibly even the Kaiser himself, who might have been expected to join the discussions and offer advice, it was Ludendorff's satellites, von der Schulenberg and von Kuhl who were invited. Their duty was to review the war situation and map out German strategy for the coming Spring.

Because the advantages brought by Russia's collapse earlier that year would eventually be nullified when large numbers of American troops arrived, now that their country had joined the Allies, Germany would be obliged to take up the offensive again on the Western Front. It was imperative that victory should be won within a matter of months, for the Summer of 1918 would see the balance of power swinging back to the Allies.

When 1917 opened, Germany had been very much on the defensive. The sheer size of forces ranged against her (three million British soldiers, mostly on the Western Front, and a French Army now a hundred divisions strong) had encouraged Allied generals to ignore the

1

ever increasing war-weariness among their troops, and mount another year of offensives. Bigger guns, enormous supplies of heavier shells, better and more reliable aeroplanes to observe the enemy and support infantry attacks, and the promise of a breakthrough led by improved tanks, resulted in the planning of offensives for Palestine, Macedonia and Mesopotamia.

Even dearer to the hearts of those Allied Commanders who believed that the war could, would, and should be won only in the West, was the intention to make attacks both around Arras and along the Chemin des Dames above Reims. Even those, as far as the British Commander in Chief, Sir Douglas Haig, was concerned, were only *hors d'oeuvres* to the main dish on his year's menu, a massive British drive in Flanders that would burst out from the Ypres salient, smash the German front and, delivering a right hook, would then drive the enemy back in disarray, capture his U-boat bases on the Belgian coast, and dislocate his war effort on both land and on sea at a stroke.

At the same time, warfare of a different kind was being planned and was taking place well behind Allied lines.

Briand's remark to Lloyd George that war was much too important a matter to be left in the hands of military men, was heartily endorsed by the new British Prime Minister, especially as his military men were Commander-in Chief Sir Douglas Haig and Sir William Robertson, Chief of the Imperial General Staff. While Lloyd George had been Minister in charge of munitions, his opinion of Haig had not affected the British Commander too much, but when, in December 1916, the fiery Welshman supplanted Prime Minister Asquith, his opposition to Haig's policy of attrition on the Western Front became almost a crusade. The British Prime Minister strongly opposed the argument that the Western Front was the only place where the war could be won; that the battle of attrition was the only possible way to win it, and that Haig himself, together with 'Wullie' Robertson and Haig's lesser lights, Charteris (Head of Intelligence) and Sir Launcelot Kiggell (Chief of Staff) were the only men to do it.

Lloyd George's vision was to turn the Western Front into a holding operation and attack elsewhere where the Central Powers seemed weaker. In that way her Allies could be picked off, Germany isolated, and the way prepared for final victory. Winston Churchill, starting to regain favour after the Dardanelles disaster, was also thinking in terms of the 'soft underbelly' of the enemy – a phrase he was to use and implement during the Second World War – and was hatching plans with locations as far distant from France and Flanders as the Balkans and the Baltic.

Haig, however, had no intention of being told by a bunch of politicians and others, like Churchill, with little experience of military command, to send his divisions to be committed to battle wherever they thought fit. He remained firm in his belief that there was only one way to win the war and that was to wear down Germany's strength on the Western Front by mounting attack after attack until she collapsed.

How then was Lloyd George to be rid of the strategy, pursued so grimly and relentlessly, that was killing thousands with no apparent gain? Certainly it was not to be done by copying Haig's own tactic of direct assault. Haig was entrenched in a strong position of personal friendship with the King (and His Majesty had as little stomach for Lloyd George as Lloyd George had for Haig) and any attempt to dismiss the Commander in Chief and his crew would anger the King, rouse Parliamentary wrath, and undermine the nation's resolve to continue the fight. It would require more subtle methods; methods, perhaps, that might call into play all Lloyd George's talent for deviousness and political machination.

He lost little time in starting his campaign at a conference in Rome only a matter of weeks after taking up the Premiership. There, in front of an audience that included a disgruntled Robertson (who, in spite of having travelled with the Prime Minister, had no inkling of what Lloyd George was going to say) he exhibited his considerable powers of oratory, set out his view of the military situation and urged priority for operations against the Austrians and Germans in Italy.

This naturally delighted the Italians, but when they realised Lloyd George was speaking without the knowledge and support of his Military High Command, they soon cooled. The conference ended by ratifying the plans already drawn up for the Spring attacks, and Lloyd George's scheme was merely recommended to 'be given further study'.

To say Lloyd George was none too pleased would be an understatement. On his way home, he fulminated to his companions against attacks that 'would drive men to the slaughter like cattle', and as those travelling companions were Robertson and Kiggell, the discussion became somewhat acrimonious. However, during the journey the new Commander in Chief of the French Army, General Robert Nivelle, boarded the train and introduced himself.

Lloyd George was captivated. Nivelle, the child of an Anglo-French marriage, and able to express himself fluently and cogently in perfect idiomatic English, endeared both himself and his plans to the Prime Minister. His Spring offensive was to be no battle of attrition. It was to rupture the German front, roll up their defences and in all probability end the war within weeks. If, by the unlikeliest of chances, the operation did not succeed, it would immediately be suspended and Haig's grand attack in Flanders could be mounted later in the year. Lloyd George, intrigued not only by the possibility of success, but also by the opportunity to delay Haig's Grand Plan – even, perhaps to make him subservient to the French Commander – at once asked Nivelle to visit England to explain his scheme to the War Cabinet.

There, too, Nivelle exerted his charm. Lloyd George and his fellow politicians became enthusiastic. The proposal was that Haig should extend the British share of the front, mount an attack to make the enemy commit his reserves, then 'hey presto', Nivelle's offensive on the Aisne would administer the *coup de grâce*. Haig, as was to be expected, had faith neither in Nivelle nor his plan. The senior French Generals, Joffre and Foch, were also sceptical. However, approval had been given, and Nivelle's arrangements were now so far advanced it would have been extremely difficult to cancel them.

Another conference took place at Calais on 28 February, this time supposedly called to find ways of improving the delivery of supplies for the coming offensives. Lloyd George chose the occasion to announce that Haig was to act under the orders of Nivelle, who would become, in effect, the Allies' equivalent of Ludendorff i.e. the commander of a unified Army. This caused immediate uproar. Robertson, leaving his usual trail of dropped 'h's, was all for the entire British military hierarchy to resign. Haig went privately to the King and offered to step down. His diary notes that, 'it would be easier if I only had to deal with the Germans'. Of course there had to be a compromise, and eventually it was arranged that Haig was to be subordinate only for the period of Nivelle's offensive, but from that time on, relations between Sir Douglas and his Prime Minister were, and continued to be, at the very best, strained!

Ever since the offensive on the Somme in the Summer of 1916, and during that Autumn when the French had retaken some of the ground von Falkenhayn had seized at Verdun, the German Army had been forced into defence in France and Flanders. As a result, by 1917 German field engineers were masters of military construction and met further threatened attacks by preparing better positions even than those that had withstood the previous year's attacks. Their troops were pulled back to man them during February and March. During this planned retreat to this massive new defence system, the 'Siegfried Stellung', the Germans devastated the country, forcing the Allied troops to follow in appalling weather through a booby-trapped wilderness. Roads to supply the advance had to be rebuilt immediately behind the ongoing line of attack, with troops working under fire and sleeping in the open. The weather was so foul and so cold that ink froze in fountain pens, and the oil on rifles and machine guns turned solid.

At the end of a full month's fighting some of the Allied troops following up the German retreat had still not reached the new Siegfried main defences.

> There were fires burning when we occupied Gommecourt, and so we tried to put them out. The junction of every road had been blown up, and everything of value 'had been destroyed. All the fruit trees had been

pulled down or the bark 'ringed' so the sap could not rise. All the wells
had been blown in, and one had been poisoned with arsenic. The only
buildings standing were the château and some we used as billets. The
château had been mined, but the charge hadn't exploded fully. The engineers took seven hundred pounds of unexploded charges out of the
cellars. (Private diary: Officer of the 62nd Division.)

This German destruction caused the Allies extreme difficulties, and
consequent dislocation to the plans for their Spring offensives. The new
fortifications, soon to be given the title of the Hindenburg Line by the
unfortunate troops who had to attack them, were carefully sited. In
front lay the carefully registered killing field of no-man's-land to be
crossed before attackers even arrived at the acres of barbed wire entan-
glements protecting the advanced positions. Behind was the first of
several mutually supporting lines of defence – in total often stretching
back for several kilometres – where deep dugouts concealed troops
ready to emerge and man machine guns the moment an enemy barrage
lifted. At the same time, over in Belgium, where constant shelling had
so broken up the water courses that the low-lying land, now little more
than a gigantic sponge, precluded that kind of defence, more and more
concrete was being mixed to build pill-boxes for the German defenders
on the ridges, overlooking and preparing to resist every move made
against them in the Ypres salient.

CHAPTER 2

A 'SWINGS AND ROUNDABOUTS' SITUATION

– The Russian collapse – underseas warfare – American neutrality abandoned –

'An intelligent Russian once remarked to us, "Every country has its own constitution; ours is absolutism moderated by assassination."'
(George Herbert, Count of Münster.)

Even as the barrage, started to 'soften up' the German line on Vimy Ridge, ready for the first Allied offensive of the year, the war effort in Russia had started to collapse. Demoralised by terrible casualties, brought to despair by the shortages of food and goods during the winter of 1916–17, the Russian people had lost their centuries-old veneration of the Tzar and their unquestioning submission to his autocratic regime. Rumours of the mystical Rasputin's influence over the royal family, extending even to a belief that he was interfering in the Tzar's personal direction of the war, worsened the situation, and by now Russia was ripe for revolution. Trouble began late in February when unrest at Petrograd (the former St. Petersburg and future Leningrad) degenerated into riots as hungry civilians were joined by mutinous troops from the city garrison.

Believing that only a new political system could save the country from military defeat and ensuing anarchy, the Russian High Command demanded the Tzar's abdication, and a provisional government was set up. When this became known, the peasants forming the rank and file of Russia's Army, half-starved, harshly treated and driven forward time after time regardless of loss with inadequate weapons – some not even carrying a rifle – to face the German guns, saw the chance to end this war that held no prospects for them other than certain hardship and probable mutilation or death. Many simply voted with their feet, and went home. Others made unofficial truces, and cases of fraternisation with the enemy were legion. The tactics of the newly-formed 'Soviets' representing the masses, eager for power and challenging any continuation of the war, were also a constant embarrassment to the Provisional Government.

Realising that this presented a golden opportunity for advantageous political meddling, Germany sent money to help the revolution, and arranged for the secret return of Lenin from his Swiss exile in a sealed train, thoughtfully provided by the German General Staff.

So the Provisional Government, trying to steer a course between the Scylla of unrest in the Army and the Charybdis of Bolshevik aspirations, found its forces virtually operating an unofficial armistice throughout the spring and early summer, a situation that Germany again used to advantage by starting to move troops back to the West.

It was clear that the vaunted 'Russian Steam Roller' was falling to pieces. In Britain, 'Wullie' Robertson was even quoted in print as having said Russia was 'about finished', while in France, Pétain, in a more than usual mood of pessimism, expressed the opinion that the Russian Army would 'fall apart if it so much as made a move'.

It made the move on 1 July. Kerensky, head of Russia's provisional government, ordered Brusilov to open an offensive, and for the second year in succession 1 July proved a fateful date in the war's history. Preparation was so sketchy that local commanders were simply told to advance if the troops would obey. Some gains were made, but when the Austrians counter-attacked, the Russian Eleventh Army was routed utterly. This was the signal for a Bolshevik uprising on 16 July. It was brutally suppressed, but when the Germans took Riga on 1 September the death of the old regime was assured even before the storming of the Winter Palace on 7 November made it certain. As the German leaders met at Mons four days later, they had the prospect of 30 more divisions being available to throw against Britain and France.

For some months Germany would enjoy numerical superiority on the Western Front.

While the politicians in London were continuing their attempts to thwart further battles of attrition by taking charge of military policy, Ludendorff, virtually in charge of German military policy, was aiming to influence German politics both at home and abroad.

After the indecisive end to the battle of Jutland in 1916, the German High Seas Fleet had skulked in harbour and her Navy's contribution to the war had been concentrated below, rather than on, the surface of the ocean. Successful U-boat attacks, even as 1917 opened, were causing severe shortages in Britain. Food queues during that bitterly cold winter were widespread – as were queues for coal – and with both food and heating in short supply, Britain's civilian population, like Germany's, was feeling the effects of blockade.

Germany's use of unrestricted submarine warfare had been halted in 1916 after diplomatic protest from neutral countries, and had been replaced by a 'visit and search' policy when ships seemed to be unarmed. Now, because several U-boats had been sunk by 'Q' ships (armed vessels disguised as merchantmen luring submarines to the surface to destroy their prey by gunfire) the resumption of the 'unrestricted' policy was being argued by the Naval Staff.

The 'pros' and 'cons' were nicely balanced. On one hand, the heads of the Navy, von Tirpitz and von Scheer, argued the case along with Ludendorff for bringing Britain to her knees by strangling the flow of food and war material; on the other, the Kaiser and the Chancellor of Germany, Bethmann-Hollweg, warned of the possible results of antagonising countries – particularly America – which had up to now remained neutral. Their argument was countered by the 'unrestricted' lobby pointing out that America had a large number of German immigrants who would surely drag their new country back from the brink of declaring war on their homeland. In addition America's Irish immigrants, whose detestation of all things British had been brought to fever pitch by the summary justice meted out to Republican 'martyrs' after the 1916 Easter Rising, would certainly oppose any move to join Britain's side.

Both sides of the argument were to some degree correct, but rather like the farm animals in George Orwell's book, some were more correct than others. The weapon of unrestricted underseas warfare, like the sword carried by the mythical Walküre, proved two-edged. Britain lost 800,000 tons of shipping in March alone, but after Winston Churchill, with the support of Lloyd George, forced the convoy system on an unwilling Admiralty, losses gradually decreased. On the other hand, American anger when American lives and property again began to be lost, turned rapidly to fury that overcame both the prejudice of Irish, and the jingoism of German immigrants. A telegram sent by Zimmermann, Germany's Foreign Secretary, to his country's ambassador in Washington, added more fuel to the flames. When intercepted and decoded by a team in England which included Oliver Strachey and Nigel de Grey (who were later to contribute to cracking the German 'Enigma' code in World War Two) American rage boiled over. In it Zimmermann proposed exploring a German-Mexican alliance where, in return for an attack on the US, Mexico was to be given Texas, New Mexico and Arizona when victory was won. The text of the telegram was published in America on 1 March, and was proved authentic.

By April, with all the potential of her resources in manpower and industrial might, America took the first step along the road to abandoning her long held policy of neutrality. Throughout two and a half years of war in Europe, the United States under Woodrow Wilson's leadership had maintained a precarious neutrality, causing splits among her German immigrant communities that started to heal only when war was finally declared by the USA.

In spite of the fact that his electoral campaign had so recently been fought on the slogan 'He kept us out of the War', President Wilson stood before Congress on 2 April and stated that the time had come for Democracy to be made safe, America was far from ready to enter the struggle. For ten years the army had been sufficiently large only to quell unlikely civil disorder or to keep the peace along the border with neighbouring Latin-American countries. There were not enough rifles to arm half the proposed army, and few plans had been made to provide more. Just as the mood of optimism in Europe during August 1914 had predicted a brief war, Americans thought their boys' presence 'Over There', in the words of George M. Cohen's popular song, would bring a speedy victory and that the 'troops would be home by Christmas'.

On 6 April, Congress voted for war against Germany. As dawn broke three days later in France, whistles blew and British and Canadian troops climbed from their trenches to start the first of the Allies' spring offensives.

CHAPTER 3

THE 1917 OFFENSIVES

– Vimy – Nivelle's disaster and the French mutiny – Cambrai – Passchendaele – Caporetto –

'Cry "Havoc!" and let slip the dogs of war.'
(Shakespeare; Julius Caesar.)

Although the German Army conceded the important high ground over-looking Arras when all four Canadian divisions, together with British troops, stormed Vimy Ridge in hail and sleet on 9–10 April, it cost the Allies more than ten thousand killed and wounded, and casualties were reckoned to be light compared to previous assaults against the position.

A matter of only 20 kilometres away, the far wing of the offensive was in deep trouble. Operations there were still dragging on into May, and in an attack on 3 May, the dead from the North of England and Australia lay in swathes in front of the Prussian-manned defences of Bullecourt. The promised tanks failed to arrive, almost all having been knocked out by shell fire. The Australians never penetrated the village's defences, leaving some hundreds of metres of the enemy line free to pour enfilade fire on the Yorkshiremen. Patrols to report German strength had failed to return, the wire was uncut and snipers caused ghastly losses. A second equally futile assault on the fortified village was made a week later and it was 17 May before the position was finally taken by the 58th Division. Liddell Hart described the whole event as, 'for its scale, the bloodiest of all trench killing matches . . . a ghastly example, tactically of what to avoid', and Sir John Monash, the Australian commander, deplored the fact that his men had been sacrificed in such a 'hare-brained venture'. The description given by one of the Royal Engineer Sappers witnessing the attack from the rear after putting down the starting tapes, was that 'it was like watching corn being mown down . . .'

The next hammer-blow, falling less than a week after the start of the Vimy attack, was delivered by the stylish, supremely self-confident General Robert Nivelle. Riding on a wave of euphoria that followed his recapture of Fort Douaumont at Verdun the previous year, he had replaced Joffre as Commander in Chief. Nivelle boldly asserted he 'had the answer' to static warfare. His Sixth Army would simply break through the German line 'by an act of brute force'.

10

Unfortunately, on the other side of the wire, Hans von Böhn's Seventh Army knew only too well what was planned. The French Press had got wind of it and aroused expectations of a victory, and details of Nivelle's operation were in far too many hands. When precise orders of battle were injudiciously distributed wholesale at company level, the result was to be expected. By 6 April, as a result of trench raids made to gain information, copies of the plan of attack for both the Fifth and Sixth French Armies were in enemy hands.

Soon, where nine German divisions had manned the line on the Chemin des Dames, there were forty, and equipment to defend the front was multiplying by the hour. The German retreat to the Siegfried Stellung, as well as wrong-footing the British, had also left the French distanced from the new defences. Nivelle remained unperturbed. The German retreat, he maintained, had merely given him the opportunity to outflank the new line and take it in the rear. The city of Laon would now fall to his forces on the very first day, and after that the Germans would be in full retreat.

Pétain and the French Government had extreme doubts. When Nivelle was called to a meeting, and heard those doubts forcefully expressed, he replied that as Commander in Chief he could not tolerate such interference and threatened resignation. The politicians gave way.

While not one of the attacks that year was to bring about the final expected breakthrough, Nivelle's was an instant disaster. In the face of the German fire-storm, Colonial troops broke and ran at the very outset, even commandeering staff cars and hospital trains in the rear to make their escape. After two days of battle a further 80,000 casualties had been added to the half-million suffered at Verdun without any noticeable gain of territory. Nivelle broke his promise to abort the action if there was no early victory. The attacks continued and his 'act of brute force' became the flash point for mutiny. Out of sixteen divisions in the Champagne area only two remained unaffected, and by June the rebellion had spread to more than half the French Army.

Most units refused to take part in further attacks, but did agree to hold the line. In some divisions there was much waving of red flags, rough handling of officers who tried to restore discipline – a few were killed – and attempts made to march on Paris. One regiment shambled up to the line bleating like sheep going to slaughter. Acts of sabotage took place. Anger was felt not only against Headquarters, but towards the various branches of the Army, each accusing the others of lack of support and of displaying an incompetence that added to their own casualty lists.

A Division of Russians brought to the Western Front and used in Nivelle's battle, increased the tension by inciting revolution wherever they were sent. Kerensky had enough divisions of a different kind at home to deal with and would have preferred to let those particular troops stay in France, so eventually a French military operation had to be mounted to surround, attack, defeat, and disarm them. They were then forcibly shipped back to Russia in the early Autumn.

Of course the politicians were soon on the scene, squabbling like gulls on a tip as they sought for scraps of political advantage. Nivelle, in the course of an extremely rowdy meeting, tried to blame his subordinates, Mangin and Micheler for the failure, but at its conclusion found himself a political and a military outcast. If his promotion had been rapid, his fall was precipitous. By 15 May he was gone.

Amazingly the situation was kept from the Germans, but the political and military consequences were felt far beyond the confines of France's Chamber of Deputies and the portals of her Ministry of War. As Nivelle disappeared in disgrace to North Africa, Pétain, his successor, departed to visit disaffected units and to listen to grievances.

There were Courts Martial in plenty, and firing squads for some ring-leaders, but if official records are to be believed, only 133 French soldiers were executed for murder, desertion or mutiny during the entire four years of war. Courts Martial records for the period are still classified material.

For the thousands who had taken part in what the court of enquiry delicately referred to as 'acts of mass indiscipline', concessions had to be made. They demanded – and were given – better conditions. Never again would their lives be held so cheaply; better food was provided, better living conditions when out of the line, and, most important of all, a far more generous leave allowance. (That concession alone meant that almost a third of French front-line troops would be out of the trenches at any one time.) Pétain also removed bad characters from the ranks, reckoning the further loss of manpower was preferable to more trouble.

All this not only placed a greater burden on the British, but also brought to a temporary halt Lloyd George's hopes of decreasing Haig's power and preventing his Flanders attack. By the time the year was at an end, under pressure from politicians on both sides of the Channel, Haig had agreed to take pressure from the French by extending his front 23 kilometres southwards to Barisis. Only weeks later, Clémenceau was demanding an extension of 50 kilometres more to Berry-au-Bac and threatening resignation if the British did not comply. Haig, short of reinforcements, replied that he would take the same action if his Government gave way, and there the matter rested.

Not content with his offensive in Flanders, which by mid-Autumn was fighting its weary, bloody way up the ridges to Passchendaele, Haig decided on a subsidiary surprise attack round Cambrai led by massed tanks across particularly favourable terrain. Elaborate precautions were taken against discovery. A screen of brushwood was set up in Havrincourt Wood to hide the artillery. All construction work was done, and troop movements made during the hours of darkness with transport travelling north using full lights, while material for the offensive travelled in 'blacked out' trucks. The special trains (36 of them) each carrying 12 of the Mark 1V tanks to be used in the attack, deposited them at specially prepared sidings at Spree Farm behind Havrincourt Wood. There they were cautiously unloaded and prepared with fuel, ammunition and stores.

Only a matter of days after Ludendorff's November meeting at Mons, this sudden attack by Byng's Third Army cracked the Hindenburg line on 20 November and advanced towards Cambrai over ground between the two canals of the St. Quentin and the du Nord against the German defenders (weakened to some degree because of the need to send reinforcements to the ongoing battle above Ypres). More than eight kilometres were gained in a single day, an unheard-of success. Church bells across Britain were set ringing in celebration, prematurely, as it happened, for the staff of the Third Army had not the means to exploit such unexpected success, and von der Marwitz's reinforcements, headed by small groups of storm troopers using infiltration tactics, reversed the Allied gains within days.

As for Haig's Grand Attack in the Ypres salient that had been maturing for almost eighteen months; once the explosion of Sir Herbert Plumer's mines had changed the shape, and his Second Army the ownership, of Messines ridge on 7 June, alerting the German Fourth Army to prepare itself to meet the offensive, Haig's struggle to reach even the intermediate objective of the Passchendaele ridge dragged on from the first main attack on 31 July into November, degenerating into just the kind of attrition situation Lloyd George feared and abhorred.

But hopes had been raised by the long awaited and longed for arrival of the Americans. While Haig was still refining his plans and issuing instructions for the coming battle, the American Commander, 'Black Jack' Pershing landed at Boulogne on 13 June to a tumultuous welcome and, in an exercise designed to 'fly the flag', mounted an Independence Day Parade through Paris. Covetous French and British eyes were cast on these first representatives of the promised thousands to come. As soon as sufficient were on French soil, Pétain wanted huge numbers to be taught 50 words of command in French and used in platoons alongside his poilus to bolster their morale. Haig proposed to lay claim to as many as possible, give them the same seven weeks' basic training as British conscripts, then send them to the trenches in the British sector.

Pershing would have none of it. His task was to produce an American Army a million strong, trained to a hair and operating under American control. While he was doing that he would ask Congress for a second million. Haig and Pétain, both struggling with politicians and searching all the time for reinforcements and replacements, could only look with envious eyes at a military leader existing in a world they could only dream about.

In the meantime, Lloyd George, still trying to scotch Haig's plans for Flanders, attempted to bring the Commander in Chief and his entourage to heel by forming a new Committee of War Policy with himself in the chair and General Smuts, Lord Milner and Lord Curzon among its members. Appearing at a meeting in London, Haig and Robertson at once had the edge over their civilian questioners. After all, they, not Curzon and Milner, were the military experts and could speak, if not fluently, at least with authority and from experience. Haig pointed out that Brusilov's July offensive 'promised excellent results'; that Germany was beginning to doubt the success of her underseas warfare and in any case was demoralised by the recent Messines attack, and that France (in spite of Haig's private knowledge of the French mutiny) would be able to strike a heavy blow against the enemy.

To all objections and reservations Robertson and Haig had answers. Yes, German strength was overestimated: yes, they had enough men and supplies to ensure success: yes, Passchendaele could be reached in a single day if the Messines offensive was any guide. When asked if Passchendaele was to be the final objective, Haig replied quite sincerely that the operation would end with the capture of the entire Belgian coast.

The flow of questions dried. It was difficult to pose more to a man who was obviously so sure of victory. To all Lloyd George's further reservations and arguments the following day – including the oft-repeated one that an offensive would be more productive in Italy – the generals produced counter-arguments. Eventually the Committee agreed, with reservations, to leave the decision to the military experts on the understanding that if the battle did not achieve its objectives quickly it would be broken off and attention given to mounting an Italian offensive. Robertson and Haig had conquered the Committee. It remained to be seen if they could do the same to the German Army.

Almost all the later attacks of the Passchendaele campaign took place in conditions that confirmed the British rank and file's belief that the Germans brought over Witch Doctors from their colonial territories in Africa who could produce torrential rain at will. That rain, coinciding with every major attempt to advance and compounding the effects of heavy artillery fire, churned the entire battlefield into a sea of mud through which Belgian and French, British and Commonwealth troops struggled to come to grips with their enemy. Foch, Chief of the French General Staff, when asked for his opinion, remarked that Boche was bad, and Boue was bad, but as for Boche and Mud together . . . and ended with a typically Gallic shrug.

In spite of the Germans having used all the previous year to turn the whole line into a fortress guarded by innumerable pill boxes and machine gun nests, and an opening barrage combined with air attacks that turned the entire area into a swamp, there was some success in August when the lower ridges round Pilckem were taken, but to reach the Passchendaele crest Haig had to mount attack after attack, and those attacks went on into Autumn. By October most of the area could be crossed only by putting down duckboards and planks on top of brushwood, an occupation made hazardous by being performed in view of German artillery observers. The salient had been fought over for three and a half years. Now the ground was pulverised into a sea of mud where shell holes overlapped, woods were mounds of tangled matchwood and entire villages had completely vanished. 'The plank road', wrote Edmund Blunden, describing 'the slow amputation of Passchendaele' in his *Undertones of War*, 'was at once the salvation and the slaughter-house of the forward area . . . To leave it was to plunge into a swamp, to remain on it was to pass through accurate and ruthless shell fire'.

The attacks went on towards Gheluveld (still uncaptured by mid-September); a kilometre or so further to Poelcapelle; on to Steenstraat; to Langemarck: from there to Zonnebeke, and at last – just over eight kilometres and five dreadful months later – up to Passchendaele where, even as the Germans were travelling to their Mons conference, the Canadian 1st Division was making a final effort to become the occupiers of a 300 metre strip of mud at the head of the salient.

It was at this point that Haig's Grand Offensive finally petered out. It cost half a million casualties, at least 150,000 dying of wounds or disembowelled by shellfire; stitched through by machine gun bullets or burnt to death by phosphorous, together with hundreds upon hundreds more who simply disappeared, drowning in that terrible mud.

Headquarters had no real idea of the sacrifices they were demanding, nor of the terrible conditions. Alike at Army conference and in statements to politician, optimistic phrases were commonplace, and any attempt to paint a true picture was given an extremely cold reception further back. When eventually Kiggell, Haig's Chief of Staff, did visit the forward areas he was horrified. 'Did we,' he is reported to have asked, 'really send men to fight in this?'

'It's worse further up . . .' he was told.

Haig argued (and continued to argue after the war) that the action was continued 'to relieve pressure on the French', but as it became more and more obvious that the offensive was grinding itself deeper and deeper into the Flanders mud, and in lack of progress and proliferation of casualties was on course to rival the previous battles of the Somme and of Verdun, so the advocates of an eastern front become more vociferous. A Robertson memo to Haig as early as mid-June had said Lloyd George, was now 'very much out for blood' and that 'matters would come to a head' before long. 'I rather hope so,' the memorandum continued, 'as I am sick of this d – d life.' Now the Prime Minister told the CIGS that he intended to turn to other consultants for advice 'at this turning point' of the war. Neither Haig nor Robertson could have been delighted when the consultants turned out to be the duo of Sir John French (whom Haig had displaced as British Commander in Chief) and Sir Henry Wilson (whose predilection for intrigue made him more of a political than a military animal and prompted his detractors' unkind remark that he had an orgasm every time he saw a politician.)

These consultants, not surprisingly, agreed with Lloyd George that strategy should be controlled by a War Council whose Representatives would allocate resources and plan overall policy and actions more effectively. These plans progressed favourably when in November France and Italy joined Britain and agreed to appoint Military Members to serve on the new council (the British Military Member to be none other than Sir Henry Wilson!) and to subject their policies to its direction. If this were so, Haig asked, by what channels was he to receive his orders? . . . and as to the Central Reserve of troops being set up by the council, where would the reserve be situated?. . . who would supply the men . . . ?

Now, as the controversy spread openly to the British Press – *The Manchester Guardian* and *The Times* openly critical of Haig, *The Morning Post* and *The Globe* condemning Lloyd George's interference – yet another battle well south of the Fronts in France and Flanders entrenched both 'Westerners' and 'Easterners' still more deeply in their beliefs.

In the space of only two and a half weeks from its initial attack on 24 October, a combined German and Austrian offensive mounted against the weakest part of the line at Caporetto utterly routed the Italian Third and Fourth Armies. Reactions were predictable; 'Easterners' maintained the disaster would have been avoided if resources had been transferred to Italy. 'Westerners' felt satisfaction that the enemy had proved himself less vulnerable on the Italian Front than the 'Easterners' had made out.

Haig took no part in the argument. Caporetto, with Italian losses of guns by the thousand, supplies by the tonne, 10,000 dead, 20,000 wounded and an almost unbelievable 275,000 taken prisoner, had no more than a brief mention in his diary. When asked on the 27th to send two divisions to help the fleeing Italians, his diary notes 'we cannot spare troops to fight their battles for them.' However, Robertson left at once for urgent discussions at Italian headquarters, and the speedy dispatch of six French and (despite Haig's wishes) five British divisions sent by the War Cabinet, helped stabilise the line.

Revulsion in Britain to the long agony of Passchendaele assisted Lloyd

George's aim of preventing another such Haig offensive in the Spring of 1918. There were rapid changes at British GHQ. Plumer departed to take charge of British forces in Italy; Kiggell and Charteris disappeared one after the other. Even Robertson and Haig felt under threat.

As German reinforcements continued to flood back from Russia to the West, Haig's forces there were becoming very much depleted. In spite of all his pleas for replacements and reinforcements, the Cabinet, prompted by Lloyd George, refused to release more from the growing reserve in Britain than they considered absolutely necessary to defend the front. In this way another Haig-led offensive could be averted. The policy would be to remain in defence until the Americans should arrive in sufficient numbers to ensure victory.

Though British troops already in France were to go through great trials as a result, this was done, and done in such a way that when a furious Parliament demanded to know why in the following Spring the war was so nearly lost, the policy was justified by a clever massaging of facts and figures.

Caporetto also confirmed the realisation that the Supreme War Council's control of policy was more important than the views held by any individual or any one country. Before Winter had turned to Spring, 'Wullie' Robertson was to read of his 'resignation' in the press – his place as CIGS to be taken over by Sir Henry Wilson – and (a nice touch of malice, this) Robertson was to become Head of *Eastern* Command in England.

The entry made in Sir Henry Wilson's diary summed up his view of the year.

1. We take Bullecourt: they take Rumania.
2. We take Messines: they take Russia.
3. We don't take Passchendaele: they take Italy.

In the west, Haig seemed to be in danger of eclipse, his forces danger-ously weakened by battle and deliberately so by lack of reinforcements. The French were still recovering from the year's traumas. What would the Germans meeting at Mons decide about the battles to come in the west during 1918?

CHAPTER 4

THE GERMAN PLAN FOR 1918

– The determination to pursue military solutions – new tactics, new weapons – Ludendorff's choice of place and time as German strength increases –

'Ay, now the plot thickens very much upon us.'
(George Villiers, Duke of Buckingham; 'The Rehearsal'.)

By the end of 1917, demands from the Vatican and from President Wilson in America to start peace negotiations had long been rejected by both sides. In Germany what, in Hindenburg's and Ludendorff's view, was the faint-hearted attitude of Chancellor Bethmann-Hollweg, who had questioned the wisdom of resuming unrestricted submarine warfare – indeed, even the wisdom of continuing the war – had brought about his dismissal. In Britain, Lord Landsdowne's similar views about initiating peace negotiations had been received with such fury that he had now been living in political isolation for almost a year.

Yet if Germany had been prepared to start negotiations in the last months of 1917, she might have gained an advantageous peace. By 15 December, Trotsky and Lenin had signed an armistice, and Russia was out of the war for good. In Italy (though the surprising by-product of the Caporetto disaster was an increased determination nationwide to continue the struggle) the war effort was still in turmoil. The French Army had not recovered fully from its mutinies, and Britain's Army, weakened by losses, needed replacements which Lloyd George refused to provide. A peace settlement at that time might have seen parts of Belgium and Poland remain under the German heel, with a permanent annexation of the much disputed Alsace and Lorraine, while Turkey and Austro-Hungary, the other members of the Central Powers, strengthened their hold on the Balkans now that Russia was looking inward to the ongoing struggle between Whites and Reds, rather than to traditional spheres of influence outside her borders. But Hindenburg and Ludendorff were not political animals, – they were military leaders. Indeed, more than military leaders they were militarists, firmly in the saddle, and the merest whiff of a threat to resign was enough to force through their policies.

Haig's position in the saddle was not so sure, 'possessing a good, firm seat' wasn't the best description to be applied to that particular cavalry

18

officer at present. However, in spite of their opposition to his methods, the politicians were at one with his determination to pursue the struggle to ultimate victory.

Realising their numerical advantage could last only a few more months, the German High Command recognised that new methods and/or new weapons would be needed if the war was to be won before their forces were outnumbered again. Even if this temporary superiority gave the chance of victory, attrition alone – if past experiences were any guide – could not bring about a quick enough result for them.

Making the same mistake as the British Commander in Chief, who earlier had described the machine gun as a much over-rated weapon, the German High Command underestimated the potential of those 'devil's chariots' that first lumbered like prehistoric monsters bucking and grinding across no-man's-land in 1916. As they met at Mons, only a few days were to pass before Ludendorff, von Kuhl and von der Schulenberg learned what a massed tank attack could do. So far, like all other new weapons, the tank had not produced the breakthrough and rolling up of the enemy line its advocates hoped for. In the minds of the German Staff were pictures of tanks bogged down in the Flanders mud to be destroyed at leisure by artillery, and of tanks used piecemeal and ineffectively at Bullecourt and on the Somme. In spite of the initial terror it caused, the new weapon was vulnerable to artillerymen with steady nerves, and to infantry with the new anti-tank rifle or even with hastily issued elephant guns.

In the past Germany had been the innovator. She had introduced poison gas into warfare. The flame-thrower, too, was first used by her troops. Those weapons brought no breakthrough, only worldwide accusations of 'uncivilised behaviour', 'frightfulness', 'typical Hunbarbarity', and subsequent justification for the use of the same weapons against her by the Allies. By the time massed tanks had flattened the Siegfried Stellung's barbed-wire round Havrincourt and brought about a change of mind, and the Germans' clumsy AK 7 had made a belated appearance, it was too late. Improved British and French models had the advantage both of speed and manoeuvrability, and even a few captured Allied machines pressed into service to swell the German force brought no real advantage.

However, the Army had devised new methods of attack. The death-blow to the Russian Government's hopes of continuing the war when Riga was captured in September of 1917, had been mainly due to revolutionary artillery techniques, the brainchild of Bruchmüller, Chief of Artillery, soon nicknamed 'Durchbruchmüller' (breakthrough-Müller) by his troops.

Bruchmüller avoided the usual lengthy barrage intended to 'soften up' defences, deny the arrival of reinforcements and cause the complete disorientation of any surviving defenders (but in doing so gave ample warning for the enemy to mass troops in the rear to prevent a break-through). Instead, he planned an overwhelming and unexpected storm of fire. The accuracy of the various gun calibres to be used in an attack was worked out well behind the front. After that, only a few ranging shots in the area chosen for the offensive were needed. The results were then transferred to the entire force, which moved up during the last hours before the offensive. The positions of the artillery opposite had already been determined by improved techniques of sound ranging and flash spotting, and aerial photographs showed the position of every supply dump and command post. Using all this information, everything could be saturated by a brief but overwhelming tornado that immediately preceded the ground attack. Such a ferocious barrage, being completely unexpected, had the same devastating effect that many weeks of shelling had produced previously.

Even before the bombardment ended, small groups of battle-hardened storm troopers were on their way across no-man's-land to arrive in the enemy trenches before the shaken defenders could even think of organising resistance. In this way the weak points were exploited; if entrenched strongpoints looked like causing trouble, they were at once bypassed. The storm troopers' orders were to cause confusion, to destroy communications, to overrun company headquarters, reserve trenches and gun emplacements. Above all, to Keep Going! – all the time continuing to infiltrate the enemy positions.

These small parties of shock troops were soon followed by larger groups using the same tactics. Strongpoints were again left to be captured or wiped out after more softening up treatment by bombardment and aeroplane attacks.

These new methods worked well. Von der Marwitz's troops had counter-attacked using them when the British had tried to stabilise the line at the close of the Cambrai offensive, and his XIIIth Corps, flanked by the XIVth Reserve and XXIIIrd Corps, took back within three days most of the ground it had taken the British more than a week to win.

The bombardment at Riga and the counter-attacks at Cambrai had proved that an enemy line could be broken. The question was exactly when, why, and where was it best to apply the tactics in the coming Spring?

The High Command did not have to ponder long over the problem of 'when'. It would have to be during February or March 1918, before the Americans arrived in strength. Already elements that were to form the US 1st Division (grandly called the Big Red One from its Divisional sign) were well into their training south of St Mihiel, working eight hours a day, five days a week learning to dig trenches, put up barbed-wire and to use grenade, rifle and machine gun. There was little rifle practice at first, as rifles were not normally used by the French Army. When French and German patrols clashed, the usual weapon was the grenade. This was not good enough for General Pershing. He insisted on rigorous training with the rifle for use in open (as opposed to trench) warfare, and was determined to achieve overall standards equal in all ways to those of West Point Cadets. In spite of French doubts, dash and aggression were demanded from commanders and dough-boys alike, while any laxity in dress or behaviour saw defaulters on their knees using toothbrushes to scrub cobblestones at Langres. Secretary of State Baker privately remarked he could not see how a man could find the time to win a war when he had his mind so firmly fixed on buttons.

The 26th Division (the 'Yankees' from New England) had arrived in France at the end of September, the 2nd (Race-Horse Brigade) was in course of formation: by March 1918, 350,000 Americans would have crossed the Atlantic.

The German 'where' and 'why' were closely linked. The principal aim of the coming spring attacks was to smash the British Army. Germany's hatred had grown from the conviction that Britain, who in the early years of the century had opposed her efforts to become a sea power, had thwarted her aim to acquire colonies and form an empire. Britain it was who had needlessly entered the war because of 'a scrap of paper' guaranteeing Belgian neutrality and British troops had been present to help end hopes of an early German victory at that remarkable turnaround of fortunes on the Marne in 1914. From then on Germany had regarded Britain as the mainspring of the Alliance against her, and by 1916 the hatred of her leaders amounted almost to paranoia. The troops were even taught to sing a Hymn of Hate composed by Ernst Lissauer, who, rejected as unfit, devoted his meagre poetic talents to the service of his country. It expressed the belief that the French and the Russians were of no account. 'We have only one enemy . . . Britain', they sang, '. . . the only one worthy of our hate . . .'

There were no arguments either during Ludendorff's Mons meeting about moving resources, and attacking on other fronts. This series of all-out Western offensives was to attack weak points, and when the assault was made and Allied reinforcements were rushed to meet the threat, another offensive would open up somewhere else. Almost in the manner of the technique used in professional tennis, smash after smash would see the defenders scurrying from side to side trying to anticipate the next blow.

Various alternatives were discussed. Von Kuhl advocated an offensive in the La Bassée – Armentières area, code-named 'St. George I'. The possibility of a 'St George II' against the Ypres salient was also proposed. The 'Mars' offensive was designed to strike the area from Arras to Notre Dame de Lorette, and last of all a huge three-pronged 'Michael' offensive was put forward for examination under the code-names of

Michaels I, II and III. The meeting ended with instructions that detailed studies of them all were to be made before a final decision was taken. It was not until late in January that the 'Michael' offensives were chosen.

CHAPTER 5

THE 'KAISERSCHLACT' MADE READY

– Preparations for the German Spring offensives continue – British strength weakens –

'Cet animal est très méchant,
Quand on l'attaque il se defend.'
(From Théodore P.K; Le Ménagerie)

About the same time that 'Michael' was approved and studies began to compute the number of divisions needed for its operation, Sir Douglas Haig and his staff were also making calculations about the strength of their forces. Not only was the front stretched by the French demand that the British sector should extend south to Barisis; there were fewer troops to do the stretching. Lloyd George's policy of holding back rein-forcements was by now starving Haig's Army so badly that drastic measures had to be taken. A complete revision of brigade structure within British divisions was begun, the first stage being completed only a matter of days before the German offensive began on 21 March. The fine-tuning in further readjustments was still taking place as late as June.

In brief, it was decided that the number of battalions in a each brigade of a division must be reduced from four to three. Even when that was done, a few divisions had to be disbanded, most of the men going to reinforce other units, while the few remaining officers and other ranks were made into training cadres.

All through February German reinforcements were moving nearer the front and being positioned in strength against the British sector, for if the British could be broken, France, weakened by the losses at Verdun and on the Chemin des Dames, would certainly fall with her. The French, it was also said with derision at German Headquarters, in any case would be in no hurry to come to the assistance of their so-called partners.

The aims and the location of the 'Michaels' operations were now fixed. Once more the chosen ground was to be the Somme; the objec-tive to smash the British defences and capture the ground between

Péronne and that river. The battleground would be extended north by a part of the 'Mars' attack round Arras, and a diversionary attack would take place further south in the region of the Oise to hold back any threatened flank attack.

The available forces for the German offensive were divided more or less equally amongst three armies, each being given more than twenty divisions. To the north Otto von Below's Seventeenth Army was deployed from Arras to Cambrai: from there almost to St Quentin the line was manned by George von der Marwitz's Second Army, and the Eighteenth Army under Oskar von Hutier was to attack round, and to the south of St. Quentin. The two 'St.George' offensives were also planned in detail in case the triple blow of 'Michael' was not able to deliver the *coup de grâce*.

Finally, on 12 March, OHL (German Supreme Headquarters) issued the following order:-

> 'His Majesty the Kaiser commands . . .
> 'That the "Michael" attack shall commence on 21 March; the first wave of the attack at 9.40am.
> 'The first objective of Crown Prince Rupprecht's Army Group is to isolate the British salient at Cambrai and to occupy a line Croisilles-Bapaume- Péronne. If the right wing of the attack progresses favourably it is to push forward beyond Croisilles. The next objective will be an advance towards Arras and Albert, the left wing remaining at Péronne and the main weight on the right flank disrupting the British line. All divisions in the rear are to be brought forward in the event of success.
> 'The Group of Armies commanded by the German Crown Prince will, as its first objective, capture the Somme-Crozat canal south of the river Omignon. The crossings over both canal and river must be seized in a rapid advance. The group must be ready to extend its right flank to Péronne, and is to study the possibilities of reinforcing the left wing with divisions from the Seventh, First and Third Armies.'

Supreme Headquarters kept control of the 2nd Garde, 26th Württemberg and 12th Divisions, and ordered preparations for the complete 'Mars' offensive and for 'Archangel' (the diversionary attack by the Seventh Army on the Oise) to continue without interruption. Those forces would be brought into the action according to the way the main 'Michael' offensive developed.

Von der Schulenberg and von Hutier differed over the way 'Michael' ought to develop, but were overruled by Ludendorff. He kept unswervingly to his doctrine. The weakest point of the enemy line was either side of St. Quentin. There it was that the British must be smashed and driven in disarray back to the Channel coast while Hutier's Eighteenth Army formed the flank to hold back any possible French counter-attack. To this end the Army Groups of Max von Gallwitz and Duke Albrecht were also held under control of OHL in case a heavy attack should be made by the French or if more divisions were needed in the battle area.

Ludendorff's decision to attack around St. Quentin was well reasoned. The Allied sectors joined there. Once the French and British were divided, the next planned attack towards Hazebrouck – the main supply depot for the Ypres salient – would drive a wedge between the First and Second British Armies.

Facing von Hutier at St.Quentin was Gough's Fifth Army. British troops hated being assigned to it. Life-expectancy there was tenuous at the best; indeed, it suffered the heaviest losses of any British army during the entire war. Given its new name only a few months earlier (it had been known as the 'Reserve' Army during the Passchendaele campaign) and time after time used to spearhead attacks, Gough's force was little more than a hotch-potch of regulars, territorials, conscripts and 'Kitchener' volunteers which time after time had been sent 'over the top'. Its staff work at times was disastrous, and despite Gough's personal charm and wit, his contributions to the Somme battle in 1916, and in 1917 to the attack on Bullecourt (which cost the Australians and the West Riding Division a total of 6,000 men) as well as to the long agony of Passchendaele, hardly marked him as a commander on whom fortune smiled.

This time the Fifth Army was given the job of taking over a new sector because of the French demands and political pressure from London. Twelve divisions, weakened by the reorganisation because of the lack of reinforcements, therefore had to be spread out along a 65 kilometres line. Against them were ranged 43 German divisions with an artillery superiority of five German guns providing Bruchmüller's opening barrage to every two British guns that would try to answer it. It was little wonder that the Germans had supreme confidence that this, their 'Kaiserschlact' would end the war.

Because of their experiences during the German Cambrai counter-attacks, Allied military minds had been grappling with the problem of infiltration, and had adopted the 'defence in depth' system. Instead of the old rigidly held front line, with its backing of second, third, support and communication trenches, there were to be 'keeps' or 'forts' . . . strongpoints with mutually supporting fields of fire. Tanks, though having proved themselves in attack, were of little use in defence against infiltration tactics. They had not the speed and manoeuvrability to arrive quickly and deal with widespread incursions. Instead it was decided to station them to act as miniature fortresses capable of some tortoise-like progression if need be.

The new defence system used zones rather than lines. Within the

Forward Zone were defences designed to slow the enemy's advance and blunt his attack. Its defenders were to make a fighting withdrawal to the main Battle Zone four kilometres or so further back. There, once the initial fury of the assault had been soaked up, the enemy would be halted by the main body of defences and defenders. Behind again was a Reserve Zone where the medium and heavy batteries were placed along with the reserves who would drive the enemy back in a furious counter-attack.

As with previous innovations in tactics, from the time that Roman Generals tried to devise means of countering the elephant menace, there were arguments about this new system's effectiveness. Among the French commanders, Duchêne opposed it utterly, whereas Gouraud might possibly be persuaded to experiment. Gough's Fifth Army staff, operating it, made the mistake of placing most of their troops well to the front; the ideal position to receive the full blast of Bruchmüller's opening barrage.

All along the entire Fifth Army Front, but especially in the recently transferred sector from the Omignon to Barisis, the defences were in a sorry state. The Reserve Zone's intended position was marked by mere scratchings in the ground and, because of the devastation of the old Somme battlefield behind, the necessary supply routes of light railways and roads were either rudimentary or lacking altogether.

There was little doubt, from the massing of German troops opposite, where the blow was going to fall. What was unsure was *when . . .*

Winston Churchill, at Montreuil-sur-Mer headquarters on 19 March to discuss the matter of tank supply for 1919, was taken by Sir Douglas into the map room and shown where the enemy was massed in strength. Not only were 110 German divisions ranged against 57 British – 40 of them against the Fifth Army – but the enemy was present in sufficient numbers to suggest another offensive further north in the Ypres-Messines sector. An artillery map indicated areas drenched by mustard gas to prevent manoeuvre, and so, by inference, showed where enemy attacks could be expected.

The French, too, were worried about the approaching fire-storm, but as Haig pointed out, the weight of attacking troops was four times heavier against his men than against Pétain's further south on the Aisne.

He complained about being obliged to take over over the additional front to Barisis, and that he was now under pressure to provide more troops for the general reserve. Because Lloyd George had kept back reinforcements, he even lacked enough men to supply his own GHQ and Sectional reserves. In reply to Churchill's comment that the entire general reserve would be his if the main blow fell on the British, he said that the former arrangement of some seven or eight reserve divisions held at a mid-point, ready to move south or north according to the thrust of an attack, had been far better.

From there Churchill went on to visit his old Division, the 9th, at the very apex of the salient. The period of waiting for the German offensive to begin was beginning to fray the nerves.

'We received a hearty welcome when we arrived after dark upon a tranquil front lit rarely by a gun flash. 'When do you think it will come?' we asked. 'Perhaps tomorrow morning. Perhaps the day after. Perhaps the week after.' We spent the whole of the next day in the trenches. A deathly and suspicious silence brooded over the front. For hours not a cannon shot was fired. Yet the sunlit fields were instinct with foreboding. We examined every part of the defences from Gauche Wood, held by the gallant South Africans, to the medium artillery positions on the slopes behind Havrincourt village. Certainly nothing that human thought and effort could accomplish had been neglected. For four miles in depth the front was a labyrinth of wire and scientifically sited machine gun nests. The troops, though thin on the ground, were disposed so as to secure full value from every man . . . The sun was setting as we left Gauche Wood and took our leave of the South Africans. I see them now, serene as the Spartans of Leonidas on the eve of Thermopylae.'

CHAPTER 6

'MICHAEL' 21 MARCH, 1918.

– Gough's Army devastated – American help offered – Pétain
prepares to pull back – the Doullens meeting – 'Michael' falters –
'Mars' delayed – questions in the House –

'If the English had any apprehension, they would run away.'
(Shakespeare)

At twenty minutes to five on the morning of that cold first day of Spring
1918, Bruchmüller's barrage opened up with a crash that shook the
whole 50 kilometre front. Gough's Fifth Army was mainly on
the receiving end, but Byng's Third was affected as well. Feint
bombardments were put down on other parts of the line to spread
confusion as to where the main attack would fall.

Before focussing their attention on the British forward positions, the
German guns first isolated them by laying down a concentration of high
explosive and gas that destroyed communications, prevented movement and fell on the artillery and control centres in the rear. After two
hours of this treatment, the forward positions were deluged by the
barrage. Mortar and artillery fire pulverised trenches and barbed-wire
along with many of the defenders, and before long some sectors
of Gough's Forward Zone were in little shape to offer any effective
resistance.

Observers described it as probably the heaviest barrage of the war,
indeed of any war up to that time. British guns firing back could
only be heard by people standing within a few paces of them, and the
constant flash and flame of explosions lighting up and colouring
the fog that lay across the front merged with the even more brilliant
flashes from exploding British fuel and ammunition dumps in the
rear.

By daybreak the battlefield was covered in a thick pall of gas and
smoke from the barrage with the addition of more dense smoke rising
from burning supplies. All this, combining with the ground level fog,
allowed the German storm troopers to cross no-man's-land without
being seen by British machine-gunners. The conditions also made it
almost impossible for any artillery still capable of firing back to
support the front line troops; not only were the guns out of touch
because of severed telephone lines, but artillery observers could not

28

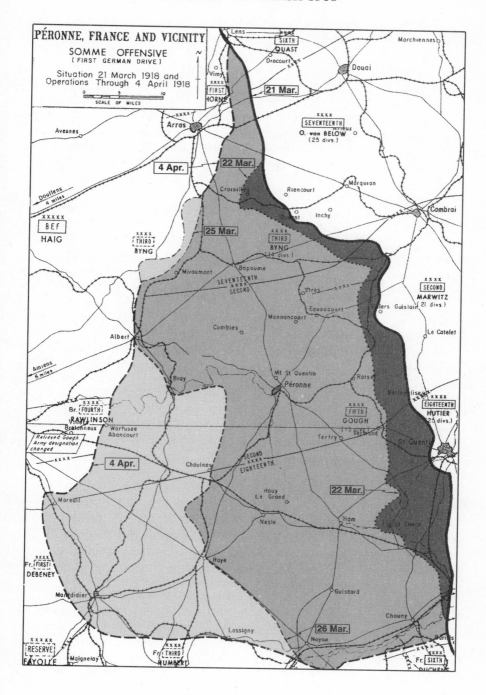

Figure 1

29

pinpoint the position of SOS rockets. Also it was practically impossible for the Royal Flying Corps' observation machines to take off.

The barrage, the lack of visibility, a weak defence and a German advantage of at least three to one, conspired to produce an almost immediate breakthrough on parts of the line held by the 21st and 24th Divisions, the 16th (Irish) and 66th (East Lancs). Some pockets of resistance fought on. Some, like one near Heudicourt where units from three separate German regiments were held back by a single company of Royal Scots, lasted until late the following day, but by evening of the 21st the German advance, particularly to the south-west of St Quentin, had forced Gough to prepare for a general retreat behind the Crozat canal.

Losses on both sides were enormous. Apart from killed, wounded and missing, the long lines of British prisoners (about 21,000 of them that day) were recorded on film as a morale-booster for the German home front. Many German casualties were caused by the Royal Flying Corps, taking to the air as soon as visibility improved around midday, wreaking havoc on the columns of advancing infantry in low-flying attacks.

As soon as news broke at his US Headquarters in Chaumont, Pershing went by way of Paris in search of General Foch. After a long hunt, he was discovered, along with Pétain and Clémenceau, in the kitchen of a farmhouse near Clermont-sur-Oise. Pershing asked to have a private word, then said – in atrocious French – that he would not fight on less than a divisional front, but would fight with all he had. Foch agreed to this, and sat down to write a press-release that changed Pershing from a man lacking any degree of skill in the French language into a polished orator. 'I come to tell you,' the official communiqué credited Pershing as saying, 'that the American people will esteem it a great honour that our troops should take part in the present battle. I ask it in my name, and theirs. There is at the moment no other question but that of fighting. Infantry, artillery, aviation, all that we have is yours. Dispose of it as you wish. Our forces will soon come, as numerous as is necessary. The American people will be proud to take part in the greatest and finest battle in history.'

When he heard about this, Clémenceau was furious. Like Pétain, he had hoped to use the American troops as reinforcements for French units. Foch and he continued to wrangle for the remainder of the war – even after it – over the way US forces should be, or should have been used.

Foch had another American visitor the following day; this time, General Bliss, US representative to the Supreme Allied Council, who, like the commander in the Tommies' parody of 'Onward Christian Soldiers' was 'safely in the rear', The General said grandly, 'Well, we came over here to get killed! Where do you want us?'

'All Pershing had' turned out to be the Divisions he considered battle-worthy – four of them – the 1st, 26th, 2nd and 42nd, listed according to their length of training. Even though an American division was twice the size of a British or a French, it was still so relatively small a force that, at Pétain's suggestion, Foch didn't mention it when he was promoted a few days later. Pershing, seeing that as yet another attempt to use his troops piecemeal, descended on Foch's Headquarters in a rage and insisted the battle order was altered to include the Americans.

The 'Michael' battle continued without pause. By the end of its second day, even faced by a continuous flow of German reinforcements, Byng's Third Army was still fighting within its designated Battle Zone, but about half of Gough's force had been driven behind what should have been its last defence line. Even if a front of sorts was established, more retreats had to be made as the flanks, outmanoeuvred, were forced to pull back. In spite of orders to hold Péronne and the river line south of the town, by nightfall of the 22nd Gough's Army was back across the Somme. Some bridges were not blown, and the Germans made particularly good use of one at Pithon on the outskirts of Ham to bring up their artillery, while their troops forded the river there, and now a gap was starting to open not only between Gough's and Byng's Armies, but between the British and French forces.

Because of the speed of the German advance, Pétain's and Haig's agreement to provide mutual help saw only a solitary French division from Humbert's Army arrive behind the British right flank on the 22nd, but coming from further north and from the rear were other reinforcements: hastily-moved British and Commonwealth divisions; more units cobbled together from bandsmen, clerks, cooks . . . indeed any man capable of firing a rifle. The Cavalry Corps, its long held aim of exploiting a breakthrough still a dream, found itself at last taking part in one organised by the German High Command, and being used as 'flying squads' to plug the gaps.

The British line retreated across the devastation of the old Somme battlefield for five whole days. 'If one had any doubt about the seriousness of the situation' (the commander of a battalion moving to stem the tide said later) 'they were soon settled. The whole area was a mass of guns of all types, limbers, ambulances, ammunition and transport . . . and moving at the rear, limping and worn-out men – many of them wounded – of the 41st, 19th, 25th, 42nd and 51st Divisions seeking their units. Too tired from heavy fighting and lack of sleep to have any idea of what was happening at the front – no news – no orders – and yet no panic!'

After a brief period of rest, some of those units turned again to face the enemy. Arthur Behrend, a captain in the Heavy Artillery, saw men of the 51st Division go past on the third day of the battle.

'I shivered with pride as I stood there watching those grim Highlanders swing by – every man in step, every man resolute. Could these be the weary, dirty men who came limping past yesterday in ragged twos and threes, asking pitifully how much further to Achiet-le-Grand?'

Sometimes help arrived fortuitously. General Sir Walter Braithwaite wrote: 'I was in a hut in Fonquevillers when an enormous figure appeared in the doorway carrying an alpenstock about seven feet high. His question to me was 'Have you any use for the hundred best machine gunners in the world?' My reply was 'Have I not?!!!'

(The man with the alpenstock was 'Tiny' Ironside, commander of the machine-gun school in France, and future Chief of Staff during the Dunkirk evacuation in World War Two; either he was lost, or the troops he was to have supported had moved. The machine-gunners' arrival was a godsend to the 62nd Division's defence of Pusieux and Rossignol Wood in the later stages of the battle.)

On the 23rd more French troops began to arrive south of the battle-front. The solitary division provided by Pétain the previous evening came into action; another, this time of dismounted cavalry, arrived at the end of the day.

By the 24th four more French divisions brought by lorry arrived, but arrived so hurriedly that two had no artillery and in all four the infantry were short of cartridges. The enemy advance was so speedy that it was impossible to form a line, and the French lost ground even more quickly than the British. By evening the Germans had advanced 24 kilometres, making their quickest gain of territory since 1914.

Gough's Fifth Army was in disarray; the Third further north in danger; and now the French reinforcements were being driven back. Pétain, making a late evening visit to Haig's Headquarters at Dury near Amiens, and worried that Haig was more concerned with protecting the Channel ports than with keeping contact between his, and the French Army, insisted this was not the main attack. It was a feint. The real offensive was about to fall on his French troops further south. In spite of Haig's pleas for more divisions to be sent towards Amiens, Pétain felt neither able nor prepared to offer further help. In fact, it became clear from from the way the French forces were regrouping, and from what Pétain said, that instructions had already been given to Fayolle to pull back his Army Group and guard Paris if the French and British forces became separated. When Haig asked if this was so, Pétain merely nodded.

At that, Haig's previous resistance to the appointment of a Supreme Commander immediately vanished. He telegraphed London, asking for Wilson, Chief of the Imperial General Staff, and Lord Milner, Secretary of State for War, to come immediately and tell the French Government that unless some really determined commander were given overall control there would be a disaster. Both, realising the seriousness of the situation, had already left.

Within a day and a half of arriving in France, Milner had finished his discussions with Haig's Chief of Staff, gone to Paris, collected Poincaré, Clémenceau and Foch, driven with them to Compiègne where they grilled Pétain about his plans. Then, bringing Pétain in tow, Milner arrived with them all at Doullens on the 26th to meet Haig and Sir Henry Wilson for a midday conference in the Hôtel de Ville.

Foch, as his Government's Military Adviser, had already produced a joint report with Loucheur, Minister of Munitions, making the case for a Supreme Command, and reinforced his view in a personal memorandum to Clémenceau on the 24th, urging on him the necessity 'to appoint one capable of directing the war – capable of giving orders and seeing they were executed'. The previous month at a meeting in London Clémenceau had told his Military Adviser to be quiet: he, not Foch, represented France. A mere week before the German attack, Foch had been described as a dotard. Now he was named as the man to meet the crisis. Clémenceau had doubts. What could Foch do, he had asked, that the others couldn't?

'Oh,' Foch had replied, 'I'd use my old methods... put a patch here... another there, and a third over there. Soon the German advance slows. Then we stop them.'

Clémenceau was impressed. 'Quel bougie!' he remarked to Loucheur.

So, while the 25th was spent in meetings between the various politicians and their advisers, it was only when they all were able to meet at Doullens next day that a decision was finally reached. At the Conference there, Pétain, ('looking,' Foch whispered wickedly to his next-door neighbour, 'like a man preparing himself for defeat') told the French President that he expected the British to be annihilated. This defeatism succeeded in stiffening the resolve to appoint a Supreme Commander. Milner, briefed by Lloyd George, anxious to see the French in charge, was delighted when he realised Haig had Foch in mind.

Foch spoke. The need was, he said, to preserve contact between the Allied Armies and to defend Amiens. The British had no more reserves south of the Somme. At this, Pétain muttered something about the French making 'a gradual relief', but he 'would not hide the fact that any units would take some time to arrive on the scene.'

Then Haig spoke.

'If General Foch will give me his advice, I will gladly follow it.'

That settled the matter. After some discussion between Milner and Clémenceau it was agreed ' General Foch is charged by the British and French Governments with the co-ordination of of the British and French Armies around Amiens. He will therefore come to an understanding with the two Commanders in Chief who are to furnish him with all necessary information.' This, after representations from Haig, and from Foch himself, found 'the British and French Armies' altered to 'the Allied Armies', and 'around Amiens' replaced by 'on the Western Front'.

Even though Foch was limited by words such as 'co-ordination', and phrases such as 'come to an understanding', the Allies were at last on the way to appointing a Supreme Commander. The mood of depression changed to optimism. Clémenceau, leaving the Hôtel de Ville, remarked that 'it was in effect a victory over the Germans.' 'It was certainly,' his aide remarked drily, 'a victory over the British.' With the exception of Haig (who, according to his diary 'lunched from a sandwich box') they all then moved to a nearby hotel. Over the meal, when Clémenceau remarked rather provocatively, 'Well, Foch, you got what you wanted!' Foch replied that to take over a battle as good as lost was hardly the recipe to fulfil an ambition.

Even as lunch was served, he was considering his plans. Situation reports hinted that the offensive against the British was starting to lose momentum. The enemy was having difficulties in bringing supplies through the wasteland of the old Somme battlefield. By now attackers and defenders were equally weary, and, as the normally well-disciplined Germans, after years of shortages and poor rations, found themselves in an Aladdin's cave of British supply dumps, the advance slowed, or as in Albert, stopped altogether.

A distraught German officer described the scene.

> 'When I came into the town . . . there were men driving cows before them . . . men carrying a bottle of wine under their arm and another one open in their hand . . . men with top hats on their heads . . . men staggering . . . men who could hardly walk . . . the streets were running with wine. Out of a cellar came a lieutenant of the Marine Division in despair. "I cannot," he said, "get my men out of there without bloodshed . . .".'

In spite of threats, and appeals to patriotism and duty, officers were unable to force men made incapable by alcohol, and indulgence in the delights of unlimited food and plunder, to continue the advance.

British resistance was now stiffening. Labour battalions, transport drivers and railway staff from the rear were formed into units that showed surprising tenacity. Outside Amiens one such ad hoc formation, with exceptional bravery, halted the advance.

Foch sent out a flow of instructions. The Allied forces were to keep in close touch; the Amiens line was to be held, forces in contact with the enemy were to hold their positions at all costs, and French reinforcements were to mass behind the British Fifth Army, consolidate the front and supply a reserve that could be committed as needed. Next he went to Gough's Headquarters at Dury, where, by all accounts, Gough had a most uncomfortable time. However, alongside all the shouting, arm-waving (Foch, although he always denied it, was well known for the habit even in his calmer moments), recriminations and counter-recriminations, was the promise that the Fifth Army's embattled troops would be relieved . Barthélemy, Fayolle's Chief of Staff – also by chance at Dury – was given instructions for his Army Commander, and the same instructions were sent to Debeney, whose First Army on the British right, was ordered to relieve General Maxse's British XVIII Corps.

Pétain, seeing which way the wind was blowing, cancelled his order of 24 March to Fayolle and sent ten French divisions, with artillery, north to Amiens.

At the end of the day the Supreme Allied Commander arrived in Paris at his flat on the Avenue de Saxe exhausted. Mme. Foch, when she heard what had happened, expressed her worries about the size of her husband's new task.

'Just pray to God,' Foch told her simply, 'that we are not too late!'

The following day saw the northern part of 'Michael' attacks start to falter. There was still fierce fighting round Bucquoy, near the old 1916 battlefields of Serre and Hebuterne, but Byng's Third Army Headquarters told Foch when he visited that day that the German advance above the Somme had almost run its course. Foch also went to see Humbert, the French Third Army commander on Debeney's right, then came back for visits to Fayolle at Clermont and on to Gough at Dury, where the situation was far less hopeful.

At Clermont, in fact, it was near to disaster. The Germans, under von Hutier, finding the weak spot between the French First and Third armies, had forced their way through, and 27 March saw them reach the town of Montdidier west of the road between Amiens and Roye, cutting one of the two main railways from Amiens to Paris. That, however, marked the limit of Hutier's Eighteenth Army advance, mainly because Ludendorff, reinforcing the northern sector, planned to destroy the British north of the point where the French and British Armies joined, rather than send his reserves further south to force back the French.

According to the German timetable, the 'Mars' attack against Arras and Vimy should have joined the 'Michael' offensives on 23 March. Because of General Byng's order to withdraw secretly some seven kilometres to new defence lines, the German bombardment fell on the abandoned positions and it took four days before the artillery could be brought forward again. This delay meant that as early as the 23rd, Ludendorff's aim of rolling up the line and driving the British Army into the sea had to be modified. The two offensives had not locked together, 'Mars' would strike as the main 'Michael' offensives were running out of steam. Because of the delay, the order sent out from Headquarters at noon that day was to exploit the gains made further south '. . . the main section of the British Army now having been defeated, our objective is the separation of the French and British by means of a speedy advance either side of the Somme.'

'Mars' at last came into operation on the 28th, but this time it was a different story. The weather was clear, the defence ready, and British artillery and machine-gun units inflicted horrendous casualties on the attackers. Most of the Forward Zone was held; the Battle Zone was not seriously affected and in the Reserve Zone the troops stood waiting for an order that never came. Twenty attacking German divisions were decimated by eight divisions defending a 30 kilometre front.

Up to 28 March the British had suffered the brunt of the action, but now Foch, whose remit included 'the strategic direction of military operations', was bringing more French divisions into the battle. Setting up his headquarters in a couple of rooms at the Town Hall in Beauvais, he was beginning to realise that the Doullens conference not only presented him with a great opportunity; its terms of reference were also limiting his ability to act decisively. Allied resistance might well be increasing, as were German problems of supply and reinforcement, but Foch needed to command rather than persuade.

Two days later, the Eighteenth German Army mounted an attack between Noyon and Montdidier, and on 4 April their Second Army advanced against Amiens. 'Both these actions,' Ludendorff admitted, 'were inconclusive. The enemy resistance was too strong . . . '.

The battle was broken off on 4 April without either of of Ludendorff's main aims being achieved. By that time, however, Foch's single aim had been fulfilled. Clémenceau had invited Lloyd George and Wilson, Pétain, Pershing and Bliss, to meet at Beauvais on 3 April, and there, in spite of Wilson's objections, Foch, although still not given the title of 'Supreme Commander,' was charged with 'strategic direction' of military operations; the only caveat being that each Commander in Chief would have the right to appeal to his Government if he thought his army placed in danger by any order received from General Foch. This, The Beauvais Agreement, effectively matched two Supreme Commanders, Foch and Ludendorff, directly against each other.

On a map, the German offensives appeared to have been successful. A huge salient starting south of Lens, ran down in front of Arras, taking in Miraumont, Albert, Lamotte-Warfusée, Moreuil and Montdidier before moving back east through Lassigny and along the Oise below Noyon back to Barisis: but a salient – even a large one – is not the best place to be with enemy heavy artillery on three sides. This salient had won very little apart from ground, and what ground! Crumbling trenches, devastated villages, wrecked woods, rusting barbed-wire, a sea of shell-craters and, overall, the unpleasant detritus of war.

'We had not gained,' Ludendorff admitted, 'the strategic advantage we hoped.'

On their way to not gaining it, the Germans had lost even more heavily than the Allies, certainly in men and in material (of which more was used than was captured), but above all, they had lost time; the time that was needed to bring them victory while they still had superiority.

Across the Channel, as realisation of the scale of the retreat sank in, and casualty lists began to be printed, there was uproar in Parliament. General Maurice (Director of Military Operations at the War Office) furious at the way reinforcements had been held back, accused Lloyd George in a letter to 'The Times' of deceiving the Commons when he stated the facts of the case. Asquith took up the issue and the matter was debated in the House. Lloyd George's oratory succeeded in convincing Parliament that his statement had been formed on information supplied by General Maurice's deputy, and he survived as Prime Minister, but political aftershocks continued for a very long time.

Lieutenant General Sir Hubert de la Poer Gough, the scapegoat of the affair, never held another command. Lloyd George and Haig, in their struggle to be in charge of directing the war, between them came very near to losing it in March 1918.

CHAPTER 7

'GEORGETTE'

– Allied gains in Flanders reversed –

'What though the field be lost?
All is not lost: th' unconquerable will
And study of revenge, immortal hate,
And courage never to submit or yield.
And what is else not to be overcome?'

(John Milton)

As the 'Michael' and 'Mars' offensives started to lose momentum, Ludendorff looked to 'George I' and 'George II' to make the break-through. He realised that if he timed his attacks carefully, Haig, having started to move his few reserves to meet the first onslaught, would be in severe straits when the second blow fell a matter of hours later. As a result, 'George I and II' were combined to form a kind of scaled-down 'George the Third', codenamed 'Georgette'.

Downing Street's policy of denying sufficient reinforcements, together with the facts that Bruchmüller's artillery was still intact and the German Army still enjoyed numerical superiority, convinced Ludendorff more than ever that defeating the British Army was the key to victory, and he started to move his forces northwards to the Lys valley below Ypres.

Haig had placed the main part of his limited forces along a line from Arras to Givenchy, so that the industrial area and coalmines round Lens could be defended. Also the heights of Vimy Ridge and Notre Dame de Lorette formed natural strongpoints. Further north the line had to be held more thinly; even more thinly than Gough's Fifth Army front had been manned at the start of the 'Michael' attacks. Above Armentières, the river Lys formed the boundary between Horne's First, and Plumer's Second Armies.

Through the last days of March and the first few days of April, Foch had been planning to launch a two-pronged offensive on 12 April that would push the Germans back from Amiens and free the main Paris railway line from bombardment. 'It would', his directive read, 'be to the greatest advantage if these two offensives could be carried out simulta-neously. The Commanders in Chief are requested to notify the earliest

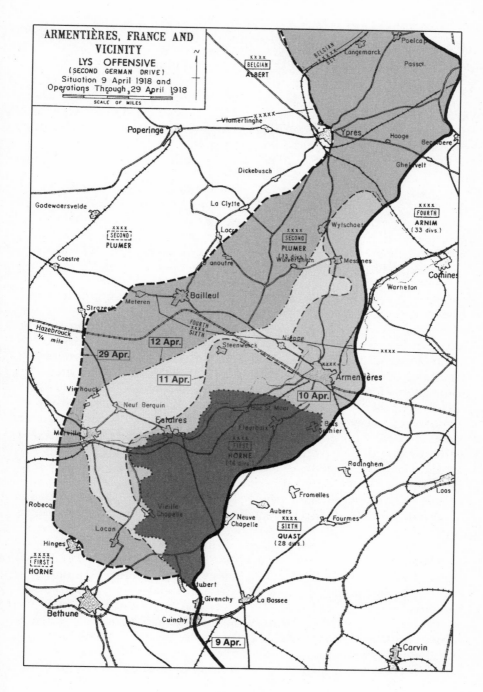

Figure 2

39

date they judge possible to start these operations.' His plans were pre-empted by the 'Georgette' offensive. Its initial objective was to take the Hazebrouck supply centre then push on to the coast. The attack started early on Tuesday 9 April.

Right at its centre was the 2nd Portuguese Division, counting its last hours of a front-line spell. Descriptions of the Portuguese have varied from 'the brave Portuguese' to 'generally recognised as being the worst troops on the Western Front'. The British rank and file, amused by their unsoldierly appearance and rickety transport, knew them as 'the geese', or more often as 'the Pork and Beans' until authority issued instructions the term was not to be used.

In the face of the Sixth Army's massed attack directed by von Quast, the Portuguese broke, leaving the 40th and 55th British Divisions on their flanks to make shift as best they could. According to the rumour that spread throughout the British Army, the sight of their blue grey-uniforms and yellow boots disappearing into the distance so maddened the troops left in danger, that machine guns were moved to the rear parapets and turned on the fleeing rabble. The 40th Division, its position made completely untenable, was quickly over-come.

Once again thick mist hampered machine-guns defending the rear, and two hours from the start of the attack German infantry were again pouring through a gap in the defence. Somehow or other the gap was plugged, and some very surprised bandsmen making their way forward to head a victorious German parade into Bethune found themselves taken prisoner. The following day, however, von Quast made more progress against depleted British units brought from the Somme to regroup in what had been presumed a quiet area, and that day also saw the second phase of the attack mounted by Sixt von Arnim's Fourth Army (four new divisions bringing its strength to a total of thirty-one) extending the assault from Armentières to the Ypres-Comines canal. There the British line was manned by elements of the 19th and 25th Divisions with only one brigade of the 29th in reserve. Ludendorff's assumption that Haig's reserves would have been rushed to the rescue of the Armentières to La Bassée sector proved correct.

Eventually Plumer's Second Army, much to the fury of Foch who counted every kilometre of mud lost as a personal insult, had to retreat beyond Wytschaete and Messines, taken at such cost the previous year. By 12 April a united front formed by the German armies had made a breach 48 kilometres wide, and they were only 8 kilometres from Hazebrouck. No more British reserves were available. There was no possibility of retreat. The normally dour, uncommunicative Haig issued his order of the day.

TO ALL RANKS OF THE BRITISH ARMY IN FRANCE AND FLANDERS

Three weeks ago today the enemy began his terrific attacks against us on a fifty-mile front. His objects are to separate us from the French, to take the Channel Ports and destroy the British Army.

In spite of throwing already 106 Divisions into the battle and enduring the most reckless sacrifice of human life, he has as yet made little progress towards his goals.

We owe this to the determined fighting and self-sacrifice of our troops. Words fail me to express the admiration which I feel for the splendid resistance offered by all ranks of our Army under the most trying circumstances.

Many amongst us now are tired. To those I would say that Victory will belong to the side which holds out the longest. The French Army is moving rapidly and in great force to our support.

There is no course open to us but to fight it out. Every position must be held to the last man: there must be no retirement. With our backs to the wall and believing in the justice of our cause each one of us must fight on to the end. The safety of our homes and the freedom of mankind alike depend upon the conduct of each one of us at this critical moment.

D. Haig. F.M.
Commander in Chief
British Armies in France

General Headquarters,
Thursday April 18th, 1918.

Haig also appealed to Foch to relieve pressure on his troops either by starting a French attack, or by sending reserves to the St. Pol area as reinforcements, but, according to Sir Henry Wilson, 'Foch would not hear of relieving us either up at Ypres, or opposite Amiens. He simply would not hear of it!' Foch, of course, was in a dilemma. Whilst realising the British were in difficulty, though underestimating its severity, his first concern was to set up a defence able to cope whatever happened, and to do that he had to keep firm control of the reserves.

He met Haig on the 14th, told him that in his opinion 'la bataille du Nord' was dying down, and it was essential the reserves should be held back to guard against the renewal of the German offensive against Amiens and Montdidier, which he expected daily. Could not the nine or ten British divisions reduced to cadre strength be reformed? When the situation permitted, a rota would be organised for battle-weary British divisions to lick their wounds in a quiet area on the French sector. In the meantime he had confidence in British ability to contain the attack, rather than risk a collapse of the front by promising relief.

That very day, when the British seemed at the end of their tether, a message arrived at Paris, to the delight of Clémenceau, approving Foch be given powers appropriate to carrying out his task. The British Government 'saw no objection' to his being given the title of Commander in Chief of the Allied Armies in France.

Although the new Supreme Commander might have been correct in expressing confidence that the British would resist, his assessment that 'la bataille du Nord' was dying down was incorrect. An ill-tempered meeting was taking place between Haig and Foch that day at Abbeville, Foch refusing point-blank to carry out any relief while the battle was in progress. This strengthened suspicions in the British War Office, among the exhausted troops struggling against bomb, bullet and bayonet, and particularly at Haig's Headquarters, that the French were preparing to fight to the last drop of British blood. 'Ce n'est pas bon du tout!' Haig asserted in reply to Foch's assertions, and threatened to invoke the new Beauvais Agreement.

In the French camp, a certain feeling of smug superiority was rife. British troops were obviously inferior to their Commonwealth counterparts, and even more so to the 'Enfants de France'. Opinions like those of Henri Desagneaux – a Captain in the 359th Infantry Regiment – were commonly held, and even more commonly voiced.

> 'The inhabitants are glad to see the French again. They have no confidence in the English any more. During the last Boche attack they lost 25 kilometres in the first day. Regiments at Amiens threw down their weapons and fled with the civilians. People have nothing but praise for the Canadians, Australians and Hindus . . . it was they who stopped the enemy advance . . .'

In the event, Foch, brought up short by Haig's threat, began to realise the danger in Flanders was greater than he had estimated, and by 16 April had gone north to assess the situation at first hand. Although he still refused Haig's request to flood the area from Aire through St. Omer to the coast, because it would mean the loss of the port of Dunkirk, he asked the Belgians to relieve part of the British line round Ypres, and did send some French troops towards Hazebrouck and a detachment from his 'Army of the North' to take over the front round Mount Kemmel, but gave orders for them not to be in too much of a hurry to come to the rescue. They arrived on 18 April, the final day of the Lys offensive.

Ludendorff, still with hopes of a breakthrough, next mounted an attack between Villers-Bretonneux and the river Luce on the 24th, and against the Flanders hills dominated by Mount Kemmel and Scherpenberg hill on 25 April. The French 28th Division (part of Foch's relief detachment) held the slopes of both those important positions in Flanders, but after suffering a ferocious gas bombardment and throwing back

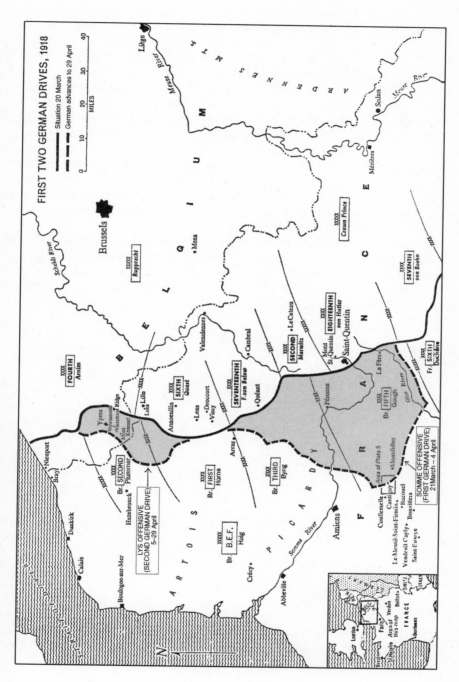

Figure 3

43

three separate infantry assaults, the troops defending Kemmel broke, leaving those on its summit and a British unit on the left to be surrounded and overcome. It was again something that did little to sweeten relationships between the Armies, and there was much discussion as to what should be done if the German attacks were to continue. Was it, Sir Henry Wilson asked, more important for Haig to guard the Channel Ports, or maintain a firm front with the French?

Foch was emphatic that he 'would let nothing go'; neither Paris nor the Channel Ports. 'Ask me the question when I am beaten, not before!' he said.

Fortunately the capture of Kemmel was the last German success, in spite of a serious 'false alarm' on the 28th that the hill line behind Kemmel had been lost. Ludendorff failed to follow up the advantage. Taking the advice of his Fourth Army staff that there was no chance of more gains with the forces available, he called a halt, and issued orders to prepare against expected counter-attacks.

The offensive had definitely run its course. But, as one weary Tommy exclaimed on seeing a group of pathetically young Germans in over-sized uniforms being hustled to the rear, 'Blimey, look what's been pushing our Army about!'

CHAPTER 8

THE CHEMIN DES DAMES BREAKTHROUGH

–'Blücher' – 27 May 1918– the Allies wrong-footed – Duchêne ignores warnings – an American success at Cantigny, but disaster on the Chemin – the Germans reach Château-Thierry – the struggle at Belleau–

'This narrow elongated plateau between the valleys of the Aisne and Ailette derives its name from the road constructed there by order of King Louis XV to give his daughters pleasant views as they travelled to visit a friend in the area . . .' (Tourist guide. c. 1900)

*   *   *

'Blücher – Gebhard Leberecht von – (1742 – 1819) Prussian soldier: led the Prussian Army at the battle of Waterloo.' (Oxford Dictionary)

Ludendorff admitted in his war memoirs that once the intensive offensives of March and April had failed to achieve a breakthrough, he and his colleagues faced 'a most perplexing problem'. The supply of reserves was beginning to dry up, causing him worries, but he still held stubbornly to his purpose of breaking the British, and breaking them round Ypres and Bailleul where there was the greatest chance of exploiting success.

'The enemy's attention,' he went on to argue, 'had first to be drawn to some other sector to force his reserves to move away from Flanders before Rupprecht's final devastating blow there could be delivered.' As a result, by mid-April the German Crown Prince's Army Group north of the Aisne and Vesle was told to prepare, maintaining the utmost secrecy, 'Blücher', the codename for an offensive with supporting attacks to either side, against the Chemin des Dames' ridge.

This meant four more valuable weeks had to go by while the supplies were gathered and the troops made ready, and all the time during those weeks the enemy strength was building constantly, but if the delay produced an ultimate victory further north for the Bavarian Crown Prince's Army Group, the risk was worthwhile.

At his headquarters, Foch, too, was refining plans with his 'famille militaire'. He expected Ludendorff to take up the offensive again where it had almost succeeded – at the point where the French and British sectors met, or for him to make another assault further north in Flanders. Foch organised his reserves, but needed sufficient of them to anticipate the expected German attack by making one of his own if possible. If he had enough strength for that, there would certainly be more than enough to throw back the Germans if their attack came first. Could he gather enough men together? The near disasters of March and April had seen Britain hurry 140,000 soldiers across the channel, but it would be some time before Haig's Army was fully recovered. Indeed, the lack of manpower in April had forced him to disband four more divisions, parcelling them out to help make good battle losses and lack of replacements from the beginning of the year . Foch's protests at these further reductions increased suspicions and added fuel to British grievances about the tardy arrival of French help during their weeks of trial, and their resentment over comments in the French Press about supposed British inadequacies. Indeed, even that Francophile, Sir Henry Wilson, wrote in his diary that 'The French mean to take us over body and soul . . . Numberless signs of increasing interference.'

This search for reserves found Foch locking horns with Pershing as well. The Supreme War Council, with the approval of President Wilson, had resolved that during the emergency American infantry and machine-gun units could be attached on a temporary basis to French and British divisions. Pershing, seeing this agreement as yet another plot to divide up his forces, dug in his heels. His task, apart from honouring his previous agreement that the infantry of six divisions was to be trained by the British, remained the same. He would continue to build all-American divisions, and use them to form an all-American army. Even when confronted by all three Prime Ministers during the War Council meeting at Abbeville on 1 May, he would not be moved, expressing his views vehemently, frequently banging the table with his fist.

Foch, thinking like Haig that Ludendorff would make another attempt to break the British front round Amiens or Bailleul, moved his available reserves north, leaving the more southerly sectors of the French Front more lightly held, and with few reserves. Pétain, apprehensive as ever about the safety of Paris, argued against the move and tried to hold back the last few units. He was overruled both by Foch and Clémenceau, the latter expressing a firm intention to 'fight *in front of* Paris . . . to fight *in* Paris . . . to fight *behind* Paris, if needed.' So as Foch's forces gathered round Amiens, Ludendorff's storm troops were secretly moving south towards the Aisne, where those British divisions scarred in the March and April battles had been sent to rest and absorb replacements. It was a quiet sector used by the French to refit their own troops, and the British IXth Army Corps, (21st, 50th, 8th and 25th Divisions), found itself holding the line above the Chemin des Dames on the right of four French divisions.

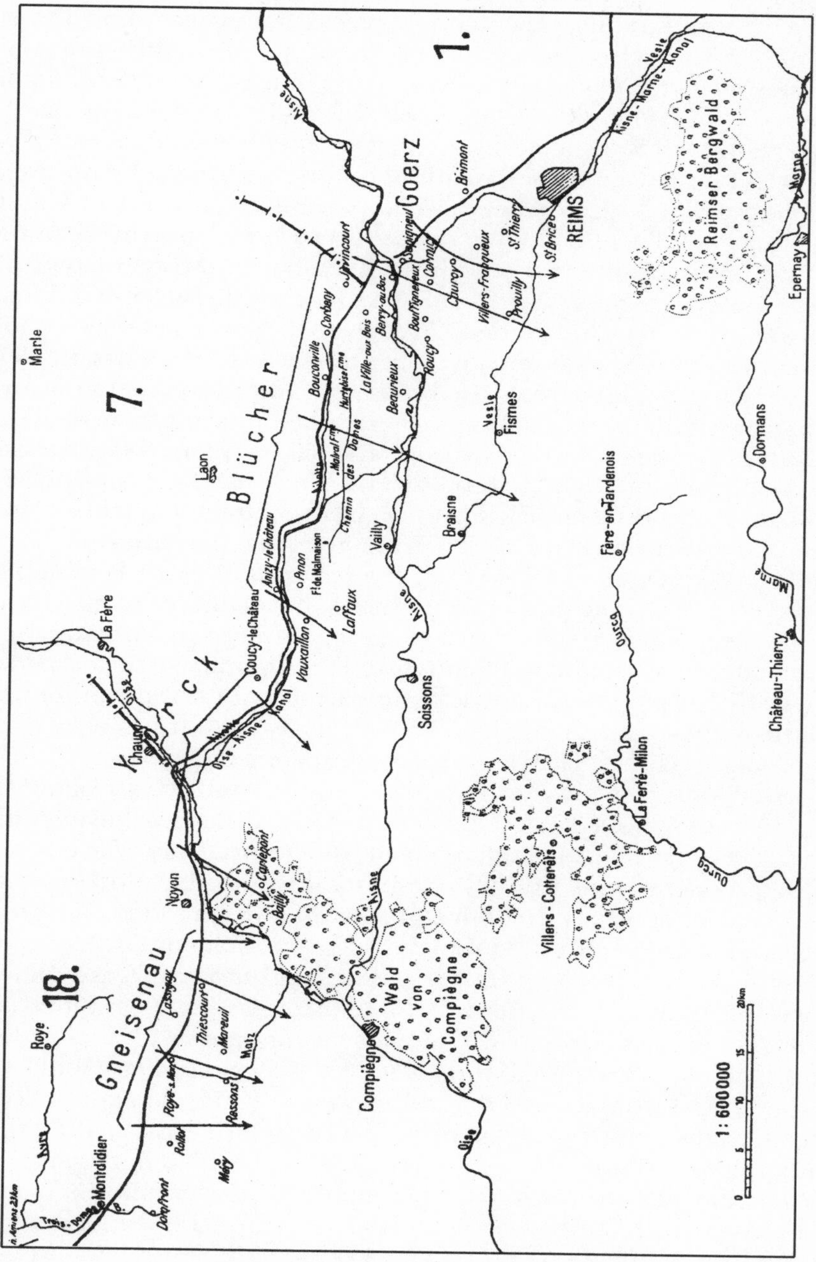
1.
7.
18.
Blücher
Goerz
Gneisenau
Marle
Laon
La Fère
Chauny
Noyon
Roye
Montdidier
Coucy-le Château
Anizy-le Château
Vauxaillon
Laffaux
Soissons
Vailly
Braisne
Fismes
Beaurieux
Corbeny
Bouconville
Juvincourt
Brimont
REIMS
St. Brice
St. Thierry
Prouilly
Villers-Franqueux
Cormicy
Roucy
Berry-au-Bac
Reimser Bergwald
Epernay
Dormans
Fère-en-Tardenois
Château-Thierry
La Ferté-Milon
Villers-Cotterêts
Wald von Compiègne
Compiègne
Thiescourt
Mareuil
Ressons
Lassigny
Roye-s.-Matz
Rollot
Mery
Dompierre
Matz
Bailly
Carlepont
Aisne
Vesle
Marne
Ourcq
Oise
Avre
Oise-Aisne-Kanal
Aisne-Marne-Kanal
Chemin des Dames
Malval Fme.
Hurtebise Fme.
Ft. de Malmaison
Anon
1: 600000
0 5 10 15 20km

Figure 4

Conditions there could not have been more different for them. The Champagne countryside, now in full May leaf, had seen little of war for some months, and after the traumas of March and April further north, it must have seemed like paradise . Before long, however, German ranging shots were increasing almost imperceptibly, and warnings came to the French from both British and United States' intelligence sources that an attack was expected along the Chemin. The warnings were loftily ignored, and continued to be ignored even when prisoners taken on 22 May told of a German build up. But then when, a few days later, a couple of escaped French prisoners tumbled into a British trench with the same story, the French Intelligence Section changed its mind. Unfortunately, the Military Operations Section did not. Indeed, French Sixth Army Headquarters told the American Intelligence Officer, Nolan, as late as 26 May it saw no signs of any preparations 'that would enable an attack to take place tomorrow'.

This, particularly in view of the attitude taken by Sixth Army Headquarters, was hardly surprising. The German preparations had been faultlessly concealed. Every axle had been greased, every wheel and every horse-hoof muffled. Storm troopers had started to move forward in easy stages a full week before the attack, always a little way at a time, always by night, always lying hidden in the woods by day. The area was sealed off, and every precaution taken against civilians passing information. The huge quantities of shells needed for the attack were brought in unmarked waggons and stored in camouflaged ammunition dumps, while the guns to provide the barrage did not move forward until the night of the 25th.

The man in charge of defending the threatened front, was General Denis Duchêne. A man cursed with a most unpleasant temperament (Pierrefeu, at Pétain's headquarters described him as having 'une humeur de dogue, un grondement perpétuel, tout de suite les gros mots à la bouche, sans raison'), he headed a staff that worked in an atmosphere of constant friction. Duchêne had ordered no raids what- soever to find out enemy intentions. His Divisional Commanders, when they found themselves well in front of, instead of behind the natural barrier of the river Aisne, and were told not to give way by as much as a step and given strict orders to mass their troops and artillery forward, making the river a potential trap, protested.

To all their complaints, Duchêne answered 'J'ai dit!' in a display of arrogance and intransigence almost rivalling the Biblical 'What I have written, I have written.'

However, early on the 26th the French took two prisoners. One, a private, said there would be an offensive within hours; the other, a junior officer, denied it. When taken into different rooms and thoroughly grilled (the French phrase 'special interrogation' possibly having hidden meanings) the officer, being told his subordinate had confessed that ammunition had already been issued for the attack, and being reminded that to give false information rendered him liable to be shot as a spy, told all he knew.

By now it was mid-afternoon. Warning of the time of attack was sent immediately to the front-line units for them to make what preparations they could in the few hours left, but back at headquarters Pétain and his staff knew it would be a matter of days before reinforcements could arrive, and then arrive only fitfully. They could do nothing but wait for the disaster to happen.

The countryside below the river Oise had been designated as far more suitable for defensive manoeuvre, and 'defence in depth' having been advised, the front above the Aisne should have been lightly held and the main strength sited further back. Again, Duchêne had chosen to ignore Pétain and d'Espéry's instructions. Not only had he placed the mass of his troops and artillery along and in front of the ridge, he had few plans to hold the Aisne line, and none at all to defend the ridge between that river and the Vesle. Compounding these mistakes, Duchêne was to fling his reserves into the battle too early and in dribs and drabs, instead of using them to form a defensive line to the rear that would steady any retreat.

Meanwhile the Germans were planning a feint attack below Amiens, 'Tarnopol' – named after an earlier German victory on the Eastern Front – to take place on the same day that von Bülow's and von Böhn's offensive was planned to start on the Chemin des Dames, hoping that this would confuse Foch as to which was the main assault.

Early in April Foch had moved the American First Division across from the St Mihiel salient to Cantigny, a village on the higher ground 6 kilometres west of Montdidier, where the German 21 March offensive had come to a halt. There, as they joined Vandenberg's battle-worn Army Corps, the doughboys were given their first severe test. The German High Command had given instructions that wherever Americans appeared in the line they were to be given 'special treatment'. The troops of 'The Big Red One' had a particularly nasty welcome of high explosive and gas. Casualties were four times those of the French on the flanks, and scenes were similar to the ones after the first gas attack in March 1915. In spite of this, Vandenberg told his Army commander he considered Bullard's men capable of recapturing the village and gave them five days' intensive preparation for the job. The Germans, believing the Americans were not capable of a full-scale attack, but suspecting they might mount a heavy raid, not only shelled the rehearsal area, but planned their own raids to take prisoners and gather information.

In the event, the German 272nd Infantry Regiment, attacking the doughboys at Cantigny, found itself driven back so speedily that United States' troops were soon occupying the German 'jumping off' positions. The following day the Americans stormed and retook the village. German units that had been pulled out to rest at Montdidier had to be rushed back pell-mell to prevent a breakthrough.

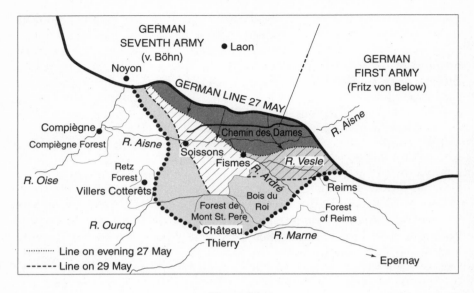

Figure 5A

At 1 am on the 27th, Bruchmüller's barrage of high explosive and gas, this time provided by more than 4000 artillery and mortar pieces, fired two million shells against a 30 kilometre length of the Chemin des Dames. The bombardment was so violent that many of those who managed to live through it were driven mad. After two and a half hours of this treatment, two German armies advanced on the few weakened Allied divisions and completely demolished them. What might have been the difficult first stage of crossing the river Aillette had been so meticulously planned that, crossing by means of footbridges specially constructed for the purpose, the attackers were occupying the Allied forward positions within five minutes of the barrage lifting. Once again, as in March and April, the Germans had the additional advantage that fog shrouded their movements, and that, unbelievably, the croaking of a huge army of frogs in the valley hid the sound of their approach.

Fifteen fresh divisions, with another seven in close support, fell upon the four French divisions and three of the four weakened British manning the front. Among them, was the 2nd Battalion of the Devonshire Regiment, a unit of the 8th Division led by Lieutenant-Colonel Anderson-Morshead. Told to hold the Bois des Buttes near Pontavert, it did just that. Surrounded, the troops fought on until late morning. A IXth Corps' Special Order signed by Bernard Montgomery (a Major on the Corps' staff at the time) included the words, 'There is no doubt that this battalion perished en masse. It refused to surrender and fought to the last'. The French Sixth Army Commander wrote that 'when the British trenches were subjected to a fierce attack the 2nd

50

Devons repelled successive assaults with gallantry and determination until a late hour . . . the few survivors of the battalion, though isolated and without hope of assistance, fought to the last man with unhesitating obedience to orders. The whole battalion – colonel, twenty eight officers, five hundred and fifty NCOs and men offered their lives in ungrudging sacrifice . . .' The 5th Battery of the 45th Royal Field Artillery met the same fate in the same area, continuing to fire until no-one was left to man its guns.

British and French observers in the rear were horrified to see German observation balloons rising from the Allied front line only a matter of minutes after the attack started, but on the British right, the 45th Algerian Division, not directly attacked, was able to form a pivot upon which the IXth Corps' line hinged, retreating under constant threat that its left wing would be turned and all four divisions overwhelmed. Fortunately the hilly country west of Reims helped a fighting withdrawal, and resistance there prevented the German breach from widening too much. The providential arrival of the 19th British Division at Chalons within a few days gave much needed assistance, but the constant struggle reduced the strength of the five British divisions now involved to that of one, indeed, the 21st Division had almost ceased to exist, and as the men retreated they found themselves under a constant barrage of invective from the area's inhabitants.

Away on the British left the French line disintegrated on the first day of the attack. The central division simply disappeared, overwhelmed by five German divisions that rolled over it on their way down to the Aisne eight kilometres away. Crossing points were captured along a 16 kilometre stretch of the river by 10 am. Duchêne's staff had failed to blow all the bridges in time, and the Germans were beyond the Aisne, almost entirely unopposed, by noon. By evening they had crossed the Vesle at Courlandon. No other advance in the war had ever taken so much ground in a single day.

Forced towards Soissons, the French tried to hold back the German right wing, but on the second day of the offensive, German shock troops were still on the move in open country, their start line 24 kilometres behind them.

In spite of Pétain's attempts to bring up reinforcements, the Allied situation continued to worsen. The tattered divisions on whom the attack had first fallen, along with the reserves first thrown into the battle, were driven across the Ourcq at Fère-en-Tardenois by 29 May. By then, Pétain, without any reference to Foch, had denuded the Montdidier area of reserves, and was asking for the Tenth Army and all the Flanders reserves. Foch could only agree to what the French Commander in Chief had already set in motion, and in the face of such a crisis, he even allocated the Tenth Army to Pétain. Fierce German assaults continued against the French below the Ourcq and by evening of 30 May, after a gap of four years, the Germans, on the Marne again at Château-Thierry and with Paris in their sights, had reached Vaux and were occupying Belleau Wood with French reinforcements from further north yet to arrive. On 31 May, Pétain was again demanding that the French reserves be sent from Flanders, and that the American units training in the British Zone be moved south.

The German élite shock troops were already anticipating a further advance, boasting to the Commander of the 3rd battalion of the 2nd French Infantry, who had been forced to surrender along with his 800 men on the evening of 30 May, that next day would see them move forward again.

'Tomorrow we march to Paris', he said laughingly to their commander.

'No, monsieur, never to Paris. Think of 1914 and the Marne', was the serious, dignified reply of the French Lieutenant Colonel.'

Kurt Heffer of the 5th Grenadiers, quoting the conversation in his diary, wrote that for an instant he almost believed the officer, 'but the elation we felt after four days' marvellous progress soon revived our spirits. In those four days, crossing the Chemin des Dames, the Aisne and the Vesle we had reached the Marne, that legendary river. We had suffered very few casualties, whereas the enemy had been gravely weakened. So, for us it was "Nach Paris!"'

Pershing, meeting with Foch that day, pointed out the possibility of striking the Germans on the flank at Soissons. Foch was too despondent even to discuss the matter. 'It was', Pershing was to write later, 'difficult to imagine a more depressed group as they contemplated what was probably the most serious situation of the war'. Only a day or two later, prompted by Foch, Lloyd George, Clémenceau and Orlando were asking President Wilson for more troops, saying that without them the war could well be lost.

However, Ludendorff's original intention to limit the diversionary offensive's advance to the high ground below the river Vesle, caused him first to pause on the 28th, then, astounded by the degree of success, to commit more reserves and continue the advances to the Marne valley, and south-west towards Paris. Once the barrier of the Marne was reached, efforts went into exploiting weaknesses between the Ourcq and the Marne, and that evening orders came to the German 36th Division, in the hills above Jaulgonne on the Marne, to pause.

'On the night of 30/31 May we received the first of the 36th Division's orders to hold the line we had reached. We didn't understand this, as we didn't know what was going on on our right or our left', Heffer admitted.

Foch, realising the gravity of the situation, was not only giving guidance to Pétain on tactics, but to be more immediately available, and in closer touch with events, was moving his headquarters nearer to the front, first to Mouchy-le-Châtel and, a few days later, to Bombon. The new headquarters was soon to become known in the French Army (because of the atmosphere of calm that prevailed there whatever the crisis) as 'The Monastery'.

It was at this desperate stage of the battle, that the two American divisions rushed to the area started to arrive. Provins, Meux and Coulommiers saw an apparently endless stream of lorries packed with cheering, shouting, singing troops, moving towards the threatened front. At Provins, Pétain's Grand Quartier Général (GQG) staff were, in Pierrefeu's dramatic words, 'feeling to be watching a blood transfusion to the mangled body of France.'

Full of confidence after their success at Cantigny, the 1st Division moved to hold the Marne crossings at Château-Thierry while the 2nd Division under General Bundy took over the Belleau Wood sector from the French and checked the advance there.

'Then, when at early dawn', Heffer reported, 'our advance posts reached the river they were met by well-directed fire from the far bank. We had in front an enemy who no longer thought of retreat.

'Later that morning I was with the regimental commander on the hills above Château-Thierry. The sun was shining and a veritable paradise extended before us. A light breeze blew along the valley and the atmosphere was one of peace, not war. Nothing could be seen of the enemy, but if one showed oneself the bullets came thick and fast. We spent most of our time trying, without success, to find targets for the artillery.'

Only a matter of days later, led by the Marines and the 3rd Infantry Brigade, Bundy's troops counter-attacked against the four German divisions holding the square mile of Belleau Wood west of Château-Thierry. All Pershing's insistence on aggression (he often summed up a man's ability by repetition of the word fighter . . . 'he is a fighter – a fighter – a fighter!' being the ultimate accolade) proved its value. It took three weeks of desperate, often hand-to-hand, fighting, almost 2000 dead and 7000 wounded to clear the position and recapture Vaux, but from then on, even the most battle-hardened troops of the German Army viewed the prospect of tangling with the Americans with some trepidation. On the orders of the French Sixth Army Commander, Belleau Wood was renamed Bois de la Brigade de Marine.

By 1 June, Pétain, instead of throwing in reserves piecemeal, was now building a large semicircular defence in the rear that, like a huge dam, would hold back the German flood.

Foch's ability – even his fitness to hold the post of Supreme Commander – was under question. Having told Clémenceau he considered the Chemin des Dames operation to be a feint (which had more than an element of truth, in view of Ludendorff's follow-up plans for

Flanders), he was now accused of being responsible for the Chemin débâcle by moving reserves north to cover Amiens. The British, too, could not help but compare treatment of them during the Lys offensive with the immediate rush of reserves south during the present crisis. Doubts on all sides were voiced as to whether Foch's small headquarters staff could cope with the organisation of complex inter-Allied operations.

However, the fiasco, as well as causing some feelings of suppressed self-satisfaction among her Allies, brought forth a good deal of sympathy for the French predicament. Amongst the French themselves, the feeling of superiority that had followed the Italian disaster at Caporetto and the precipitous British retreat in March, which had bolstered the belief that they themselves were the only ones capable of repelling a German attack, quickly vanished. Derisory jokes and comments about their Allies' lack of fighting power suddenly became muted, and there was a distinct sense of unease about the fate of the British units in French care which could not be erased entirely by the award of the Croix de Guerre to the 2nd Devons and to the 45th Gibraltar battery.

Even though Ludendorff's spectacular advance had come to a halt and his troops found themselves in yet another salient, he had at least achieved his aim of forcing the Allied reserves away south and allowing the planned 'Hagen' offensive to fall upon the unsupported British. Foch had needed 6 French cavalry, 35 Infantry, 5 British, 2 American and 2 Italian divisions to stem the attack. Besides, another German advance would soon improve their situation, and psychological and political as well as military factors were now affecting French morale. Her capital was now within range of, and being bombarded by, the Germans' monster 'Paris' gun. Soon she might well see a repeat of the collapse and humiliation suffered half-a-century before when Paris had been besieged by Prussian troops.

The French capital was certainly a tempting prize that was well within Ludendorff's grasp now his forces had reached the Marne. 'Our surprise attack against a thinly defended front where few Allied reserves were available, was completely successful', he wrote. 'The initial goal was not too ambitious, but the quick and clever exploitation of our far-reaching initial success brought a rich gain in area as well as enormous booty. The chances of a successful attack being made in Flanders *and of further gains south* were greatly enhanced.' (Author's italics.)

But it would have been better for him to have discontinued the action once he knew French reserves were on the move, and to have set the Flanders offensive in motion.

Foch obviously expected him to do just that, but also knew, as the Aisne battle entered into the dangerous first days of June that, if he made the wrong decision about committing his reserves the Allies could lose the war. Pétain, his thoughts still on Paris, wanted them moved south, but Foch could not afford further to denude the north. There

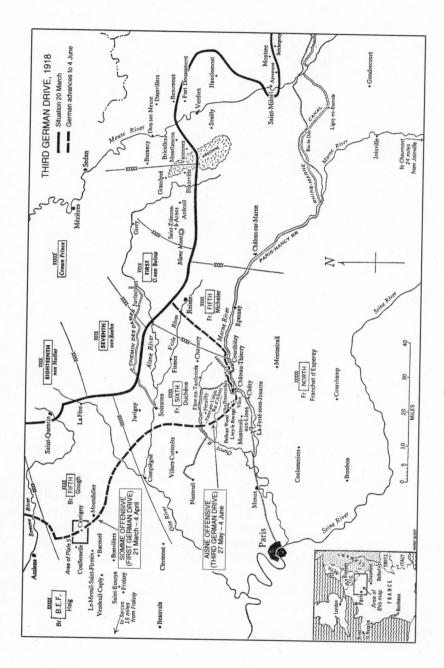

Figure 5

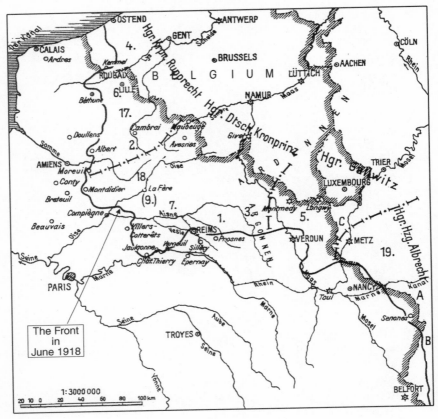

Figure 6

thirty divisions commanded by the Bavarian Crown Prince waited only for the word that would set them on the British again. He held on to his reserves and asked the Belgians, not under his control because their country's constitution forbade it, to take over the Flanders sector as far as Ypres. This they agreed to do. That, in its turn, increased Haig's strength round Amiens. French reserves already moved south were replaced by US divisions still in training; Pétain was even allowed to take some troops out of the line in quiet sectors. That so alarmed General Edouard de Curières de Castelnau in the eastern sector of the front, that he protested he would be forced into retreat if any attack were mounted against him. Foch, furious, said there must be no more such talk. Resistance was to be given à l'outrance – if necessary, step by step.

By 4 June the enemy advance was halted. The crisis, for the time being, was over.

CHAPTER 9

'GNEISENAU'; THE MATZ; 9–13 JUNE 1918

– Ludendorff's attacks continue – Foch anticipates the Matz offensive – reappointment of Mangin – 'Gneisenau' broken, then countered – increasing German problems – Foch gathers resources for a Soissons offensive – more German preparations – Flanders, or Marne ? –

'Beware of desp'rate steps. The darkest day
(Live till to-morrow) will have passed away.'
(William Cowper.)

As the Allies hung on, holding back the German attacks, and any thoughts of victory were banished to 1919, Erich von Ludendorff – comparing the rapidly mounting Allied strength to his own declining numbers because of a lack of reinforcements and the early stages of the influenza pandemic spreading among his troops – knew that if Germany were to win, the victory would have to come by August at the latest. There was no alternative for him but to carry on the attacks.

Foch was also very well aware of this. On the very day that the Aisne offensive was halted round Château-Thierry, he had warned Haig that if the Germans resumed their attack towards Paris it might well mark the start of the war's final battle, and had advised British Headquarters to make contingency plans to move their reserves south. Haig, knowing Rupprecht's divisions were poised ready round Arras and Amiens, Ypres and Bailleul, and considering his forces would be endangered by such a move, protested vehemently and asked his government to step in and invoke the Beauvais agreement. At the War Cabinet meeting on 5 June, Sir Henry Wilson backed this appeal, saying Foch was not only inviting a disaster to happen, but inviting it to happen to the British Army.

Wilson and Milner crossed the Channel to come to a conference in Paris on 7 June, where they again backed Haig in no uncertain terms. Clémenceau and Foch were left in no doubt about the extreme alarm felt both by the Army and Downing Street regarding any British move south when another German attack on the Lys or the Somme was extremely probable. This was not the only storm to be weathered by the

French leaders in Paris that day. There was outcry from Parliament, press and public, all demanding that those responsible for the recent Chemin disaster, whether in army or in government, should be sacked. It was such tempests as these that brought out the best in Clémenceau and earned him his nickname of 'The Tiger'. He stood squarely behind Pétain and Foch, giving them complete and unflinching support, demanding that they must remain at their posts, being 'so happily complementary to each other.' Still, scapegoats had to be found, just as they had been on previous occasions. Denis Duchêne was the first, deservedly, to be dismissed. He was replaced by General Jean Degoutte. Others soon joined him in disgrace. Pétain's Chief of Staff, Anthoine, disappeared along with many of his underlings, and Pétain's fury at this was not lessened when the up-and-coming Buat – a strong supporter of Foch's policies – was nominated as replacement. Louis Guilloumat was brought back from Macedonia and given the tasks of defending the capital and of acting in place of Foch or Pétain if either was taken ill, was injured or died.

When the British representatives had finished their tirade against his proposals, Foch pointed out that he had merely called for forward planning, and would not ask for an actual move of British reserves south unless an attack looked certain; in future, he added cannily, he was sure that Haig would protest only if 'des imprudences' actually took place, in which case he would be the first to agree with the Field Marshal. 'Does not a large orchestra,' he commented later in his memoirs, 'take a certain time to tune its instruments? And when it is formed from diverse sources, is there not also the problem of musical pitch?'

Lord Milner then tried to reconcile the two men. Had Foch, he asked, any intention of withdrawing more American troops from the British sector? Foch replied he did not. In that case, Haig broke in, why were both French and American units taken south during the Chemin des Dames crisis without him even being informed? 'I never saw old Foch so nonplussed,' Milner reported later. 'He simply had not a word to say!'

Clémenceau reprimanded the Supreme Commander, saying that such an occurance must never be allowed to happen again.

Now, after three major offensives, the Germans were in the uncomfortable position of occupying three separate salients. The most likely way for them to improve their position was to smash the French front that projected towards Noyon, between Compiègne and Montdidier. The large forests round Compiègne and the lack of rail links down to Château-Thierry made an attack from the Marne area unlikely, and Foch concluded the next attack would be far more likely to be made between Noyon and Montdidier. At last he started to move his reserve, only a single division at first, but soon he was asking Haig for two more, replacing them with two of the British divisions that had suffered such grievous loss in the Chemin des Dames attack. Some battle-weary

French and some untried American divisions were sent to Lorraine to prevent any surprise attack in the east.

Foch was right. On 9 June Ludendorff launched his Eighteenth Army against the very sector that had been predicted, while the Seventh Army joined the offensive south-west of Soissons. This time the French resistance was far better organised. Humbert and Debeney, commanders in Fayolle's Army Group, had been told by Pétain to operate a 'defence in depth', and despite their reservations about the new method, had placed a hidden line of machine guns as the only means of meeting the initial attack. Behind this line lay a zone some two or three kilometres deep bristling with strongpoints. An attack would have to overcome both sectors before it came up against the main defences, still five kilometres further back.

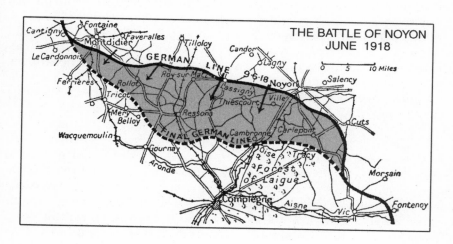

Figure 7

Apart from its obvious open invitation to defenders manning the front line to commit suicide, the system was designed to cause maximum enemy casualties and give time and space both for flexible Allied manoeuvre and precise commitment of reserves. The defence was only partially successful because the French commanders, not completely convinced of the new strategy, were able to plead that they had complied with Foch's original instructions to defend the ground 'step by step', and as a result the Germans were able to occupy ten kilometres of the second zone by mid-morning before being halted by French reserves. However, Fayolle, commanding the Army Group, was already preparing a counter-stroke to drive back the the enemy troops before they had time to consolidate.

Foch reinstated Mangin as a Corps Commander to deliver it; an extremely bold step on Foch's part. Mangin the fiery – Mangin 'the Butcher' – one of Nivelle's subordinates in the Hurtebise disaster the previous year who had been sacked along with his chief, and even, like an out-of-favour courtier in the times of the *Ancien Régime*, had been forbidden to live within striking distance of Paris, was given four fresh divisions and told to attack east towards the Matz valley. Fayolle knew that some units and their supporting artillery could not arrive before the evening of 10 June, and tried to postpone the attack for a couple of days, but Mangin, with the support of Foch, refused to delay. His divisional commanders were rushed to the front before dark, shown assembly areas and objectives to be reached, and told to bring their troops forward during the night.

On 11 June, the Germans, having arrived at the hilly country in front of Compiègne, found themselves under a heavy counter-attack, particularly towards Méry, lasting for two days, that recaptured two villages and took a thousand prisoners. By then it was obvious that the German Seventh Army was having no more success round Soissons than von Hutier's men around Compiègne, and to continue with the assault would only cause useless casualties. Ludendorff therefore told von Hutier to move to the defensive, and as German resistance stiffened, Foch, in spite of Mangin's impetuous demand to continue his counter-attacks, ordered a halt.

In almost twelve weeks that had passed between the third week of March and the middle of June, attack following attack had gained the Germans a great deal of ground, but very little of this ground gave them a strategic advantage. At OHL there was growing disillusion that victory still was beyond reach in spite of all the huge sacrifices of life and material. Now, along with his other problems of increasing influenza and dwindling replacements, Ludendorff was haunted by the fact that the enemy forces were larger than when he had mounted his first attack against them in March. Three quarters of a million Americans were now in France, and units were beginning to arrive from other fronts: from Salonika, from Italy, from Egypt...and at last a constant flow was coming from Britain, previously held back to thwart more battles of attrition. Older men were taking over supply and maintenance, releasing younger soldiers for the front. France, her Army's confidence restored after the 1917 mutinies, was again ready to play a full part.

In spite of doubts about his abilities being voiced after the Chemin des Dames disaster (Foch had to threaten resignation before Lloyd George withdrew yet another attempt to place the planning of military policy into the hands of the Supreme War Council) the Generalissimo started preparations not only to resist another Ludendorff offensive, but to mount his own counter-stroke. Heartened by the Americans' success at Cantigny, their attack at Belleau Wood, and by Fayolle's halting of the German Matz offensive, Foch – only a fortnight after the débacle of 27 May – was writing to Pétain that he 'had the honour to invite his attention to the net of German communications around Soissons.'

The 'defence in depth' policy was examined even more closely. Particular attention was given to the quality of troops manning the second and third positions where most damage was to be done to the enemy. The thorny question of how reserves should be allocated was finally settled. Foch insisted both Haig and Pétain must be prepared to move to the assistance of the other if needed. Pétain, protesting, said the British had by now had ample time to recover from their battering of March and April and ought to be well able to look after themselves. He, too, invoked the Beauvais agreement and appealed to his Government against the order. Clémenceau not only backed Foch, but withdrew Pétain's right to invoke the Beauvais agreement in future.

Not only had the Supreme Commander control and distribution of Allied forces in his hands; he was also responsible for their supply and maintenance. Haig and the British Government were constantly reminded of the need to reconstitute the divisions broken up because of losses and lack of reinforcements. Because of Foch's urgings, all but two were eventually reformed, but the task was still going on into July.

There was also the need to equip the growing American Army. It had been agreed that US troops sent to France during May and June should consist of of infantry and machine gunners. During those two months Britain shipped more than 500,000 men across the Atlantic and a General Staff section was set up in Paris solely to deal with US needs. Each ally met the others' shortages from its own wealth of supplies. The French provided the Americans with artillery, the Belgians with vehicles and the Italians with shells; Britain was sending tanks to the French, heavy artillery to American batteries and aeroplanes to the Belgians. American pilots flew French planes, while consignments of American steel were being shipped across the Atlantic to make still more guns and tanks.

Ludendorff was certainly making ready for another attack. The question was whether it would come in Flanders from Rupprecht, or the German Crown Prince's Army Group attacking round Reims, crossing the Marne and advancing on Paris. From air observation and intelligence reports Foch favoured the Marne, continued to plan his counter-stroke against the German flank at Soissons and asked Haig to send four of his divisions south to help. Whitehall, alarmed by this further move south, once again invited Haig to appeal, but Haig very courageously backed his Chief of Staff, Lawrence, who had agreed to the move, even though Flanders and Artois were still menaced by Rupprecht.

The German Crown Prince's forces were in a pocket between the Aisne and the Marne and supplies by rail had to come through the yards at Soissons. If Soissons could be recaptured, Foch reasoned, or even if its rail network could be brought under fire, German supplies would be disrupted and Ludendorff sooner or later would have to retreat. He therefore ordered Pétain to use the Tenth and Sixth armies to capture the heights around the town.

On the river Vesle at Fismes Ludendorff's Grenadiers were already rehearsing for their Marne crossings and being issued with the best equipment possible at that stage of the war. They were given new uniforms, extra rations and – an unheard of luxury after four years of blockade – new leather boots. All that could be done in the four weeks before Ludendorff's date for the start of his 'offensive for peace' arrived, was being done.

Nevertheless, Rupprecht's force stood ready and waiting in Flanders. His still might be the first blow to fall.

CHAPTER 10

'FRIEDENSTURM'; THE PREPARATIONS

– Ludendorff plans his 'offensive for peace' – Foch for a defence of the Marne and a counter-attack – British and American involvement –

'Qui desiderata pacem, praeparet bellum'
(*Vegetius – C4th. B.C.*)

Once 'Gneisenau' had run its course, both sides used the rest of June and the first weeks of the following month to prepare for their next move. At German Headquarters the staff 'expected great things before the end of July', while on the Allied side hopes were stirring that eventual victory, even if delayed until 1919, would be theirs, for the balance in France and Flanders was tilting more and more quickly in their favour. The rebuilding of the British Army after its March and April maulings was nearly complete; Franchet d'Espéry had been dispatched to Salonika to organise an offensive there (much to Sir Henry Wilson's chagrin; he had hoped to limit the extent of Foch's authority to France and Italy while he himself was placed in charge of all other theatres of war). Italy, rejuvenated after Caporetto and prompted by Foch to take up the offensive again, had given Austria a thrashing on the Piave in mid-June, bringing that country even nearer to collapse; by now France was almost recovered from her traumas of 1917, and the number of American troops was growing day by day.

In contrast, German strength continued to decline. From the opening attack on 21 March to the end of the Gneisenau offensive, almost 700,000 men had been lost, and the next age group to be called up was not large enough to make the losses good. Even though on paper, Ludendorff's strength had been swollen to nearly three and a half million by prisoners returning from Russia, and half a million more men were in reserve, the shortages of matériel, and, more importantly, of front-line quality troops, was becoming apparent. Away from the Western Front, the weakness of other members of the Central Powers made the situation even worse. Large numbers of Germans were tied up trying to bolster Turkey and Bulgaria, who, like Austro-Hungary, were near to throwing in the towel, and of the half million German reserves, many were wounded or still convalescing. Older men were released from policing occupied territory and were brought in to meet the shortfall, but they could hardly be described as front-line battle material.

Living conditions in Germany by now had gone from the extremely difficult to the almost impossible, and front-line morale was not helped when letters from home and soldiers back from leave told of the true state of affairs. The Spring Offensives had not brought the hoped for results, and brooding on the losses suffered, when victory seemed as far off as ever, encouraged a feeling of despondency. Disaffection began to spread. Many back from Russia, feeling they had made enough sacrifices, refused to return to the front and became deserters hiding away in the forests. There was a short-lived mutiny in the Navy. Influenza had thinned the ranks of some battalions to less than 500, and the average German private began to compare his rations and living conditions not only to those of the enemy, but to those enjoyed by his own officers.

More comparisons were being made on the other side of the lines. Pétain, after studying Germany's military strength closely and comparing it with that of the Allies, and Foch from some inner gift of prediction, realised the tide was turning in their favour. Pétain even said that once June was past, another Allied offensive might see a speedy German decline, with Ludendorff being forced to pull back to a shorter line and trying to gain time by starting negotiations; and that, instead of giving him a breathing space, might produce an immediate German collapse.

However, the German Quartermaster-General still had enough men and material to crush the French, move on Chalons-sur-Marne and Paris; then, when Allied reserves were rushed south to meet the threat, to send his aircraft north, load his artillery onto Flanders-bound trains, unleash Rupprecht's force, destroy the British and capture the Channel Ports.

> 'In spite of everything, Field Marshal Hindenburg and I maintained stout hearts. We had to surprise the enemy at some weak spot. If this could be done, a German victory on the Marne and in Champagne – even as late as July 1918 – would have changed the war-situation in favour of the Fatherland . . .'

And so he ordered his fifth offensive – what he was pleased to call his 'Offensive for Peace' – to be planned against what appeared to be the lightly-held front between Château-Thierry and Verdun.

> 'Our second attack by the Crown Prince's forces was now planned for July on each side of Reims. This would improve the Seventh Army's tactical

position: von Böhn's flanks, resting on the Vesle, were exposed as the centre of the Army advanced to the Marne. The offensive was also designed to draw more Allied reserves south from Flanders and so to make more certain the success of Crown Prince Rupprecht's further offensive against the British.'

In this battle which was destined to become the turning point of the war, the German Crown Prince's Army Group would mount yet another pincer attack in the classic German mould. Almost two and a half million men and a huge number of guns were brought together on either side of Reims, and once more the Kaiser (who had previously watched the opening of the May offensive from the California Position above Craonne) was invited to see the spectacle of its opening barrage before leading a triumphal procession into the shattered city of Reims.

So while Haig steeled himself to meet Rupprecht's blow round Hazebrouck, the French were busy organising their defence around Reims and along the Marne. Maistre, the Central Army Group Commander, had Berthelot's Fifth Army west of the city and Gouraud's Fourth to its east. Fayolle, commanding the Reserve Army Group, had Mangin's Tenth Army holding the line from Soissons, down to where Degoutte's Sixth guarded the Château-Thierry corner and held the Marne banks, where they joined de Mitry's Ninth further along the river. All were responsible to Pétain, French Commander in Chief, who in turn was responsible – as was Haig – to Foch.

The Supreme Commander had difficult decisions to make. Both the Flanders and Marne sectors guarded vitally important objectives. On the one hand, Haig feared for the Channel Ports . . . on the other, Pétain for Paris. The decision where to place Allied strength was Foch's alone, and a correct choice was crucial. With responsibility for the entire battle-line from Belgium to Switzerland, he and his staff sifted information coming to Bombon from aerial observation, from front-line reports and from information sent by spies in German occupied areas. Indications pointed more and more to the coming German attacks being made round Reims and along the Marne rather than in Flanders. If von Böhn's Seventh Army west of Reims made an attack that could be held, the whole of the German salient from there to Soissons would be at risk.

Foch decided to provide only enough troops at the base of the salient to stem the advance, and secretly to move his divisions in strength for his own attack on the German flanks. Even while he was sending out his orders to halt, then to counter the Matz offensive in those first days of June, he was already intending that Mangin should lead his proposed attack against the western flank . . . Mangin, in whom he had first shown renewed confidence by proposing, 'To Mangin, a Corps', and now, after the period of probation on the Matz had been completed successfully, ordering, 'To Mangin an Army.'

Mangin's plan was back with Fayolle by 16 June, with copies to Foch and Pétain. The Tenth Army would first mount limited assaults to improve its positions, then tanks and artillery would smash the German line in a surprise attack. Follow-up operations would capture the Chaudun plateau and the heights above Villers-Hélon (midway between the roads leading to Soissons from Château-Thierry and Villers-Cotterêts). The loss of the Villers-Hélon positions would rob the enemy of his observation posts. After that, the offensive would move east. At least eight divisions would be needed to reinforce the thirteen allocated for the attack; seven spearheading the assault with massive artillery support. The reinforcing divisions would exploit the breakthrough, their minimum objectives being the high ground round Chaudun and the area around Violaine, further south.

By mid-June, Foch and Clémenceau were at Chaumont, asking for Pershing's help, even though his Americans were still heavily engaged at Belleau Wood and Vaux. Requesting a list of divisions available, Foch merely said 'studies were being made'. There were to be no more wrangles about an Independent American Army. Neither was Clémenceau told about what was intended. Surprise being of the essence, if the faintest whiff of Allied intentions reached the Germans because of a political leak or press speculation, the results would be disastrous.

The US 1st and 2nd Divisions south of the Marne, Pershing told him, had received reinforcements and were now back to strength. The 3rd and 28th, still absorbing replacements, would soon move into line – the 3rd along the Marne from Château-Thierry to Varennes – and the 42nd east of Reims. The 26th was poised to break out north east from Belleau, and the 4th, 32nd and 77th had almost completed their training.

Two weeks later, Foch sent back his proposals. The 42nd was to help defend the sector from Reims to Verdun. Now that Belleau Wood and Vaux had been recaptured in the first days of July, the rested 1st and 2nd Divisions were to go to Mangin, while the untried 28th was sent as reserve behind Degoutte's Sixth Army below the Marne, waiting there for the German attack.

Degoutte set up a half-moon defence line from Château-Thierry to the east of Dormans, its left resting on the American 26th Division. It then curved south as far as the valley leading to Paris, then back again to join the left flank of Maistre's Army Group above the river towards Reims.

East of the city, Gouraud, pressured for a full week by Pétain to adopt 'defence in depth', and eventually persuaded to abandon the previous French policy of holding every step of ground, gave his Fourth Army instructions to operate the new scheme in terrain that was ideal for the purpose, while in Berthelot's Fifth, west of the city in the hilly, wooded Montagne de Reims where there was far less room for manoeuvre, the

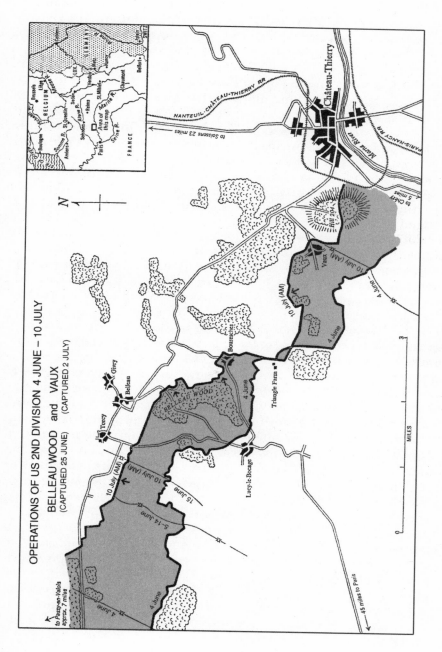

OPERATIONS OF US 2ND DIVISION 4 JUNE – 10 JULY

BELLEAU WOOD and VAUX
(CAPTURED 25 JUNE) (CAPTURED 2 JULY)

Figure 8

French 14th and 20th Divisions, Ist Colonial Corps, and Italian troops manned the line.

On 22 June Fayolle approved Mangin's use of the entire Tenth Army for the counter-attack and added two complete regiments of light tanks. Before the month was over Foch sent out secret orders detailing the divisions needed and, during its last few days, an exploratory attack by a joint Franco-British force north of Soissons captured some ground.

Mangin believed that if his attack started without the usual warning of a lengthy artillery barrage, the Germans would find themselves in difficulties comparable to those of the Allies on the Chemin des Dames. By 9 July Foch was enlarging his plans to include Berthelot's Fifth Army west of Reims in his own pincer attack to retake the Marne salient. These alterations and additions would inevitably delay the counter-stroke for a few days, but if the German offensive opened first, Foch told Pétain on 13 July, their attack must be allowed to develop before Mangin and Berthelot fell upon their flanks.

Eventually, 20 divisions and 350 light tanks were gathered, and hidden in the forests round Villers-Cotterêts for Mangin's use. Foch took them from Pétain, who had earmarked them to guard the French capital. The eight division strong French reserve in Flanders had also gradually been brought south. Soon Foch was asking for more. To the further disquiet of the British Government, French troops and five American divisions training in the British sector had already moved towards the Marne, and now, in the second week in July, Haig was asked to move four British divisions below Amiens, allowing the French troops manning the line there to move south towards the expected German attack. Lawrence, Haig's Chief of Staff, agreed, ordering a hastily cobbled-together British XXIInd Corps under Lieutenant-General Godley to take on the task, and in spite of grave doubts about the French ability to mount any major offensive and fears about the threat posed by Rupprecht, the decision was ratified next day by Haig when he returned from England. However, when hard on the heels of that request came a second, that those four divisions should now be placed completely under Foch's control, be sent to the battle area and be replaced by four more, alarm bells began to ring both in Whitehall and at Montreuil-sur-Mer Headquarters.

Lloyd George, thoroughly unnerved by the depletion of forces in the north when Rupprecht stood so near to the Channel with thirty one divisions ready to fall on a British force half its size, personally telegraphed Haig offering to invoke the Beauvais agreement (the second time this had been threatened by the British Government since the beginning of June) on the grounds that Foch was putting the British Army in jeopardy.

Haig himself, equally concerned, and worried that Foch had not read the German intentions correctly, nevertheless courageously agreed to the Supreme Commander's demand, but asked the second move be delayed at least until their planned meeting at Mouchy on 15 July. By the time Foch had gathered all his forces, Fayolle and Maistre, Commanders of the French Army Groups involved, would have all the French Tenth, Sixth, Ninth, Fifth and Fourth Armies, together with the XXIInd British Corps, two Italian divisions and the Americans supplied by Pershing under their control.

In July German Intelligence estimated there were 22 American divisions in France, and half a million US troops actually fighting or ready for combat. An American division, moreover, was twice the size of a British or French. Ludendorff's initial conclusions from combat reports were that the Americans were 'not very well trained, but extremely eager, and even too rash, with apparently inexhaustible nervous energy'. German headquarters hoped these new conscripts would not have the quality shown by the American regulars at Belleau, and that their officers would not be able to control such large numbers of men in actual war conditions.

On the edge of the Marne in the front line, the American 3rd Division had been preparing its defences from Château-Thierry to Varennes for more than a month. The rumour was that Mondésir, the neighbouring French commander beyond Varennes, was already packing ready to withdraw. Dickman, commanding the 3rd, opted for defence in depth; – then, to avoid an international incident, moved his front line to comply with Degoutte's instructions that the troops must have 'one foot in the water', and moved them back to their original positions as soon as the Sixth Army Commander had left.

Muir's 28th Pennsylvanian National Guards sent to Degoutte as reserves were not so lucky. First of all Degoutte placed them behind the 38th Infantry of the American 3rd Division and the French troops guarding Varennes, then changed his mind. They were moved nearer the river, then some of them were used to fill gaps between French battalions. Finally, on 14 July four companies of the 28th's 55th brigade were sent to the very edge of the Marne on Dickman's right.

On the west flank of the salient round Soissons, the preparatory attacks had continued, improving the line ready for Mangin's assault, now fixed for 18 July. These caused such havoc that one of von Eben's Ninth Army officers noted on Bastille Day (the day before Ludendorff's offensive was to start) that four of his divisions had been so hard-hit that 'any heavy demands in battle are no longer possible. They should be withdrawn and replaced by four fresh infantry divisions.' This was impossible; there was no quiet sector where they could recoup, so for the time being they were to be given as much rest as possible and used only as second wave troops to follow up attacks. Indeed, before being used as storm troops again, time to re-equip and reorganise completely was requested, 'so they could face future engagements with dash and courage rather than experience failure in their present vulnerable state.'

Foch still was hoping his offensive would start before that of the Crown Prince, but again repeated his order that any German assault was to be held, then countered by Mangin's attack against their line between Soissons and Château-Thierry, capturing the high ground below Soissons and enabling artillery to shell the rail complex there. Such a success would cut their supplies and isolate von Böhn's Army, but a surprise assault of that size in such extremely hilly country, Fayolle admitted, would need 'first class troops'. On the Reims side of the salient, it was becoming obvious that Berthelot would need reinforcements if the Fifth Army was to make a breakthrough.

Towards Verdun, on the eastern side of Reims, the heavier part of the double attack was to be made by the German First and Third Armies under Fritz von Below and Karl von Einem. They would break the 40 kilometre French line and aim for Chalons-sur-Marne. By now German shortages of material and food were so severe that orders permitted any plunder taken during the advance to be shared by the attacking troops, but all booty taken at Chalons-sur-Marne itself was to be the Property of the State.

At the base of the salient from Château-Thierry to Epernay, the six groups of von Böhn's Seventh Army were to push south, crossing the Marne on a wide front, link with von Einem and von Below's advance, then move on Paris through the Surmelin Creek valley. Once his river crossings were secure, von Böhn would send some artillery and troops back north to support Rupprecht's 'Hagen' offensive round Hazebrouck. By that stage Allied reserves would be on their way south.

'H' day, first fixed by German Headquarters for 10 July, was delayed until midnight of 14/15 July to allow the final gathering of equipment. The fact that their intelligence section's prediction that Foch would strike on the 14th proved unfounded, encouraged them to believe their own plans had not been discovered.

CHAPTER 11

'THE OTHER SIDE OF THE HILL'

– Each side continues to search for information about the other's
position – the German plan of attack is captured –

*'All the business of war, and indeed all the business of life, is to endeavour to find
out what you don't know by what you do; that's what I called "guessing what was
on the other side of the hill."'*

(Arthur Wellesley, Duke of Wellington.)

Ludendorff's losses on the Chemin des Dames – even if difficult to
replace – had been moderate compared with the Allies', and his storm
troops, flushed by relatively easy success and a rapid advance, were in
good heart. Von Böhn's first obstacle was, of course, the Marne itself.
Over countless years the Marne has dug deeper and deeper into the
land, producing a valley bordered by extremely steep slopes. Near
Château-Thierry, the river is about eighty metres wide, and runs swift
and deep. There are thickly wooded hills, orchards, vineyards and
pastures on both banks. North German troops thought it all bore a
remarkable resemblance to their own river Weser that runs deep and
wide at the Westphalian gate.

By early July the 5th Grenadiers, to be amongst the first to cross, were
in rest at Fère-en-Tardenois, 20 kilometres above the river. Already
rumours were spreading that the attack would be on the 15th. It was to
be a repeat of the 21 March assault; exploiting areas that offered least
resistance, protected by Bruchmüller's rolling barrage.

French Intelligence knew their exact position.

'In the night we heard a dull sound followed by several seconds of silence,
then whistling became louder and louder then an explosion struck our
ears . . . We rushed out of houses that offered no protection against the
heavy railway artillery of the French and scattered in the fields, not
returning until daybreak when it was more calm. Life wasn't pleasant and
we buried many before we received the order to attack.' (Leutnant Kurt
Heffer).

The first assault would be made by infantry and machine gunners
using rafts and boats. Artillery and transport would cross later by
pontoon bridge. The rehearsals on the Vesle at Fismes meant infantry

71

billeted round Fère-en-Tardenois were faced with a march of 18 kilometres each way in hot weather, choking on the dust that rose tree-top
high in the woods above the town.

> 'We returned tired out day after day, only to be subjected to French
> artillery fire during the night . . . and all this only a few days before the
> attack!'

Inevitably, although the Germans made every attempt to keep their
plans secret, the French and Americans took prisoners and questioned
them closely. German deserters provided more information about the
build-up. Ammunition columns were still on the roads at nine in
the morning even though French observation planes were airborne at
first light.

Though the exact date of the attack still wasn't known, all these jigsaw
pieces helped build a picture that confirmed Foch in his conviction that
the first attack would come round Reims and on the Marne rather than
against Haig in Flanders.

The German Intelligence Section also was using spotter 'planes,
balloons, interrogating prisoners, and sifting information to produce
reports that listed the changing pattern of Allied divisions right up to
the moment of the attack in the first minutes of 15 July . . .

Report of Intelligence Officer, Army Group German Crown Prince.
'Attack front up to 9am July 15th.

> 'First Army (east of Reims): Statements of prisoners confirmed our
> assumption of the enemy order of battle . . . 163rd Division in sector E of
> Prunay (a few kilometres from Fort de la Pompelle), and the 124th
> Division is confirmed present north of Prosnes. Our 124th Division
> brought in prisoners from 27th Division who say their Division is in rest
> at Mourmelon le Grand . . .'

The French 132nd was also located, holding positions opposite the
coming attack.

> 'Seventh Army: Changes in enemy order of battle along the Marne attack
> front ascertained through prisoners . . . 125th Division in the sector south-
> west of Dormans. 51st Division, formerly 20th Division, in the sector E of
> Dormans.'

The 125th Division was plotted on the German Intelligence maps
south-west of the town.

Above the river, and in the Montagne de Reims, the French 8th
Division was identified south of Olizy and Violaine, and the 8th Italians
had the 120th French in support round Chambrecy.

Even from as far away as Senlis, reports came that the 40th Division had just arrived. A complete battle order of Allied divisions on the Marne's south bank was mapped and distributed . . .

. . . but of Mangin's forces gathering in the forests of Villers-Cotterêts and of Retz below Pierrefonds, the Crown Prince's Intelligence Officers made no mention . . .

Ludendorff's troops received their orders on 12 July. Only regimental and battalion commanders with a few company officers were allowed forward to see the start lines and to note approach routes, vehicle parks and supply areas, in case the enemy was alerted by a sudden increase in activity.

The German 10th and 36th Divisions camped in the woods about five kilometres back from the river for the last few days before the attack. Hostile artillery fire was only light and spasmodic, the weather was pleasant: warm with an occasional shower. The 5th and 6th Grenadier Regiments, who had fought side by side in the Chemin des Dames attack, were to cross the Marne together between Jaulgonne and Chartèves, linking the two divisions.

Opposite them, Dickman's American 3rd Division held the crossing and guarded the Paris-Nancy railway. Behind the railway was the Paris aqueduct, and to the right, 'Le Rocq' plateau . . . an ideal place for the Germans to regroup once they had gained a secure foothold. Dickman planned to use it to break their attack, and placed his 4th Infantry Regiment towards Château-Thierry, then the 7th, the 30th and finally the 38th up to Varennes.

In spite of Ludendorff's initial, somewhat dismissive assessments, word of American aggression at Cantigny and Belleau Wood had spread through the German Army, and there was some apprehension when the Grenadiers realised who was opposite . . .

'I was working on the orders for attack when a very agitated Grenadier came in. Respectfully he asked if it was true that the Americans were in front and that the attack had been made known to them. I reassured him, but discreetly enquired as to the general opinion about the attack. There was confidence in the command, but also an indefinable sense that the attack would not succeed. The enemy had taken prisoners from amongst us, among whom was an officer who, in spite of all instructions to the contrary, had important maps in his possession. Here and there there had been desertions.

'Hostile fire grew stronger day by day, and when we went to our jumping off position on July 13th, thick clouds of gas lay in the Jaulgonne forest.' (Kurt Heffer.)

In the days leading to the offensive, both sides had patrolled vigorously, searching for prisoners and information.

During the evening of 14 July Gouraud's troops captured an enemy major, who, in spite of all instructions to the contrary, was carrying the complete plan of attack. Gouraud not only could give his Fourth Army six hours advance warning of its exact time, but knew to a nicety the positions of the German assembly areas. West of the city and below the Marne, Foch's artillery also prepared to saturate the German start lines just before Bruchmüller's bombardment opened.

The first waves of German troops moved to their positions during that Sunday evening of 14 July. They massed in the woods about 500 metres away from the river bank. Again, not to alert the enemy, no trenches had been dug : small flags marked the start line, and as darkness fell, they were difficult to find. That intensely dark night caused more problems. Some units became lost and when they finally arrived they were tired, had lost some of their equipment, and stragglers still had to catch up, but at last everyone was in place.

Well to the rear of the battlefield, the Kaiser was escorted to the wooden grandstand built to give him a distant view of the opening bombardment. With him was Karl Rösner, correspondent of a Berlin newspaper, later to chronicle the entire events in a somewhat emotional but detailed account of the Imperial Visit in his book 'Der König'. Present when the All-Highest was met at the railway station by Hindenburg and Ludendorff, Rösner went with his idol to the observation post (on the way there, the Emperor spoke 'in kindly fashion' to two Aryan blonde-haired, blue-eyed adoring nurses) and keenly watched, ready to note down His Highness's reactions to Bruchmüller's bombardment.

By now, only a few hours before the start of the offensive, Ludendorff is on his way to German Supreme Headquarters at Avesnes. Foch is with his staff at Bombon. At Provins, Pétain worries that the moving of his Paris divisions to Mangin will bring about a German breakthrough. East of Reims, Gouraud hopes he has not been fed false information encouraging him to expose his own artillery positions by anticipating Bruchmüller's barrage by a full three hours.

At British Headquarters, the general opinion is that the French might possibly defend the Marne, but any counter-attack will be out of the question. In spite of Rupprecht, Haig has made plans for Godley's XXIInd Corps to move south to the French front.

In Russia the group of Bolsheviks holding the Tzar and his family prisoner are finalising their plans to execute them *en masse*.

Mangin is planning the last details of his counter-stroke in the forest of Villers-Cotterêts.

A burial party has collected the remains of aviator Quentin Roosevelt, son of the former American President, Theodore Roosevelt, shot

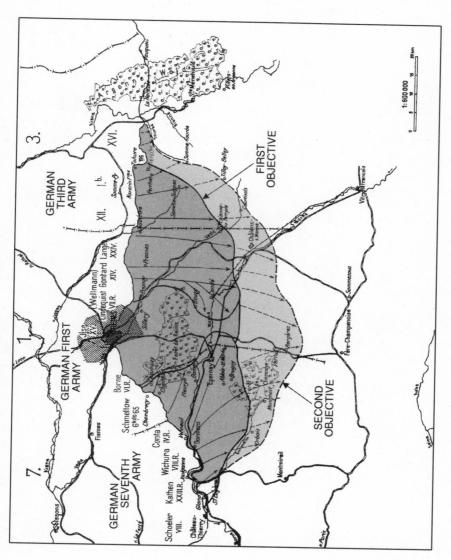

Figure 9

75

down that day. And on either side of the lines millions of men sweat, pray, fear for the morning, brag, write letters, or, like some of Heffer's Grenadiers, 'settle down to get some sleep: things were not due to start yet . . . '.

CHAPTER 12

OPERATIONS BEGIN; MONDAY 15 JULY 1918

– The Germans attack – the 'fog of war' descends – the advance is held at Château-Thierry

'. . . if she found a blade of nutgrass in her yard, it was like the Second Battle of the Marne . . .'

(Harper Lee – 'To Kill a Mocking Bird')

The captured battle plans, together with information from deserters, confirmed Foch in his analysis. At ten minutes past midnight on 15 July, the German guns would stand ready loaded, the word 'Feuer!' would be shouted, and by 1.30am their first troops would be crossing the Marne.

Initial reports arriving at the Crown Prince's Headquarters in the small hours were promising. Von Eben's Ninth Army Headquarters spoke of medium artillery fire reported by the Corps holding the right and central sectors north of the Aisne, while its heavy feint barrage south of the Aisne was 'drawing little Allied response, with the general situation mainly unchanged'. Some skirmishing had taken place in the southern sector, where 'two hostile companies that advanced last evening against the left of the 42nd Division were driven off. Our front-line attacks on the east bank of the Savières brook, north east of Corcy, have not yet succeeded in driving out the enemy, who is offering stubborn resistance. One officer and eight men, said to belong to two different units, were brought in as prisoners last night'. There was even time to pass the information to Headquarters that conditions were 'changeable . . . cloudy . . . falling weather . . . 16 degrees C'.

Von Böhn confirmed his Seventh Army troops were in position and the 'barrage opening on time'. A later report said that the improving weather was giving better conditions for directing artillery fire. Enemy shelling was 'much stronger', but reports were starting to come in of a successful attack across the river above Varennes. Reinforcements were being brought up, and the rolling barrage would be followed according to plan. Prisoners had been taken from the French 51st Division opposite Trélou, and though progress reports from the Château-Thierry area had not yet arrived, it was known that the 87th Division had already sent back some American prisoners.

All of this was unduly optimistic. By midnight, shell after shell was falling on the assembled storm troopers as Allied gunners south of the river hastily reloaded time after time.

> 'Suddenly there was a tremendous burst of artillery fire. I looked at my wrist watch: it was midnight. Our bombardment wasn't due to start until ten past.' (*German time was an hour ahead of Allied, and Heffer's diary notes 'one o' clock'. His, and other German timings have been altered to match those of the Allies for clarity's sake*). 'I climbed out of my shell-hole to look. It was enemy artillery fire, and proved even more intense than our own . . .'

. . . and Bruchmüller's was spectacular enough. Perched on his wooden tower well to the rear,

> 'the Emperor listened to the terrible orchestra of our surprise fire-attack and looked upon the unparalleled picture of projectiles raging towards the enemy positions.' (Karl Rösner – 'Der König')

At the receiving end, men on both sides had little time to admire 'the unparalleled picture' of either barrage . . .

> 'In a short time all our telephone lines were cut. By 12.50am we were being pressed from the rear for news. Half an hour later we passed back what we knew. Two companies in the 175th Infantry on our left had been completely annihilated by French fire. There was no news yet about the crossing of the river . . .' (Heffer: 5th Grenadiers)

In spite of the fusillade, some of the attackers had managed to keep to the timetable, crossing on schedule. They were the élite of the Army: the very best: many of them veterans with experience of the Somme, Passchendaele and the Spring Offensives . . . They crossed by boat and raft under a hail of rifle, mortar and machine gun fire. Waiting for them from Château-Thierry to Varennes, were Dickman's 3rd US Division, a mixture of Reid's Pennsylvanians and French troops round Varennes itself, and more French divisions extending the line from there towards Epernay.

Opposite Dickman, the German 10th and 36th Divisions waited for the order to attack. Barrage and weather had both hindered their move to the jumping-off line. Rain and a light fog combined to produce a particularly dark Summer night. 'It was difficult,' Heffer recounted, 'to see a hand in front of the face.' Both Divisions had suffered in the shelling, the 10th particularly round its headquarters and on its artillery positions. The 398th Infantry was on the right nearest Château-Thierry, the 47th

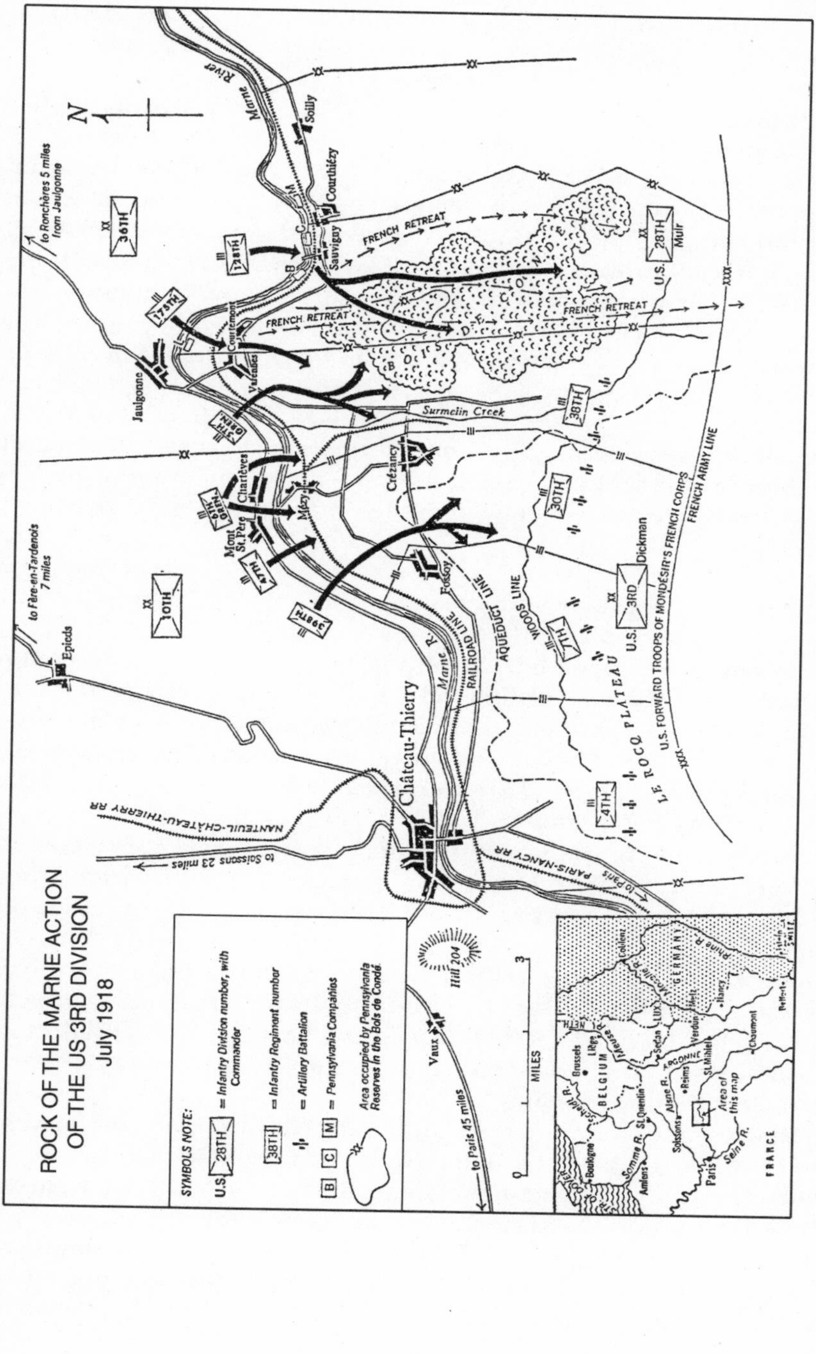
ROCK OF THE MARNE ACTION
OF THE US 3RD DIVISION
July 1918
SYMBOLS NOTE:
U.S. 28TH = Infantry Division number, with Commander
38TH = Infantry Regiment number
= Artillery Battalion
B C M = Pennsylvania Companies
Area occupied by Pennsylvania Reserves in the Bois de Condé
MILES
to Paris 45 miles
Vaux
Hill 204
Château-Thierry
to Soissons 23 miles
NANTEUIL-CHÂTEAU-THIERRY RR
PARIS-NANCY RR
to Paris
Epieds
to Fère-en-Tardenois 7 miles
to Ronchères 5 miles from Jaulgonne
Jaulgonne
Marne River
Marne R.
RAILROAD LINE
AQUEDUCT LINE
WOODS LINE
LE ROCQ PLATEAU
U.S. FORWARD TROOPS OF MONDESIR'S FRENCH CORPS
FRENCH ARMY LINE
U.S. 3RD Dickman
U.S. 28TH Muir
10TH
36TH
Mont St. Père
Chartèves
Mézy
Crézancy
Fossoy
Varennes
Courtemont
Sauvigny
Courthiézy
Soilly
Surmelin Creek
BOIS DE CONDE
FRENCH RETREAT
N
BELGIUM
GERMANY
FRANCE
Paris
Area of this map

Figure 10

in its centre, while the 6th Grenadiers on the left flank joined the 5th Regiment of Grenadiers on the right of the neighbouring 36th Division.

The 10th German Divisional War Diary for 15 July gives some idea of their immediate difficulties.

> 'Weather rainy..light fog, clearing later. Heavy enemy harassing fire concentrated on north bank of Marne during night . . . especially on battery positions of 1st and 2nd batteries of 162nd foot artillery battalion. Our barrage opened, but at the same time enemy fire was being directed against the gorge at the Divisional Battle Headquarters. 12.20am all communications disconnected. 12.45am 47th infantry arrived: one battalion routed by the bombardment from the enemy. The battalion had got into the fire falling on the gorge near Divisional Headquarters: first aid was administered to casualties by the Divisional Medical Officer. 1 am. 20th brig. reports 1st battalion 47th Infantry in position – also 2nd and 3rd battalions of the 398th Infantry. Wireless message dispatched to Group 'Assembly of Infantry completed according to plan' By 2.00am all our repaired telephonic communication completely shot to pieces. Enemy artillery intermittently bombarding Divisional HQ and ground behind it.'

McAlexander, commanding the US 38th Infantry opposite, had placed three companies ready to meet the 10th and 36th Divisions' attack, leaving the siting of defensive positions to his company commanders. On the left, where the US 38th Infantry joined the 30th – the very point on which two German Grenadier Regiments were to converge – four American platoons guarded the river's edge. Captain Jesse Wooldridge was in charge. Two companies extended the line to the French positions at Varennes, while another, commanded by Captain Reid, was dug in deep, ready to rush to defence positions in slit trenches facing Varennes when Bruchmüller's barrage had rolled past. They knew their right flank would be exposed, but were confident they would be given support.

About 250 doughboys of the 3rd Division, and one of the four companies of the 28th, placed there by Degoutte, bringing the total to 500, were lining the bank just where the Grenadiers' and the 175th and 128th Divisions' attacks would converge. (Degoutte had wanted 2,000). The first German objective was to take the ground enclosed by the loop of the Marne opposite Jaulgonne. The other 38th Infantry troops were behind in support . . . the 1st Battalion behind the railway line with its reserves deployed to protect the flank. The 3rd Battalion lay hidden, guarding the guns on the far right of Dickman's position.

Behind Reid's slit trenches, a 'Hill 231' was marked on the maps . . . really only a mound, but nevertheless an important machine gun position. Reid would have to defend the flank if the French retreated.

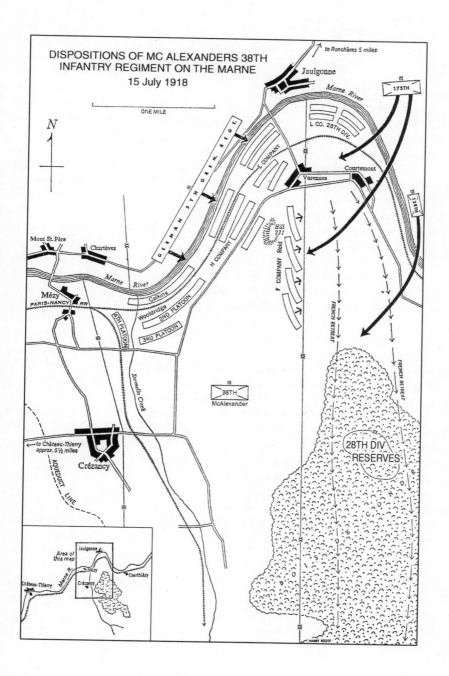

Figure 11

(McAlexander suspected the French would keep casualties to a minimum by doing this, but told his men that it was their task so to impress the Germans with their fighting ability and, above all, with their *desire* to fight, that their enemy's morale would be shattered.

Heffer's companions in the 5th Grenadiers' first battalion were also mauled by shellfire as they came down one of the ravines leading to the river. The boats they were to have used had been abandoned some way back, and the crossing point was already under a hail of machine-gun bullets, coming from the first of Wooldridge's platoons, commanded by Lieutenant Calkins, placed in thick bushes at the river's edge with instructions to fight until overrun. Two more were behind, with a fourth on the railway spur running down between Crézancy and the Surmelin creek to join the main Paris to Nancy line. The other companies on Wooldridge's right had also placed platoons on the bank to meet a frontal attack; those further back extended Wooldridge's positions along the railway.

Left of the 5th Grenadiers near Jaulgonne, a battalion led by Captain Plehwe had managed to cross the Marne and reach the railway embankment. Heffer's company still waited for the order to advance. All the men could do was scrabble for cover and put on masks, as gas was now mixed with the shrapnel and high explosive coming at them in the dark. Finally it was checked that all were armed, and the order was given to advance.

'We came down,' Heffer's diary continues, 'through valleys raked by fire, but it was the only way to get to the river. The light artillery with us had no means of avoiding the shellfire. As the ammunition exploded, guns were dismounted: men and horses killed.

'We found some abandoned boats and carried them forward. Then came another salvo. More were killed and wounded by machine-gun fire as we struggled at the launching point.' There were shouts that more boats were lower down. Even so, there were only two where there should have been six. The first set off, overloaded. Immediately a machine gun started up, but fired too high. The far bank was reached, and the troops scrambled out. They had been told to expect few survivors and little resistance following Bruchmüller's barrage. Now, after being shelled all the way from their start line, they found Americans ready and waiting for them.

> 'At the river's edge we had first come up against barbed-wire which hadn't been made out through field glasses. Behind, was a trench. One of our men felt something soft in front of him. The enemy had sheltered there from our artillery and there was hand-to-hand fighting before we could continue the advance.'

Calkins was wounded and captured at 2am. Corporal Connors destroyed 20 boats before the platoon ran out of ammunition and had only grenades left. Connors continued to throw them until he was shot in the act of hurling another grenade and was blown to pieces by his own weapon. A few men struggled back to the railway embankment, but the two Grenadier regiments had been forced to change direction because of their stand.

In spite of the ferocious defence at the river's edge, a battalion of the German 398th Infantry, right of the 10th Division, gained a toehold on the railway embankment between the American 30th and 7th Infantry positions. Soon after 4.00am, Leutnant Schedler of its advanced construction squad, had released a carrier pigeon carrying the information that two battalions were now overcoming American resistance in front of the railway, and three companies were on the embankment itself. Half an hour later these troops mounted an attack on the 7th American Infantry's flank.

Two American platoons immediately charged full tilt straight at them.

Behind the embankment, Lieutenant Butcher managed to hold back his men who were all for joining in, and they settled down to an all-day skirmish without being dislodged. The Germans recoiled in disarray from the American charge, and the 7th Infantry was able to redeploy its flank to face any further attacks.

Numerous messages now started to arrive at German Headquarters reporting the true state of affairs. The 5th Grenadiers were in difficulties; the 6th Grenadiers now fighting off strong counter-attacks from the woods south of Crézancy, and though part of the railway station was held by a few men of the 398th, the attack was held up with both flanks 'in the air'. Reinforcements were needed urgently.

Some idea of the increasing confusion can be gained from the German 10th Divisional War Diary.

'2.50am: the staff of the 398th infantry proceeds to the Marne. Report received 3.00 am that staff of 398th have advanced : No reports yet in regarding progress of infantry. Enemy artillery fire has abated. 3.15 Regiment Grussdorf has reached assembly point without losses. 3.20: Advanced construction squad has reached the Marne. 3.50: Twentieth brigade reports 398th staff at Marne. 3rd Battalion 398th infantry has crossed, also greater part of second battalion. 1st battalion routed by shellfire. Strong enemy machine gun resistance. Concentrated fire of our own artillery, apparently, is too far to the south. The Americans are said to be opposite us. The crossing goes on by means of ferry. 4.00am ... 20th brig reports orderly officer 47th Infantry just returned. Reports that the bridge at X 1 will be completed in about 20minutes. 4.10. 2nd Leutnant in charge of Construction squad reports all of 3rd battalion 398th infantry has crossed. About an hour ago the 2nd battalion 398th and 1st battalion 398th were crossing. Enemy machine gun nests, trench mortar and artillery barrage. Flare signals were not observed. 4.20 am 20th brig.

reports 47th Infantry has come up. 4.22.. 2nd Leutnant Schedler (advanced construction squad) sends following message . . .'398th Infantry reports from N bank 2nd and 3rd battalions 398th already meeting with resistance, which will be broken, on this side of the railway. 1st battalion 398th shelled when assembling. Parts of it have crossed. Battalion is being reorganised. 6th, 8th and 11th companies have just reached the railway embankment.' Flash message from Grenadiers received at same time ' 1st battalion crossed at 3.40am . . . suffered slight losses. 2nd battalion following. Right wing of 36th Division, according to reports, encountering difficulties.' Corps HQ informed of events by mounted orderlies, and at 5.00am by carrier pigeon. 4.55. 6th Grenadiers reports strong enemy counter attack from small woods S of Crézancy at about 4.15; parts of railway station being held. Reserve battalion brought into action. No connection with right or left. Reinforcements needed urgently. Enemy was prepared, attack having been betrayed eight days since. 5.05 . . . 398th infantry says part of regiment has reached railway station. At this moment very heavy machine gun fire from enemy on left. No contact with 6th Grenadiers. 5.24 . . . Orderly officer of 1st battalion, 47th infantry reports from bridge L 1 that battalion is under machine-gun fire from small wooded sectors. 6.25 20th Brigade reports 1st battalion, 37th Infantry S of Marne, bridge finished . . . 3rd battalion 47th Infantry in process of crossing. 5.30 Americans attack near the 398th infantry. The attack comes to a stop. Regiment is without contact to left or right. 5.33. Divisional staff officer in charge of operation informs adjutant of situation of 398th infantry. 47th infantry must be directed to press 398th infantry to attack, and to attack the Americans in flank. 47th infantry troops in contact with right wing of 6th Grenadiers to attack the position previously given to the left wing of the 398th. The 47th infantry must be directed to come up along with the rolling barrage.'

By now Headquarters was sending a series of orders to its 47th Regiment that show the mood of increasing panic. 'Reinforce the 398th: attack the Americans on your right: keep in firm touch with the 6th Grenadiers on your left: join in the attack: keep up with the rolling barrage. . . '!!

Too much was being asked: from there down to Château-Thierry, the German attack was held.

A little further east, towards Varennes, the fighting was just as vicious. Von Böhn had given the German 2nd Guards Division the task of breaking the Yankees. The Brigade's 5th and 6th Grenadier Regiments had crossed the Marne between Mézy and Varennes, while specially chosen Infantry attacked the French positions around Varennes itself.

The six French divisions holding the line from Varennes almost to Epernay fought desperately for a time then, without warning, retreated

ABOVE: German troops 'following up' after the initial 27 May assault – the first time since 1914 that the Chemin des Dames was crossed. *(Q23769 Imperial War Museum)*

BELOW: Captured British soldiers of the IXth Corps in what had been a six-foot-deep trench. The devastation gives some idea of the ferocity of Bruchmüller's barrage. *(Q23849 Imperial War Museum)*

ABOVE: A French column retreating past the unarmed remnants of a British military band. The location is probably somewhere below Jonchery. *(Q6676 Imperial War Museum)*

BELOW: French and British troops withdrawing. The different cap badges and occasional weaponless, or hatless man point to a forced march. *(Q6677 Imperial War Museum)*

ABOVE: The Destroyed Bridge at Château Thierry: an area defended on 15 July by the 3rd American Division and the focal point of their attack to retake the town on 21 July. *(Q581201 Imperial War Museum)*

BELOW: The revolutionary Renault FT 17 tank that spearheaded Mangin's counter-attack. Rear-engined, and equipped with radio, it had a revolving turret and was crewed by two men. *(Q11120 Imperial War Museum)*

ABOVE: Devons of the 62nd Division taking a prisoner in the Bois de Reims. (A propaganda photograph taken after the event?) *(Q11086 Imperial War Museum)*

BELOW: British, French and Italian troops examining a captured machine-gun, and one Italian officer examining the camera! They are from the 11th Italian Corps, the British 62nd Division and (probably) the French 77th Division in the Ardre valley region. *(Q11107 Imperial War Museum)*

ABOVE: British troops in action in the Bois de Reims. This gives some idea of the conditions of 'open warfare' in the woods bordering the valleys. Note the shot-scarred tree and the British casualty – obviously past medical help. *(Q11110 Imperial War Museum)*

BELOW: British stretcher-bearers prepare to move a wounded German outside Marfaux, 23 July. The Germans were driven from the village after a bitter struggle the following day. *(Q6855 Imperial War Museum)*

ABOVE: British carrying a German stretcher case. The arm hanging limply over the stretcher side and the lack of interest shown by the watching French shows the commonplace nature of such events. *(Q6875 Imperial War Museum)*

BELOW: The pity of war. French wounded – possibly tear-gassed – and a British soldier make their way back to a dressing-station. The screens on the left are to prevent enemy observation. Unfortunately the signpost is illegible, but the lie of the land suggests the flank of the salient below Soissons. *(Q6864 Imperial War Museum)*

ABOVE: An American official photograph of the 148th Field Artillery on the move at Vaux (just west of Mareuil en Dôle) in the latter stages of the battle. One of the thousands of horses killed in the war lies at the roadside. *(Q69950 Imperial War Museum)*

BELOW: Men of the British 34th Division returning after the final capture of Hill 158 above Beugneux on 1 August. The number of German forage caps and the flanking guards suggest prisoners in the column rather than British troops wearing souvenirs. Note the kilt cover worn by Scottish members of the Division. *(Q8191 Imperial War Museum)*

ABOVE: The Highland Division receiving Berthelot's recognition of their struggle as they take part in a march-past on 1 August. *(Q9172 Imperial War Museum)*

BELOW: Also on 1 August, an American Infantry Regiment attacks across open ground at Choloy. *(Q69955 Imperial War Museum)*

headlong, not stopping until they reached Degoutte's main defences. This stranded a company of the US 28th Division: it was surrounded and its headquarters' staff taken back across the river as prisoners. The Second in Command of the left flank formed his men into a fighting square that forced its way back to Regimental headquarters after a four hour long battle.

The 28th Division' 'C' company presumed its wiring party sent to the river's edge had been wiped out when the German barrage opened, but seven survivors set off to fight their way back, gathering men as they went. Thirty-six hours later the twenty strong group reported to Headquarters.

No warning was given by the French that they were going to retreat. McAlexander asked the 28th Division to take over their abandoned positions in Bois de Condé on the 38th Infantry's flank. The Pennsylvanian National Guard not only held them, but with French troops who had rallied, counter-attacked and drove the enemy back.

The next objectives given to Heffer and his men were to join the fighting on the railway embankment, capture it, then keep up with the rolling barrage and break Degoutte's half-moon defence line. By now the rolling barrage had started.

'We looked at our watches. God! We must keep up! "Advance!" We were given new objectives as the original plan could not be carried through. My group reached the railroad. The railway station at Varennes was captured after a short fight. The Moulins to Varennes road was crossed. We were now a kilometre south of the Marne, and started to climb the steep slopes behind the river, but from our right came shouting and a fusillade of fire. Through the morning mist we could see assaulting columns in brown coming through the wheat; more Americans!

'The commanders of our second battalion and the neighbouring rifle battalion, Captains von Plehwe and Eben saw the danger. Everyone who could fire faced right . . . The enemy certainly showed courage: they didn't stop until our machine-guns and rifles had caused bloody losses, but the situation was critical...we had to pull back . . . Where were the 6th Grenadiers? What was the artillery doing? It just kept on firing according to plan . . .'

In fairness, the artillery was hindered by the mist covering the area. On reaching the railway, attacks had to be made in waves until enough men were below the embankment, sheltered from American fire, to storm the position.

There was more hand-to-hand fighting as the US platoon led by Lieutenant Phillips on Wooldridge's right struggled with more Grenadiers east of Heffer and his comrades. Though wounded, Phillips bayonetted the German captain, who, dying, shot Phillips through the head . Phillips' platoon sergeant then took charge, led a rush down the embankment and counter-attacked.

As early as 6am McAlexander had committed his second-line troops, and was bringing up his third. Battles were now taking place in the woods...in the wheatfields . . . on either side of the railway . . . in ravines leading up from the Marne . . . on the Rocq plateau itself.

Wooldridge knew his right flank had to be secured before his men were wiped out. Twenty set out to deal with a troublesome machine-gun. Only Wooldridge and a private came back, bringing the remnants of the machine-gun crew as prisoners. Because of many such actions the two Grenadier Regiments were unable to join up when the French retreated. A Brigadier and a Colonel of the 6th Grenadiers had both been shot, and 'it was suicide to raise your head above the ears of wheat.'

Wooldridge killed the Staff Major of the leading battalion, who, when wounded in his right hand, tried to draw with his left. The German Adjutant was bayonetted by the platoon's water cart driver. Another officer tore up his battle orders even as a pistol was jammed into his ribs. To his astonishment, in the thick of it all, Wooldridge found he had been joined by a pair of Irish-American cooks who ' just felt they were missing out'. The fighting was becoming so confused that at one point McAlexander was trapped between Wooldridge's platoons and the Germans.

Laurence Stallings reported their conversation, shouted through the noise of battle.

'Colonel!' Wooldridge yelled. 'Don't you know nothing can live out there?'

'Well, while we've anyone left alive,' McAlexander shouted back, 'let's give 'em hell!'

On the 38th Infantry's right flank, Reid used his last reserves of cooks and water cart drivers late in the afternoon. The earlier part of the day saw the Grenadiers on both flanks and to his rear held back by McAlexander's troops in slit trenches. Reid was under the impression the troops streaming south were Frenchmen. In fact they were German. He could not rely on his support from his second line, as it was fighting for its own survival, but replacements arrived a few at a time. Reid promoted men in the field to lead counter-attacks. The last one, around five o' clock, was made up of a force of clerks, orderlies and typists led by the company cook. Reid was 'just too busy' to join in himself.

Further west in the direction of Château-Thierry, the 30th Infantry and their supporting artillery suffered all day under shelling and sniper fire from across the river. A Lieutenant taking messages between the 30th Infantry and its artillery (Dickman had placed the guns forward to give close support) had seven horses shot from under him in the course of the day, and both guns and gunners suffered losses. The surviving crews moved across, took over artillery left by the retreating French and manhandled it into position behind Reid's troops

By nightfall the 6th Grenadier Regiment had been virtually wiped out; half its number killed or wounded, the others taken prisoner. Most of the prisoners were taken in the Surmelin valley where they should have joined up with the 5th, whose remnants were forced back to the river's edge at the end of the day.

One company of the 6th Grenadiers did manage an advance of almost four kilometres up the Surmelin creek valley between American infantry advancing on their right and the artillery firing on their left, believing the other companies were only temporarily held up. Eventually they were spotted, but managed to hold out until nightfall when a few survivors made their way back in the darkness.

'We realised the attack had failed. July 15th saw our most severe defeat of the war. I've never seen so many dead; never such a frightful sight. The Americans completely annihilated two of our companies in close fighting. Hidden in the wheat they mowed down our men from a distance of about 40 paces. We knew them to be cold-blooded, but this was sheer bestial brutality. People who haven't had to fight them can talk about indifferent leadership, American bragging, and so on, but it was because of them we lost sixty percent in killed and wounded that day.'

CHAPTER 13

MIXED GERMAN FORTUNES

– Success for the Germans as the Marne is crossed between Varennes and Epernay – their attack is once more brought to a standstill east of Reims –

'Those skilled at making the enemy move do so by creating a situation to which he must conform. They entice him with something he is certain to take, and with lines of ostensible profit, they await him in strength.'

(Sun Tzu)

From Varennes, eastwards through Dormans and Port-à-Binson to Boursault, the Germans had far more success, placing some 75,000 men on the south bank, and establishing a front about five kilometres deep almost to Epernay. This didn't appear to disturb Foch too much. When Berthelot reported he could not hold the attack and the enemy was about to cross the river, Foch merely told him to contain their advance as much as possible.

It was nevertheless a day of great stress for the Supreme Commander. The first reports from the far side of Reims were more than satisfactory, so he set off for his meeting with Haig at Mouchy. However, Pétain, faced by seven German divisions on the south bank of the Marne, fearing the threat to Paris and possible further mutinies sparked by more casualties to add to the 400,000 since March, seemed to lose his nerve. He ordered Fayolle (whose divisions defending Paris had been allocated to Mangin) to suspend the planned Tenth Army attack and bring the troops back.

Pétain had never been fully behind Mangin's planned counter-attack; French Headquarters certainly tried to delay it, arguing it would be more effective when the German reserves were fully committed.

Foch, on his way to Mouchy, stopping at Fayolle's Noailles head-quarters, and finding him in the process of obeying GQG's order to prepare all available French reserves to go south, took decisive action. He immediately countermanded everything, told Fayolle that Mangin's attack was to start as soon as possible, pressing for the 17th, but finally agreeing to a day's postponement.

French Headquarters protested vigorously, but at half-past-midday Pétain had a telephone call from Foch at Mouchy telling him there could be no question of slowing, much less of halting Mangin's attack.

'In case of extreme need you may take only those troops you consider to be absolutely indispensable, informing me at once.' Having done this, he started his meeting with Haig.

In the meantime, intense arguments raged at Provins. Buat (who had replaced Anthoine as Major General of the French Army much against Pétain's wishes) spoke in strong support of the Mangin counter-stroke, and in the end the French Staff agreed to obey Foch's orders.

Ludendorff's troops were now advancing deeper and deeper into French territory, causing more and more perturbation at Provins, yet moving deeper and deeper into a net and in increasing danger of being cut off by the coming counter-attack.

And more troops were now on their way to strengthen that counter-attack.

The four British divisions Foch had asked for were already travelling south or preparing to move. The 62nd (West Riding) Division was making slow progress round Paris that day, preceded by thirty-four trains carrying the men of the 51st (Highland) Division who had fought by their side at Cambrai. As they jolted south, 40 men (or eight horses) to a railway truck, the Italian sector on the French Front west of Reims gave way, and a German advance started from Bligny down the Ardre valley towards Epernay aiming to join with the forces east of Reims, capturing the entire area, and dominating the Marne valley.

The 51st Division was at once rerouted to Nogent sur Seine, and that evening the troops were immediately moved by lorry to the Marne's south bank. The 62nd arrived south of Chalons the following day.

The Corps' other Divisions – the 15th (Scottish) and the 34th -had been ordered to move to an 'unknown destination' which eventually turned out to be the area north of Paris on the west of the salient. The Scots travelled by train, wet to the skin from a thunderstorm, arriving at Clermont on that day. The 34th, given only a few hours' notice of the move, arrived at Senlis the next day.

British Headquarters believed the Chemin des Dames disaster had affected French morale so badly that their ability to deliver a strong counter-attack was doubtful. In close touch with Provins, and knowing Pétain's defensive attitude only too well, Haig worried not only about the depletion of his reserves, but also that Pétain would use them to bolster his defence of Paris instead of giving extra power to Foch's offensive. After all, the only success to Foch's credit was the stemming of the Matz offensive and Haig knew any disaster on the Marne that put Paris in jeopardy might see Foch's plans for a counter-attack overruled by a combination of Pétain, the Grand Quartier Général staff and the French Government.

Back in Paris, Foch, in fact, was yet again under a cloud. When Berthelot reported the Germans about to cross the Marne, and Foch merely told him to 'limit their progress', Clémenceau was furious, raging that Foch was not the man he had been, and talking of sacking him. With German bridgeheads established on the south bank, the attaché to the War Council, Colonel Grasset, thought Foch finished. However, using a map to show the opportunities opening because of the German advance, he asked that any decision about Foch's future should be delayed a few days.

Nevertheless, the four British divisions were on their way south, and that night when General Smuts arrived, yet again offering Haig Government support if he thought Foch was pressing too hard, Haig replied that he 'would take the risk, accept the responsibility, and act in the main interest of the Allied cause'. He even gave this to Smuts in writing with the comment 'if Foch proves to be wrong, the blame will rest on me. On the other hand, if he is right, the credit will be his. With this,' he added pointedly, 'the Government should be well satisfied!'

Possibilities were opening up for the Allies. '. . . it was now necessary,' Foch recognised, 'to transform my rôle of co-ordination into one of management . . .'."

Among the German forces on the south bank of the Marne, wild rumours started to spread.

> 'Even though our attack up to Varennes had failed, we hoped that results on other parts of the front might be better. There were stories that Reims had been captured – that the Bavarian Division east of Varennes had made a spectacular advance of seventeen kilometres. They were nothing more than the usual rumours that go like wildfire through an army, and were, as so frequently happens, completely false..
>
> 'Everywhere it was the same story: heroic attacks: enormous losses: no significant result: We accepted this, and only hoped to be able to hold on to our position. Also we hoped to rest. A day like July 15th breaks body and nerves for weeks. Our ranks had been decimated. Everyone was despondent . . . – we'd left many comrades on the far bank of the river we'd left unburied. There was a sense of foreboding that time was running out for us as well . . . '

On the eastern flank of the salient 15 July had a very different story to tell.

Gouraud's Fourth Army was employing the 'elastic defence in depth' so scorned by Duchêne and suspected by Degoutte. Its thinly held front line, causing heavy German casualties as it retired, was to lure the attackers from the protection of their own artillery into a zone where a ferocious counter-barrage would hit them just as they reached Gouraud's main defences. If the information gathered by the Allies proved false, all the French batteries by now would be registered and soon subjected to the most appalling punishment.

At Chalons-sur-Marne, Gouraud and his Chief of Staff waited

anxiously. Precisely at the time predicted for the German attack, a huge shell arrived, destroyed the nearby generating station and put out every light in Headquarters. Both men heaved a sigh of relief. The information was obviously correct.

Despite the First and Third German Armies having been under heavy fire for three full hours before their own attack started, initial reports from German First Army Headquarters, like those from von Böhn, had been promising. Its Infantry Groups Lindequist, Gontard and Lange had been able to make their way to the jumping-off positions without trouble, their own artillery preparation and infantry attacks had started as ordered, and 'according to reports so far', the infantry was making good progress overall. The 3rd Guard Division was seen by an artillery observer reaching the old Roman road west of Mourmelon le Grand, and little reaction was reported from the French. Prisoners confirmed the French 124th and 163rd Divisions had moved back to their original positions. Air reconnaissance squadrons could not take off because of low cloud and ground mist. Also, all the observation balloons used by the German artillery to register targets had been shot down in air attacks.

The French bombardment had caused severe casualties among the assembling troops, the force of 20 tanks was knocked out by field guns firing over open sights, and before long, these reports of progress gave way to admissions that the advance was running into severe difficulties. Gouraud's front line caused the Germans severe losses, and when the defenders had been eliminated or driven back and the Germans were out of range of their own artillery protection, they came under fire from the main defences as Gouraud had planned.

The Third Army identified the 42nd American National Guard (The Rainbows) fighting in the second defence zone north of St. Hilaire au Temple. Its 165th Infantry Regiment from Manhattan was brought into the changing line of resistance a few companies at a time, always under control of their commander, General Mencher. Time after time they mounted fierce counter-attacks, and, knowing they lacked battle experience, the Germans used various ruses in an effort to break them. Dismounted Uhlans, wearing French uniforms and shouting in French accents, were immediately mown down. The same trick was tried again during the night. This time the Manhattans welcomed the Uhlans with open arms, then bayonetted them.

All this was not without cost. The Rainbows suffered almost 1500 casualties between the 15th and 18th.

However, the Germans not only lost heavily: they gained precisely the amount of ground Gouraud intended. By noon of the 16th, well under two days from the start of the offensive, von Below and von Einem, having occupied some one hundred and fifty square kilometres of useless territory littered with dead, and with abandoned equipment, obeyed Ludendorff's instructions 'for the First and Third Armies to suspend the offensive and re-organise into defence by withdrawing certain divisions for this purpose . . .' Indeed the 50th, 86th Divisions, and the 8th Bavarians of von Below's Army were so badly cut up they had to be pulled out completely to be replaced by fresh troops from Jäger regiments.

Both armies were still 30km north of the Marne, and back on the defensive.

Ludendorff admitted that the attack round Reims ' did not succeed at its first onslaught', and that 'the offensive was stopped the following day to avoid useless waste of strength.' But he maintained that the failure of the Marne offensive as a whole was due to one thing, and one thing only . . . to Allied foreknowledge of the attack; not to insufficient preparation, mistakes in planning or command, nor to a lack of fighting power, or demoralisation among his troops. Everything was due to treachery.

> 'The Americans obtained from treacherous German prisoners what we were preparing and where it was to take place'. . .

Leutnant Kurt Heffer was a little more dispassionate:-

> 'Why didn't the attack succeed?'

He went into the reasons in some detail: the bottom of the salient was restricted and under threat; communication with the rear was sketchy; the night attack made the location of enemy positions difficult, particularly as the Marne formed a natural barrier. As to the preparations: success was to be expected only if absolute secrecy prevented the enemy from rearranging his forces; if all means were taken to ensure constant progress of the infantry with minimal losses, and finally if the assaulting troops were morally and physically fresh and capable of attacking at maximum effort for several successive days. 'When we examine the attack from this point of view,' he ended, 'one must come to the conclusion that serious faults in planning were committed.'

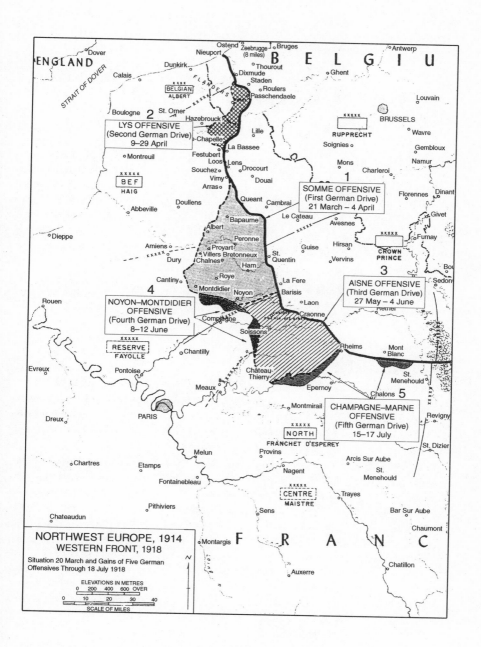

Figure 12

CHAPTER 14

TUESDAY 16 JULY, TO EARLY MORNING, THURSDAY 18 JULY

– After the failure east of Reims, Ludendorff plans to withdraw from the Marne's south bank – British troops start to arrive – ongoing preparations for the Allied counter-attack –

It needless were to tell what deeds were done,
Nor who did best, nor who did worst that day,
Nor who made head, nor who began to run,
Nor in retreat what chief was last away . . . '
(George Gascoigne – 'The Fruits of War')

Only thirty-six hours after his 'Offensive for Peace' started, Ludendorff realised that the eastern attack had failed. 'Once the decision to abort the Reims attack had been taken, it was pointless to attempt to advance further below the Marne or to leave our troops on its south bank. We had to make arrangements at once for a move back across the river.'

Expecting the Marne crossing to have been a major breakthrough, the High Command had provided transport to bring up large numbers of reinforcements, and this, together with the bridges set up across the river to supply the advance, was to be equally effective once it was decided to pull out the troops from the south bank. The retreat was fixed for the night of 20/21st.

The decision to withdraw was, of course, highly secret, and heavy French counter-attacks went on all through Tuesday and Wednesday, trying to dislodge the German bridgeheads. The French divisions driven back between Varennes and Boursault, though still in some disarray, were turning to attack the German positions, and tanks were on their way to make these attacks more effective.

German Headquarters was also having to cope with Allied pressure on other sectors of the salient. North of Soissons, the scene of fierce exploratory assaults during the previous days, attacks against the Ninth Army were still going on. 'It was, however,' von Eben reported, 'easier to contain them.' Ever since 11 July, reinforcements had been needed to stiffen those of his divisions that had suffered the most, and by now the exhausted 3rd Reserve Division would definitely have to be withdrawn. During its three weeks' spell in the front line it had suffered the greatest losses out of the four most under attack, and was completely used up. Permission for this being given, Group Headquarters implemented the move at once, but nothing could be done to relieve the remainder of the Ninth Army.

East of Reims the German rearguard tried to slow the advancing Allies while work went on at a furious pace to set up strong defence lines to the rear. Day and night long, the German First and Third armies were deluged in an unceasing heavy bombardment of high explosive and gas

One area, however, still gave Ludendorff hopes of some success. In spite of Allied counter-attacks, the Germans were still advancing down the Ardre valley from Bligny towards Marfaux west of Reims, and there was still a possibility of them joining up with their comrades to its east, cutting off the city, occupying the area and dominating the entire Marne valley. In fact, pressure on the Napoli and Salerno, Brescia and Alpi Brigades making up the IInd Italian Corps was so severe that their sector of the front was likely to be completely driven in, and the whole flank placed in danger. At present it looked as if Foch's plan for a two-pronged attack by Mangin and Berthelot on each side of the salient would have to be limited to Mangin's intended thrust.

To help stop the advance along the Ardre, and to push back the Germans already across the Marne, two divisions of the British XXIInd Corps (the 62nd and the 51st) had been routed towards Epernay. The 51st Highland, which still kept its reputation of being 'a bonny fighting machine' in spite of the reorganisations common to every British division, and was still entirely composed of Scottish units, set up Divisional Headquarters at Moussy, a little south-west of Epernay, and only a few kilometres from the German positions below the river at Boursault. Moussy was now a front-line town, with hundreds of Scots added to the crowds of French, Senegalese and Italians in its streets. Two enterprising members of the Division (guarded by a colleague with fixed bayonet to prevent trouble, – and to keep an eye out for the Military Police) finding a wine cellar in an abandoned house, disguised themselves as French peasants and sold off the lot, making a profit of 2,000 francs before being put out of business by resentful comrades.

The 62nd (West Riding) Division had eventually arrived at Mailly-le-Camp, over 40 kilometres south of Epernay. Reporting to Chalons-sur-Marne headquarters, General Sir Walter Braithwaite was told his Division was to be attached to Berthelot's Fifth Army. The West Ridings, who throughout their entire war service never gave up land they had once captured, were coming to terms with the further reorganisations and absorptions that had taken place in June, and with

95

men from Hampshire, Devon, Durham and even from New Zealand in its ranks, by now had lost all resemblance to its original formation as a Kitchener Volunteer division.

The two divisions were destined to fight their way together on either side of the river Ardre towards the Montagne de Bligny, while the other divisions of the Corps (the 15th and the 34th) were sent to join Mangin's Soissons attack in an attempt to 'pinch out' both German flanks.

The 34th Division, one of those disbanded in the April reorganisations and reformed only in the last days of June, was a hotchpotch of units from India, Egypt and Palestine together with some Gallipoli veterans, dispatched south to Senlis only a fortnight after its final draft reported for duty. Also travelling south, the 15th, like the 51st Division, was still completely made up of Scottish units: the Black Watch, Gordon Highlanders, Camerons, Royal Scots, Argyll and Sutherlands, Seaforths and the Cameronians all being represented. It eventually arrived at Clermont on the 18th.

Meanwhile, back at British Headquarters, heartened by the offer of Government support General Smuts had brought the previous evening, members of staff, because of the threat from Rupprecht, were urging Sir Douglas to invoke the Beauvais agreement and demand the immediate return of the XXIInd Corps to the British Zone.

Wednesday 17 July

Ludendorff's decision to pull his troops back across the Marne produced a flurry of activity and planning meetings taking place all morning at German Headquarters. About the same time at Bombon, General Du Cane (British liaison officer at Foch's headquarters) was given a letter to take to Haig recommending he start to deploy his reserves as a precaution against Rupprecht's threatened attack. As Du Cane was accompanied to his waiting car by General Weygand, he was quietly told, 'General Foch also gives you permission to tell Sir Douglas that Mangin's Army will start its attack with 20 divisions first thing tomorrow morning.'

Arriving at Montreuil-sur-Mer, Du Cane found that the letter demanding the immediate return of the XXIInd Corps had been written, and was waiting only for Haig's signature. In spite of the verbal message he had brought from Bombon, Haig still signed and sent it, but gave Du Cane along with it a personal message for Foch that if the British divisions were needed to exploit success, 'they should, of course, be used.'

By 5.00am that Wednesday the 62nd Division was starting to move towards the battle. The troops supporting the Divisional Infantry (Engineers, Signallers and other units), given no transport, were faced with a long, hard trek of 30 to 40 kilometres in a mixture of steamy heat and thunderstorms. As a result, the Division did not become fully operational until the 19th.

The British troops were only a small part of the forces moving to mount the counter-attack. Mangin's XXth Corps, made up of the 1st and 2nd American and the 1st Moroccan Divisions, was moving into the forests near Soissons. The red-fezzed Moroccans, reckoned to be the best shock troops in all the French Army, were to be chanted into battle with an accompaniment of prayers from their Mullahs. Because of their previous heavy casualties, three battalions of Senegalese and a battalion of Foreign Legionnaires were with them. The American Divisions were either side of them.

Opposite, quite unaware of the build-up, the German IXLth Reserve Corps (Group Staabs) had three divisions astride the Aisne between Autrêches and Cutry. From there the 13th Württenburg Division (part of Group Watter) took over the line. Mangin's XXth Corps faced the left part of Staabs' and the right part of the sector held by Watter's Corps. The 2nd US Division would be attacking the point where Watter's 14th Reserve Division and the 42nd Division joined.

Below the 2nd Americans, the XXXth Corps of the Tenth Army took over the line down towards Château-Thierry, where the XIth and IInd French Corps were to attack. Round Château-Thierry itself, just to the west of the salient's tip, Edwards' US 26th Division from New England were with Degoutte's veterans, and along the Marne, Dickman's 3rd American Division, having halted the German crack Grenadier storm troops two days earlier, was preparing to counter-attack.

Altogether some 150,000 Americans were alongside the French troops in the salient. Muir's 28th Division was with de Mitry's Ninth Army, while the 42nd Division 'Rainbows' under Mencher, having already helped Gouraud halt the German attack east of Reims, were following up the German withdrawal with the Fourth Army.

The German defences between Soissons and Château-Thierry consisted of outpost zones guarding the main line of resistance where machine-guns and infantry at battalion strength were dug in to form strongpoints. Beaurepaire farm in the Vierzy ravine south of Chaudon was one such. About a kilometre and a half further back, the first line of artillery waited, with more troops in support, ready to mount counter-attacks. The main artillery positions were behind again.

That night Ludendorff set off from his Avesnes Headquarters to meet the Bavarian Crown Prince's staff, for the time was now almost ripe for Rupprecht's hammer-blow to fall against Haig in the north. 'I myself went to the Headquarters of the Army Group of Crown Prince Rupprecht to review once more the state of their preparations. The attack was intended as a continuation of that which had been suspended at the end of April. It was to be made by the Fourth and Sixth Armies

97

north of the Lys, its objectives being the possession of the commanding heights between Poperinge and Bailleul, as well as the high ground round Hazebrouck.'

By now the bulk of Mangin's force was buried in the forests of Retz and Villers-Cotterêts, the last elements making their move up to the attack line through a heavy rainstorm during the night.

Also by now the bodies of the Tzar and his family had been buried in the Russian forests near the scene of their imprisonment.

Because of the storm, the night of the 17th again was very dark; no lights were allowed, and the troops were making their way along paths that wound through tunnels in the forest lit only by the flashes of lightning above the interlaced branches. Roads had a narrow strip in the centre that was paved, and soil verges concealed drainage ditches on either side. Breakdowns and vehicles damaged by collisions had to be pushed over the edge to clear the route, much in the same way that kept the supply route of the Voie Sacrée from Bar le Duc clear during the Verdun battle.

Major Berthier, an officer on Mangin's staff, had fought over the ground back in 1914, and was able at least to give the Americans some idea of the lie of the land. Much later – almost at the end of the 1920s – General Giraud said orders for the American attack had been drawn up after comprehensive air reconnaissance. The 2nd Division's commander, Harbord, when he heard this, strongly disagreed.

The barrage was to start at 4.35 am with the infantry and tanks immediately following up, but many of the troops didn't know exactly where the start line was. It was vital to be there on time to keep up with the rolling barrage. Wet through, inadequately guided and frequently lost, French, Moroccans, Senegalese and Americans, all flanked by troops speaking a different language, were about to attack positions the Germans had been preparing for five weeks.

Bullard, commanding the two Divisions making up the American Ist Corps, was acting under the orders of the French XXth Corps Commander, Berdoulat. His subordinates, the Divisional Commanders Harbord and Summerall, were desperately trying to duplicate and distribute last minute orders. Harbord didn't even know where to find the ammunition dump supplying his 2nd Division. His men found one nine kilometres away intended for the 1st Division, and commandeered it. When two of Harbord's 23rd Infantry battalions eventually managed to find their places, the third, having become entangled with men of the 9th Infantry, was still missing. After that two battalions of Marines caused further delay by cutting across its front. By the time it was found at last, and its French guides were given proper directions, the 3rd battalion troops were drenched to the skin, minus machine guns, confused by two changes of direction, and had a full two kilometres to go to their first objective. They emerged from the forest just after the barrage started and had to make a 300 metre dash to catch up.

Mangin's attack was literally 'up and running' . . .

CHAPTER 15

THE MORNING OF MANGIN'S COUNTER-ATTACK; THURSDAY 18 JULY 1918

– The German line between the Aisne and Marne broken –

'Voilà le commencement de la fin.'
(*Charles-Maurice de Talleyrand*)

The first messages warning that the salient was under threat arrived at the Crown Prince's Headquarters shortly after a quarter to four that morning. The American 26th and French 167th Divisions were advancing around Belleau Wood, with the New Englanders, enhancing the American reputation for ferocity, charging strongpoints headlong regardless of casualties. The struggle was so bitter and losses were so heavy that messages were sent back by trios of 'runners', a minute apart, in hopes that at least one of them would get through to Divisional Headquarters. By 9am that morning the Germans had been driven from the villages of Torcy, Givry and Belleau, above Belleau wood.

Less than half an hour later calls for help were coming from the opposite end of the battlefront. Gouraud's Fourth Army was putting down a very heavy sustained barrage east of Reims. It was so fierce on the sector held by the First Army's Guards Ersatz and 199th Divisions that it seemed almost certain there would soon be an attack.

Instructions to meet these threats had scarcely gone out, when at 4.35 am the entire sky from Soissons to Château-Thierry lit up as more than two thousand guns opened up together to pound the German line.

Exactly twenty-five minutes later, another extremely heavy bombardment started both in the Montagne de Reims area and along the Marne. Everything pointed to the imminent start of a major assault, but where would it fall? Between Soissons and Château-Thierry? Along the Marne up to Reims? Perhaps east from Reims to Ste. Menehould? This was one of the longest battle fronts of the war. Ground and air observation were equally impossible because of thick fog across the salient; for once the weather was favouring the Allies. There might even be multiple attacks.

A signal was sent off to General Ludendorff, away from the action with Rupprecht at Tournai, saying it was strongly suspected French troops were hidden in the woods around Villers-Cotterêts, and were almost certainly backed by strong reserves.

Above Soissons, von Eben's troops had already suffered serious casualties during the past days; the blow might well fall there! Degoutte's joint force of Americans and French was already on the move below the Ourcq, and more American Infantry threatened the Marne crossings as far as Dormans. From there, eastwards to Epernay, the German divisions across the river were fighting off counter-attacks by de Mitry's Ninth Army; already the French 1st Cavalry Corps, advancing behind the artillery barrage there, had driven the German line back a kilometre. Then, by mid-morning in the Forêt de Reims, Nanteuil la Fosse had fallen to a 14th Divisional attack, and the Germans were retreating in the Bois de Courton. Finally Gouraud's line, so recently alive with vicious counter-attacks, again threatened action: its artillery barrage on the German positions from Reims towards the east could well herald a new Fourth Army offensive.

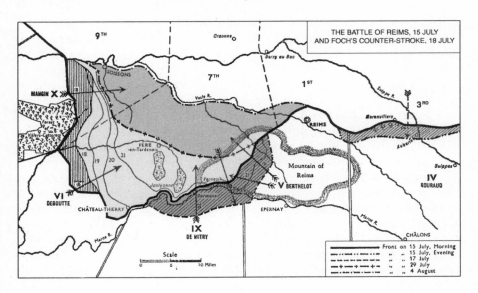

Figure 13

These, however, were not the attacks that made the breakthrough that day, for the positions held by the Sixth, Ninth and Fifth French Armies below the Marne and in the Forêt de Reims, and additionally in Berthelot's case a lack of reinforcements, did not permit spectacular advances. The honour went to Mangin. His preparatory moves had established excellent positions, and the Tenth Army, lying in wait in the forests, was to give the Germans their biggest shock since the previous Autumn. Now that the Germans were across the Marne the salient's flank was vulnerable, and the massed tanks and twenty infantry divisions were ready to strike that flank without warning. Leaving his command post before daybreak, his final orders given, Mangin was at hill 255, an observation post 4 kilometres north east of Villers-Cotterêts.

After pounding the front line, Mangin's rolling barrage started to move east, its curtain of fire saturating the rear areas. As it moved, more than three hundred Renault FT-17 light tanks clattered out of the forests, followed by troops of the Ist, XXth, XXXth, XIth, IInd and VIIth Corps of the French Army, breaking down the wire defences, isolating, and wiping out the German advance posts.

Above the Aisne, on the extreme left of the Ist Corps, the 162nd Division, told by Mangin to remain in their trenches when the barrage opened, started to advance against Fontenoy at 5.20am. From Vingré, near Nouvron, its troops, and the men of the Corps' 153rd and 11th Divisions, with the 72nd in support, took up the attack almost to Missy aux Bois below the river, where the 253rd Division on the Corps' right flank joined up with the troops of the 'Big Red One', attached to, and fighting on the left flank of the XXth Corps. It was vital the Aisne flank should be strongly held against any possible counter-attack, and more reinforcements were sent across next day when the XXth Corps' 69th Division was transferred to the area.

Their left flank secure, the central Divisions of the Tenth Army between the Aisne and the Savières brook, were soon advancing quickly towards the important objectives of the Chaudun plateau and the heights round Villers-Hélon. Here, the XXth Corps (the 1st and 2nd American Divisions either side of the 1st Moroccans) were crossing a plain broken by hills and ravines, making quickly towards the Crise valley. If the heights overlooking the Crise were taken, the important rail network at Soissons could be brought under artillery fire.

The US 1st Division had been in position with an hour to spare, and started to advance immediately behind the French tanks. In spite of suffering heavy losses, every objective they had been given for the end of the day was taken by 10am. On the other side of the Moroccans, the troops of the 2nd Division's 23rd Infantry (the ones forced to run to catch up with the rolling barrage) still managed to gain their objectives by 8am, though also, like the 1st Division, suffering heavy loss.

Nearer Château-Thierry, further south, the divisions of Degoutte's Sixth Army along the Ourcq, having surprised the enemy outposts, tackled the main line of defence. This was broken by a violent artillery bombardment, and the advance resumed a few minutes after 6 am.

German Supreme Headquarters had, of course, given exact and detailed orders about the setting up of defences between Soissons and Château-Thierry, and these had been meticulously carried out, but the speed and ferocity of the unexpected attack completely overwhelmed everything. Behind the lines, troops taking advantage of the quiet spell, had even started to harvest the crops for their own use. In the confusion that was everywhere along the entire 45 kilometre front, men caught like that could only fight where they stood, hampered by chest-high corn, circled by light tanks whose revolving turrets were spitting fire. After them came the infantry – wave upon wave – thousands of confident, well-armed French and Americans.

Von Eben and his Ninth Army Staff, also forced into retreat, tried to rally the confused troops in the rear. Panic began to spread; thousands surrendered, their usual fighting spirit broken by the speed of the attack, in some cases by battle fatigue, and for many, by the first stages of influenza. Survivors said that those who surrendered reasoned that 'they had done as much as could be asked of them.'

In spite the sudden overwhelming shock, some units rallied and set up positions further back in the woods, managing to slow the Allied advance a little. They were mainly veterans with experience of defensive fighting on the Aisne and in Champagne during the 1917 battles. Without them, the German retreat could well have become a full-scale rout.

The German High Command concluded from reports that reached them in the next days that many of the front-line units had surrendered *en masse*, and they sent out denunciations of the many who shouted 'Kamerad' and put up their hands, or those who had fled without trying to use the country's natural defence features. Ludendorff, in particular, condemned the mass surrenders, saying theirs was not at all like behaviour in the past when German troops had endured day-long drumfire without flinching.

Indeed, it was not. In no way could 18 July be compared with the situations Ludendorff described. First of all to be comprehensively shelled, then trapped without adequate cover while hordes of enemy infantry overran their positions and tanks fired at them from the rear, was enough to cause a complete breakdown of morale.

By 7am, the Tenth and Sixth Army Command Posts at Bonneuil-en-Valois and May-en-Multien knew everything was going exactly to plan, and at Provins, when news of the opening successes reached French Army Headquarters, Pétain ordered the 12th Division to be brought across from Lorraine, and the 19th Division to move from Nanteuil to take position behind the Reserve Army Group. At the same time, a telegram ordered the Highland Division to join the West Ridings and relieve the Italian IInd Corps, now in danger of complete collapse. If the British did not arrive quickly, Reims might well be lost, and Pétain also hoped that giving both divisions to Berthelot, would not only halt the German thrust, but would also enable him to move over to the offensive.

Once he knew that Pétain, in spite of his distrust of the counter-stroke, was taking decisive action, Buat, the new État Major Général at Provins, left for Bombon to discuss the battle's next stages with Foch. Pétain also contacted Bombon to confirm the 62nd and 51st Divisions would join the battle as soon as possible. The other British Divisions (the 15th and 34th), together with any others made available for Fayolle's Reserve Army Group, were to go towards Villers-Cotterêts but would not be sent into battle without Foch's approval.

In spite of the promised counter-attack having started, Rupprecht's continuing menace in Flanders was still worrying British Headquarters intensely, and General Du Cane arrived at Foch's Headquarters with Haig's letter saying that an estimated 31 divisions now seemed poised to strike, that the British Second Army could muster only 16 divisions at most, and it was imperative the British XXIInd Corps should immediately return north.

Foch replied at once by telegram, refusing the demand. Because of the successful start to the battle, and particularly in view of Haig's verbal message that had come with the letter, the 15th and 34th Divisions were under orders to move to the Villers-Cotterêts sector. Once the telegram was on its way, he sat down, explaining his reasons more fully in writing. Although, he told Haig, he was completely aware of the danger in Flanders, the enemy was now under attack by all available forces along a 130km front running east from the Aisne. Any major German attack against the British front was impossible for the time being. If, however, some limited action should take place, British reserves brought from quiet areas would provide resistance and, even if he were in a position to order immediate release of the British Corps, all the transport available was needed for the Marne battle. It would be six to eight days before Haig's four divisions could possibly be back in the British Zone, 'where they would make little difference to a show of strength, while their departure from the Marne would definitely cause difficulties. A return to the British Zone would risk not only the success of the present battle, but that of later attacks.'

This meant that during that morning French Headquarters could tell Fayolle that six more divisions, (the 12th, 52nd, 25th, 62nd French and the 15th and 34th British), were to be sent to exploit the success. Fayolle himself ordered the 7th Division and the 87th (moved behind the front by car to Vivières) to join his reserves, ready to strengthen the attack. From the extra divisions supplied by French Headquarters, the 15th and 34th British and the 87th French were allocated to Mangin, the 52nd French Division was moved behind the Sixth Army and the other three provided by Pétain (the 12th, 26th and 62nd) were brought up immediately behind the battlefront. The light tanks of the 501st Regiment of Artillery of Assault were also ordered to join the heavy tanks and attacking infantry of the XXth and XXXth Corps.

All that day Foch chivvied Pétain to find reinforcements for Fayolle's attempt to cut off von Böhn's vulnerable Seventh Army. A special directive ordered every available unit south of a line from Château-Thierry to Reims to reinforce Mangin and Degoutte, and Maistre's Headquarters was telephoned and told to make the French 52nd and American 42nd Divisions ready for an immediate move back west. By evening, a telegram ordered troops of the 52nd Division to Meux by car and lorry. Once there, Fayolle sent them straight on to Marolles and La Ferté-Milon. Another telegram from Headquarters ordered the Eastern Army Group to send the French 25th and 62nd Divisions west by rail the same evening.

Early that morning, when the Tenth Army attack had opened, General Robillon, commanding the IInd Cavalry Corps, had been with Mangin at Côte 255. At 7.15am Mangin had ordered him to move his mounted troops up through the infantry and spearhead the attack. Fayolle, at his Lamorlaye Command Post, was also planning cavalry strikes towards Fère-en-Tardenois 'to cut off the last of the enemy engaged on the Marne.' Knowing the danger to Mangin's Army of a flank attack from across the Aisne, he issued the first of what were to be many warnings during the battle for the Tenth Army Commander always to have a division in reserve, guarding the left flank against any such move.

Before the thick fog that had so helped the initial success had cleared completely, the Germans, with no time even to ask for a counter-barrage of gas, had lost their advanced positions in front of the Ourcq and first lines of defence along both Ourcq and Aisne. Nothing like it had happened since the Allied attack at Cambrai in 1917, and again it was made possible by the use of massed tanks – this time the much improved Renault T17 light model. Its speed, manoeuvrability and revolving turret formed a weapon that completely overwhelmed the defending troops and utterly bewildered their commanders.

As soon as the fog began to thin around nine, air patrols were aloft in force to harass the Germans and monitor progress. They spotted the XXth Corps at Missy aux Bois (the American 1st Division), at Chaudun (the Moroccans), and on the edge of Vierzy (the 2nd Divisional Americans), while to the south the 38th Division (XXXth Corps) was almost at Montramboeuf and the 48th at Villers-Hélon. German reconnaissance planes, also airborne at last, reported enemy reinforcements coming up in strength.

Among the confusion of reports coming to the Crown Prince's headquarters, a message arrived from Ludendorff demanding 'the rash attack headed by French tanks south-west of Soissons be broken up'. This drew the rather tart reply that in view of the seriousness of the situation, it might be better if the Quartermaster General returned to Avesnes at once. This gave Ludendorff his first doubts about ordering the start of the 'Hagen' attack. If the enemy offensive below Soissons forced von Böhn to withdraw, might not a similar attack come on the Reims flank and cut off the entire salient? The original plan of switching offensives from one sector of the Western Front to another would have to be rethought because of this intensive counter-stroke; and if Rupprecht's 'Hagen' assault had to be given up – even postponed for the time being – could the forces needed ever be brought together again?

> 'During the discussion at Crown Prince Rupprecht's Army Group Headquarters on the morning of the 18th, I received the first news that, by means of an unexpected tank attack, the French had pierced the line southwest of Soissons . . . I concluded the conference (naturally in a state of the greatest nervous tension) and returned to Avesnes.'

By mid-morning the Allies were on the plateaux round Dommiers with French artillery in close support, and by 10.55am the railway yards at Soissons were under fire. Further north-east, resistance was stiffer, and two more days' fighting would be needed before the Paris to Soissons road was cut beyond Missy aux Bois and the ravine behind it taken at bayonet point. The XIth French Corps further down the line was also meeting fierce resistance below the Savières brook. The 128th Division, which should have broken out north of the buisson (thicket) de Hautwison, was struggling forward only slowly, the 5th Division's move up to the line had met unexpected set backs and the 41st Division was at a complete halt in front of Ancienville.

Back at the centre of the XXth Corps, the Moroccan Division's attack began to lose momentum, so the American Divisions moved to cover the gap and continued the advance...so rapidly that the troops on the flank of the 9th Infantry were unable to keep up. As the Corps reached the northern part of Vierzy ravine about midday, American Marines bringing back prisoners were accosted by a crowd of Senegalese attached to the Moroccans. These coloured troops were held in awe by their Allies and in dread by the enemy. A few days later on the far side of the salient, enquiring what burial rites should be used for a Senegalese casualty, a British chaplain was told, 'killed in battle – not buried....eaten!' Stories of torture and mutilation of prisoners had spread through Allied and German armies alike, and these particular Senegalese were obviously intent on annexing the captured Germans to make a few experiments. The Marines refused to give them up, and the Germans, borrowing weapons from their captors, lined up side by side with them to defy the Muslims.

CHAPTER 16

THURSDAY 18 JULY 1918.
THE AFTERNOON AND EVENING

– The end of the Germans' last advance – the Allied attack
continues –

'Voilà le commençement de la fin'.
(Charles-Maurice de Talleyrand)

In an attempt to stem the advance, German Army Group Headquarters ordered a counter-attack from Saconin to Mont Castile (the hill south-east of Villers-Hélon), but before it could be mounted the full seriousness of the situation became known, and the orders were changed. Three divisions were sent to the Seventh Army to prepare a defence line between Soissons and the hills north of Château-Thierry with the clear understanding that troops were to occupy this new position only in case of absolute necessity

Another position, still further back, was being set up from Bucy-le-Long on the north bank of the Aisne, and with these new defences in mind, fresh orders transferred Group Borne from the Seventh Army to the First, and Group Watter from the Ninth to the Seventh. In addition, in order to support Groups Winckler and Watter which had suffered heavily – the one at the hands of Degoutte's troops, the other from Mangin's attacks – headquarters hastily assembled a new group, Group Etzel, from the 10th and 19th Reserve Divisions, brought the troops up in lorries behind the threatened front and ordered them to mount an immediate counter-attack.

In its initial attack, the French Sixth Army above and to the west of Château-Thierry, had driven back Groups Winckler and Schoeler to Chouy and the west of Monthiers before being halted. A heavy artillery barrage in the early afternoon prepared a second wave of heavy attacks led by tanks with air support. These, however, were more isolated and spasmodic. Group Watter, again under attack from Vierzy through Chouy to south-west of Neuilly-St-Front, was pushed back to some extent, but Group Schoeler's 4th Ersatz Division defeated all attacks against the hill east of Lice-Clignon, and the 87th Division even regained some ground. The fact that these afternoon attacks were isolated persuaded German Headquarters Pétain had momentarily lost control of the situation and had missed the chance to smash their defence. For the rest of the day and all that night, German heavy artillery drenched the Allied lines and rear areas with a mixture of high explosive and gas.

Because of the previous night's storm damage and the log-jam of supply waggons in the Villers-Cotterêts forests, Robillon's Cavalry did not arrive on the Tenth Army front until two in the afternoon. Its 4th Division was utilised north of Vierzy round Dommiers and St- Pierre-Aigle, on the left of the 2nd Americans, its 6th (forced to dismount) used to reinforce the 38th division's stalled attack at Montramboeuf and in the Bois de Mauloy west of Vertes-Feuilles, and its 2nd Division at Coeuvres. A battalion of infantry also arrived by lorry from Mortefontaine and Vivières to support them, but it was now certain there would be no cavalry charges terrorising disorganised units with lance and sabre behind the German lines that day. At Vierzy, the troopers were even unable to get across the plateau on horseback, and eventually had to arrive in small groups on foot.

Meanwhile, stout German resistance continued north-east of Chaudun round Vauxbuin.

By two in the afternoon Mangin was urging the XIth Corps to 'mount the agreed operations with dispatch', and exhorting General Penet to press home his XXXth Corps' attack towards Villers-Hélon 'with the utmost resolution'. Reinforcements were on their way, Penet was assured. The British 34th division was already marching through Largny to join him.

About the same time that Mangin's messages went out to the XIth and XXXth Corps about increasing their pressure, Ludendorff arrived back at Avesnes. He was to write later:

> 'I arrived at two in the afternoon. The General Field Marshal (i.e. Hindenburg) met me at the railway station. In the Command Room we immediately discussed the serious situation on the left wing of the Ninth Army and the right wing of the Seventh. The picture of a huge battle and speedy enemy advance became clear, and equally clear that round Soissons, the enemy had planned and prepared for this. The railway line forming our communications, and which had to be held, was at risk.'

As early as March, the German High Command had intended a follow-up assault on Reims and had earmarked reserves for it. Now, having deployed them there, and with the other forces in position ready for the intended 'Hagen' offensive, the troops available to stem the Soissons advance were either with Rupprecht, or at the wrong side of the salient.

However, within half an hour decisions had been made. At 2.30pm two divisions were taken from Rupprecht's force to join the German Crown Prince's Army Group : at 2.49pm an order went to both the Army Groups that heavy artillery and mortars intended for 'Hagen' were to be placed on standby for use by von Böhn's Seventh Army. The 5th Infantry Division was transferred from the Eighteenth Army at Laon, and three groups of fighter 'planes and three other air squadrons were placed under the German Crown Prince's command. The Fifth Army's 76th Reserve Division was also to be brought across from La Ferté .

Plans for the Reims attack were immediately put on hold. Hindenburg had already informed the Kaiser of this decision, assuring him that 'it would definitely be resumed as soon as the enemy push against the salient's flank could be halted, and our line re-established.' Meanwhile, the troops who were south of the Marne were ordered to stand fast 'as long as possible'. New defences would be prepared on the north bank. The coded order went out that afternoon, but the situation was now causing such concern that a second quickly followed it, ordering the withdrawal to start that very night.

Opposite Jaulgonne, the divisions of Degoutte's Sixth Army on the river's south bank were making tank-led attacks against the German 113rd, 36th and 10th Reserve Divisions. These were held, but further east above the river, Group Conta's 2nd Guard Division was driven out of Tincourt, and Group Schmettow's 185th Division was forced into the southern part of the Bois du Roi above the hamlet.

> 'On July 18th the enemy attacked us far more energetically with tanks, but without any greater success. The order to recross the Marne was received as a message of deliverance . . . also we had news that things were going badly behind on our right. The enemy attacking in force from Villers-Cotterêts had advanced 16 kilometres that day. We had no option other than to make a withdrawal back to the north bank of the Marne. We clenched our teeth: we now had to use our strength in stopping the march of assembling forces. The men were patient and silent, retaining their honour as they copied the example of the veterans of 1914.' (German 36th Division diary.)

Ludendorff later painted a rosier picture.

> 'In spite of these disappointments we had succeeded in weakening the enemy's front in Flanders by forcing him to move reserves from there. It was decided to send some of our troops in the Reims area, no longer needed for the next assault, to Rupprecht in the north to launch the long-planned 'Hagen' attack there as soon as it was feasible.'

The French VIIth Corps, between the IInd Corps and the Americans, gained more ground during the early afternoon but the IInd Corps advance came to a halt after its 33rd Division fought its way into the buisson de Cresnes by mid-morning. Further progress could be made neither there, nor against the heights of Marizy-Ste.-Geneviève. This in turn held up Mangin's right flank, and so joint attacks by the flanks of both Corps were planned against the heights of Chouy and Noroy-sur-Ourcq for the middle of the afternoon. Mangin transferred the 1st Division to the XXXth Corps at 3.15pm with instructions to take Louâtre. As the 5th Division had now by-passed the 128th, he told the XIth Corps to move the 128th Division back into reserve.

The situation was becoming increasingly dangerous for the Germans. Their lines of communication were being disrupted by the French heavy artillery bombardment, and there was no possibility of reinforcements arriving before the next day to slow, if not to halt, the Allied advance. The presence of fresh troops might have altered the whole course of the battle.

About 7pm, the Allied Headquarters knew considerable gains had been made. Air reconnaissance reported grenade battles taking place in Oulchy-le-Château, but this was not confirmed. On the heights round Villers-Hélon, Louâtre, and in the buisson de Hautwison the Tenth and Sixth Armies were still meeting stiff opposition, but more fierce attacks brought some success. Villers- Hélon and Louâtre were bypassed by the 48th and 1st Divisions, the buisson des Aubissons and Deborday by the 128th and the 5th, Ancienville and Noroy-sur-Ourcq by the 41st and 33rd . . . and now, when the Tenth and Sixth Armies successfully linked up on the Ourcq, it meant the Germans were faced with setting up a new defence line 9 kilometres back from the centre of Mangin's start line, and 5 kilometres on the middle sector first attacked by Degoutte's Sixth. By the end of the day, the German line ran from Fontenoy, through Vauxbuin, Vierzy, Villers-Hélon, Noroy-sur-Ourcq, Marizy-Saint-Mard , Breuil, Licy-Clignon, down to Belleau and Bouresches.

By then the Tenth Army advance had gained almost 12 kilometres in places, and an overall advance of around 5 kilometres had been made along a front of 45 kilometres. From that moment to the end of the war, the Allies continued to advance and the Germans to fall back.

More Allied troops were arriving. The 15th (Scottish) Division detraining at Clermont, Liancourt and Pont-Ste-Maxence, caused some excitement, as it was the first time the civilians there had seen the fabled 'ladies from hell'. Late that night the Division was ordered to move at dawn to join Berdoulat's XXth Corps with the Americans and Moroccans fighting below Soissons.

That evening Fayolle sent orders that 'the battle begun with such fortunate results, will be pursued during the night.' Mangin's centre was 'to continue to push towards Hartennes and Fère-en-Tardenois, while the right wing invests Oulchy-le-Château, and attempts to encircle the plateau of Chouy.' No chance was to be given for an enemy counter-attack, and the 87th Division went to Mangin 'to reinforce the advance'. In return, he was to send the 2nd Cavalry Corps, having made no headway, back into the reserve.

The Sixth Army was to continue its advance in the general direction of Neuilly-St-Front, but also extend its line to the right to link up with the front down towards Château-Thierry.

When these instructions arrived, both Army Commanders had given their orders for the next day's attacks and they could not be altered in time. Both, however, repeated their early evening orders to take up the offensive again at 4.am the next morning.

That night, too, the 51st Highland Division, because of the day's success round Soissons and the opportunity now to 'pinch out' both flanks, received Pétain's orders to join the 62nd Division in the Forêt de la Montagne de Reims.

Even in the prevailing mood of euphoria, the Allies were inclined to caution. Though July 18th had brought an amazing initial success, German tenacity in defence was well known, and the opportunity to 'mop up' the Marne's south bank that night was missed through lack of decisive action, when enemy divisions were already withdrawing in secret.

> 'Our troops recrossed under fire on previously-constructed bridges during the night of 18/19 July without much loss. The enemy obviously was not aware of the move; so much so that our patrols were able to remain for several hours on the south bank before rejoining their regiments and commands without interference.' (5th Grenadiers' battalion diary)

Ludendorff did not give up hope. In a telephone conversation that evening he told von Kuhl 'We hope to replace the divisions we had to take from 'Hagen' as soon as the situation on the Ninth and Seventh Army front quietens.' When the artillery could also be reallocated was still unclear. It was still needed to contain the French offensive. For the time being Ludendorff would 'demand a determined defence of the right flank', and when the present situation was remedied, it was 'almost certain' that 'Hagen' would be resumed.

Obviously his mood of that morning, approving the plans at Tournai for the Flanders offensive against Haig, had changed considerably. It was now only 'almost certain' that 'Hagen' would be resumed.

A final German victory was also starting to lack certainty.

Almost as a postscript to the day, the Americans were confirmed in their belief that cavalry charges could not themselves break the German defence. Pershing, at Cambrai as an observer, realised cavalry had had its day in a modern war. During the late afternoon of the 18th, French cavalry, breastplates polished and pennants flying, had blocked ammunition supplies as its forage train dawdled across the Americans' supply route. Now, in the day's very last minutes, Harbord and his 2nd US Divisional Chief of Staff set up headquarters at Vertes Feuilles Farm.

'There now appeared,' said Harbord, 'a French Cavalry Division Commander. He was a man of years . . . so many years in fact, that his bearded chin trembled as he spoke to me about riding in with his Cavalry Division behind the Germans at Château-Thierry and ending the resistance at a stroke. He spoke of his lack of artillery, and I offered to supply it. He mentioned his lack of reserves, and we offered him the 6th Marines in trucks, ready to follow his cavalry. He hesitated, and decided to wait until morning. I told him of my intention to move my headquarters a mile forward to Beaurepaire Farm. He was to have an officer there to meet me to arrange for the artillery I would lend him in the morning. When he departed, I asked Preston Brown if he thought we would see him again. "Yes," Preston Brown commented. "When we all come together at the end of the war to be decorated, he'll be there . . . "'

CHAPTER 17

FRIDAY 19 JULY 1918

– Operations to clear the Germans from the Marne's south bank –
attempts to cut off the salient continue –

*'a whole empire walking very slowly, dying in front and pushing forward behind.
And another empire walked very slowly backwards a few inches at a time, leaving
the dead like a million bloody rags . . . '*

(F. Scott Fitzgerald)

All that day attack and counter-attack went on, Foch determined to keep
up the battle's momentum; Ludendorff equally resolved to regain the
initiative. To slow the Allied advance and stiffen the flank between
Soissons and Château-Thierry, the natural reaction was to use units
massed for the Reims offensive and rush them west across the salient.
Hindenburg later gave his opinion, with the advantage of course of
hindsight, that they would have been better used to make a counter-
attack across the Aisne on Mangin's flank. Still, this reinforcement of
the flanks, and Ludendorff's constant determination to hold them,
meant the main body of troops, when eventually forced to withdraw, was
always protected.

As reports started to arrive at Bombon that morning from the various
Army Groups, Supreme Headquarters' staff began to map the previous
day's gains and assess the battle's progress. Foch himself left for Provins
to discuss its future stages with Pétain. At the end of their meeting they
sent out this joint order:

> 'Our objective is the destruction of the enemy forces south of the Aisne
> and Vesle. Fighting must be conducted with the utmost vigour and speed
> to exploit surprise. The Tenth and Sixth Armies must continue their
> advance towards Fère-en-Tardenois; the Ninth's task is to throw the
> enemy from the Marne's south bank, and the Fifth, moving over to
> the offensive as soon as possible, must establish a line from Châtillon
> to Bligny prior to cutting the road from Ville-en-Tardenois to Verneuil'.

Back in Paris the general opinion was that there was little hope of an
immediate German collapse. Every half-hour, shells arriving from the
German monster 'Paris' gun brought their daily toll of damage and
casualties, and the meetings of politicians, army staff and technical
advisers went on planning for the battles of 1919 and for the immediate

113

moving of munition factories and vital supplies further south if the Germans advanced again.

After issuing the joint order with Foch, Pétain telegrammed his detailed instructions to Maistre's and Fayolle's Army Groups. Two telegrams to Maistre's Headquarters recommended the Ninth Army should 'pursue the attack with vigour, forcing the enemy to abandon the south bank of the Marne'; the one following saying that because the British operation to take over the Ardre valley sector was bound to be complicated, that 'their advance should take the form of a surprise attack in conjunction with French troops'.

In other words, those of Fayolle's units south of the Marne, Maistre's entire Ninth Army, and the elements of the Fifth in the Forêt de Reims were all urged to move over to the offensive. Even though Berthelot now knew he could bring up the Highland and West Riding Divisions to relieve the Italian IInd Corps, he was still faced with serious problems because the British artillery had not arrived, but below the Marne, the Ninth Army had already started to probe the German defences. Fayolle's divisions towards Château-Thierry were also preparing to use tanks, break the enemy line, throw von Böhn's troops back across the river and send the IIIrd Infantry and Ist Cavalry Corps after them in hot pursuit.

However, the retreat planned by Ludendorff had already started. Group Kathen's three divisions recrossed under heavy artillery fire, and Groups Wichura and Conta also pulled back to the north bank, with plenty of time to spike the captured French guns before they left. There was bitter talk among the troops in the south bank bridgeheads as rumours spread about the disaster round Soissons. 'We, who had already endured so much, would now have to use the rest of our strength in stopping the enemy advance . . .' (Heffer).

The German retreat across the Marne was the most significant move that day: the Allies made little progress elsewhere. Berthelot, waiting for the arrival of the British artillery, realised any attack along the Ardre would be practically impossible without its support. The weather also was not helping. Across the whole salient heat and humidity were causing violent thunderstorms to break out, hampering all efforts to bring up reinforcements and supplies. In particular, the lower part of the Ardre valley was – indeed after all these years still is – not easy of access from the Épernay area, and the British artillery not only was faced with a journey through difficult country, but was having to clear storm felled trees as it made its way. Indeed, by the end of the day Maistre had telephoned GQG, apparently without reference to Berthelot, saying a Fifth Army offensive could not possibly begin before the morning of 21 July.

In spite of his pessimism, British Infantry had been on the march since early morning. Berthelot, expecting them to arrive that night, sent orders for them to take up position behind the Italian IInd Corps and start their attack along the valley towards Fismes next morning at 8am while his French Colonials and Italians on the flank made for a line towards Olizy-et-Violaine. However, when the planning conference at Italian Headquarters ended, the British commanders were faced with a long journey to their own Corps' Headquarters at Vertus to have their part in the attack approved, and orders to start the offensive next morning at 8am could not be distributed until late that evening.

The operation of this British relief was typical of the problems faced throughout the entire battle by the multi-national Allied force when taking over sectors from each other. The plan was for the 62nd Division to attack along the right bank of the river Ardre and the Highlanders along the left. Away on the far flank of the West Ridings, the Italian 2nd Division was to join the advance. Two of the West Riding's three brigades met with immediate difficulties. Its 187th could not understand their Italian guides, and the 185th had a forced all-day's march that saw the troops arriving exhausted at midnight to be led forward from Courtagnon. That was not the end of their troubles . . . the French guides became lost, and the weary men had to make their way through thick woods under shellfire to reach their positions just before 8am. The 186th, more fortunate, received orders in ample time for them to reconnoitre the area between Germaine and Courtagnon and to be in position some hours before zero.

In sending copies of his orders for the attack directly to Pétain, rather than using the normal method of sending them via Maistre for the attention of the French Commander in Chief, Berthelot obviously had taken issue with his Superior Commander's report that he could not mount any attack before the 21st. Maistre, affronted, complained that Berthelot had gone over his head, but when Pétain brought the matter to Foch's attention, Foch supported Berthelot, although adding his weight to Berthelot was hardly needed (Berthelot weighed seventeen stones), for the orders entirely agreed with Foch's own aims.

The attempts to free the Marne's south bank went on all morning, and when towards midday it seemed the enemy was likely to withdraw, new instructions from Group Headquarters ordered a corps of Cavalry and one of Infantry to be transferred to Berthelot's command, to attack the German flank, try to cross the river and so open the way for a Ninth Army advance. At 4.30pm, Maistre told both Armies to move at once. De Mitry immediately brought the Ninth Army artillery up to the river and ordered aircraft to take off and check that all German crossing points were under fire. Both his Army and Berthelot's Fifth were now ready to attack along their entire fronts at daybreak the following morning.

On the west of the salient round Soissons, Mangin's Ist and XXth

Corps continued to press hard, but now that the attacks were expected, tanks had not the same unnerving effect as on the 18th and any ground taken was won only after bitter fighting by massed infantry. Indeed, the men of the 1st American Division, assaulting the positions held by Groups Staabs and Watter, still had not reached their objectives by evening. Attempts to outflank the German positions stretched the line until every man was needed, with field guns firing over open sights and engineers used as front-line infantry. Fractional progress was made by the French and Moroccans on either side of them, the Moroccans gaining a foothold in the ravines of Chazelle and Léchelle.

Opposite Group Watter's left flank, the US 2nd division, in spite of all twelve of its battalion commanders becoming casualties, succeeded in capturing the strongpoint at Berzy-le-Sec , A fresh division was brought up to relieve the the battle-weary Moroccans, and together with the Americans these new troops cut the Château-Thierry road before being brought to a halt in front of Buzancy. It took the 1st American Division two more days of hard fighting to come into line with those new gains. By nightfall the 2nd Divisional Marines (the ones promised by Harbord to support the French Cavalry officer) were at Tigny ready to block a German retreat along the Château-Thierry road. There again, unsupported artillery protected the flank, and engineers were used as front-line troops. French Dragoons in the rear were unable to join in the action because of the difficult terrain. Harbord set up his positions to overlook the most likely German withdrawal route. In a two days' advance of more than seven kilometres, capturing 3,000 prisoners and 75 guns, the division had suffered almost 5,000 casualties. 'It is time', Harbord said, ' we were relieved.'

The Germans, too, needed fresh troops to fight off the Allied attacks, for their losses had also been heavy. Although Group Watter had been pushed back to a line from Tigny to Berzy-le-Sec, its 20th Division re-captured Villemontoire, while the new, hastily assembled Group Etzel repulsed successive attacks east of Parcy-Tigny.

Having taken Noroy by first light, and fighting its way above Ferté-Milon, Cameron's 4th American Division's next objective was a ravine 3 kilometres beyond, near Chouy. By 5.30am it was in their hands; just in time for them to be deluged by a French barrage, Degoutte having omitted to tell the artillery about the changed timing. The Germans, knowing the ravine was lost, also plastered the area, and caught in the middle, the Americans suffered more than five hundred casualties. Later in the day at the point where the French Tenth and Sixth Army sectors joined, operations had more success. The XIth and IInd Corps reached the plateaux of Chouy and Neuilly-St-Front, and that evening the 38th Division took Mauloy wood, extending its line left to Blanzy.

Just above Château-Thierry, Group Schoeler, though forced to retreat west of Monthiers, mounted a counter-attack and using its 87th

Division, along with units from the neighbouring Group Winkler, broke an assault spearheaded by tanks and retook the hill south-west of the village causing heavy Allied losses. Further attacks by the Allies that evening simply went to pieces. Even so, German Army Headquarters decided both Schoeler and Kathen, the most southerly Groups, should be given priority to pull back to a line between Billy-sur-Ourcq and Brasles during the night. A little to the north-west of Château-Thierry, the French VIIth Corps struggled forward a kilometre and a half against fierce resistance round Courchamps, Belleau, and Bouresches.

German reconnaissance 'planes reported more Allied divisions were moving up. Among them was the 15th Scottish, on the march after a hot, dusty twelve-hour journey by lorry through towns, villages and hamlets packed with jubilant French and Americans celebrating the first day's success. Even if the Allies had gained less ground the previous day, the Germans would have had to pull back because of the pressure on their flank and the threat to their rail links. If the front were breached, slow-moving columns of troops and transport would be caught with the Vesle at their backs. Once on the move, the German artillery alone took up 600 kilometres of road space. Ludendorff therefore had to stiffen the flanks as the salient contracted, making Foch reorganise, and so lose time and initiative. Certainly, there could be no retreat below Soissons: every forward step there brought the Allies closer to the Fère-en-Tardenois railway.

Late that evening, Fayolle again ordered the setting up of defence lines in the rear to guard against possible counter-attacks. Realising the cavalry was having little success, he pulled out its IInd Corps to regroup round Orrouy. Mangin made no changes to his plans that evening, telling his Corps Commanders, 'Attack tomorrow – same objectives', and similar orders were issued by Degoutte, who ordered the 63rd Division to be ready to check any counter-thrust while his attacks continued next day. After two days of battle conditions, his tank squadrons had to be pulled out for repairs and to rest the crews.

CHAPTER 18

THE NEXT TWO DAYS; SATURDAY 20 AND SUNDAY 21 JULY 1918

– Attacks against both flanks continue – attempts are made to cut off Château-Thierry –

'The offensive alone can give victory: the defensive gives only defeat and shame.'
(*General Robert Nivelle*)

'Along the Marne, and where our Seventh Army's left joined the right wing of the First, attacks on a wide front were now experienced. After a short artillery preparation, French and British divisions attacked Groups Conta, Schmettow and Borne. These attacks were renewed during the afternoon, but apart from minor hostile gains of ground, were thrown back. Today's battles made us realise that while we suffered some loss of terrain, the enemy's aim of cutting off the divisions fighting in the salient had been defeated. If the flanks could be reinforced we could expect the front to be held. To do this, exhausted divisions, especially those of Groups Staabs, Watter and Etzel, would have to be relieved by fresh troops.' (War Diary – German Crown Prince's Army Group.)
    'Fayolle told his Tenth and Sixth Armies to follow Pétain's telegrammed instructions, and urged, with the opportunity of cutting off the retreating Germans, that the enemy should be given no rest.' (French Official History.)

From early morning, the tanks of Maistre's Central Army Group attacked the long German defence line running from the west of the Montagne de Reims down to the Marne and along its banks. Any remaining Germans were to be forced back across the river as soon as possible. De Mitry received a telephone call a few minutes after 9 that morning that told him to 'push his Ninth Army forward to the river with all despatch and, together with the left flank of Berthelot's Fifth, to capture the crossing points.' If resistance prevented a rapid advance, the XXXVIIIth Corps would join with Degoutte's Sixth Army in an advance on Verdilly, Château-Thierry, and Épieds. This insistence on throwing the Germans back to the north bank of the Marne – certainly more for political reasons than from military necessity – used troops who might have been better used in the attacks further north that offered greater strategic possibilities, for the Germans had evacuated the south bank during the night, and the French blow, falling upon their abandoned positions, exposed them to enfilade fire from across the river, caused them heavy casualties and left the enemy untouched.

'Saturday. During night of 19/20th, remainder of divisions were withdrawn from the Marne's south bank. The enemy again did not pursue. In the morning, enemy even started strong infantry attack accompanied by masses of tanks against the abandoned positions, in which he suffered great loss from enfilade fire from the North bank.' (War Diary – Crown Prince's Army Group.)

The Germans, too, were rushing fresh troops to the area. Four new divisions were on their way. Following a meeting with von Lossberg at Avesnes the previous day, Ludendorff had ordered the move, really wanting them to go to Rupprecht, but if necessary using them to strengthen the link between the Seventh and Ninth Armies. However, as the Seventh Army, receiving orders to withdraw to the Aisne-Vesle area, started to make its preparations, those four divisions did not need to be committed by von Böhn, and remained available for Rupprecht's offensive.

The Ninth and Seventh Armies' defence line now ran south of the river Aisne below Courmelle as far as Villemontoire – then slightly south-west past St. Remy and Billy-sur-Ourcq through Nanteuil-sur-Ourcq and Sommenlans before finally moving back east from Courchamps. The French Tenth and Sixth Armies, whose attacks had gone on late into the previous night, started early morning assaults again against Groups Etzel and Winckler, Schoeler and Watter, and by afternoon Group Staabs was also involved. The Germans put up a fierce resistance, giving way only step by step, and they even mounted counter-attacks that retook some ground. Group Watter suffered heavily, but managed somehow to hold on. Group Etzel threw back one attack, but another against its 19th Ersatz and 9th Infantry Divisions broke through, and forced the line back a kilometre. A joint attack by both wings of the Tenth and Sixth Armies on Group Winckler's centre also broke the line, and by afternoon the Germans had lost the hill above Sommenlans, (*below the present D973 road*), although the line from the Ourcq through to Latilly remained firmly in their hands.

By afternoon Pétain was sending detailed instructions by telegram and urging greater efforts.

119

'Because of the successful start to the offensive, the combined Reserve and Central Army groups are to cut off the Château-Thierry pocket. While its Ist Corps guards the flank, the Tenth Army is to use its right wing to wheel further north towards Fismes in an attack southeast of Belleu (*a village just below Soissons, not to be confused with Belleau near Château-Thierry*) with the fresh 69th Division. While the XXth Corps' Moroccan division is being relieved, the advance is to continue towards Maast and Violaine.' (*in a line with Hartennes, just west of the present D6.*)

The XXXth and the XIth Corps were ordered to capture the important heights of Arcy-Ste-Restitue (*2 or 3 kilometres north east of Beugneux*), and the Bois d'Arcy and Saponay. To this end, the 73rd and 18th Divisions were brought up, with the 4th Division in support. The Sixth Army was to make for Fère-en-Tardenois; the Ninth to cross the Marne, while the Fifth, coming from the south-east, was to advance on both sides of the Ardre towards Fismes, to meet up with the Tenth.

'Everyone', the telegram ended, 'must understand these objectives must be wrested from the enemy.'

Air raids were ordered on bottle-necks of retreating troops in Arcy-Sainte-Restitue, Oulchy-le-Château and Fère-en-Tardenois. The noose round Château-Thierry was drawn tighter as Group Schoeler's left flank was driven back round Bonnes and Monthiers, and by evening the Germans had to evacuate the woods round Château-Thierry itself. This placed von Böhn in an extremely awkward situation as his entire line from south-west of Oulchy-la-Ville through Rocourt down to the west part of the large forest round Mont St Père was now in danger, and the French, seeing the possibilities that were opening up, redoubled their efforts.

Pétain was sending across reinforcements as quickly as he could. The Fourth Army, having broken the left claw of the German pincer east of Reims, was told to menace the German positions, but to make no advance. Any troops surplus to holding the line were to go back into the general reserve. The American 32nd Division and 42nd US National Guards were among those sent back across the salient. The 32nd moved behind Mangin's front, and the 42nd went to Lizy-sur-Ourcq behind the Sixth Army. Realising by now that de Mitry's eastern flank had no chance of reaching its joint objectives with Berthelot, and his western one was being left behind by Degoutte's rapid advance, Pétain decided to reinforce success, acted on Maistre's earlier orders and placed the XXXVIII Corps completely under Degoutte's control, giving him charge of all operations round Château-Thierry and along the Marne as far as Jaulgonne and Ronchères.

Meanwhile, Maistre had ordered his troops to increase pressure north of the Marne. On Berthelot's left, four divisions of the XIVth

Corps crossed the river together with Cavalry units, the Corps commander leaving only a single division on the south bank between Troissy and la Cave. Berthelot hoped this move would lead to success in his central sector next day, for his Vth Corps commander could now commit all his reserves, knowing that the fresh troops of the XIVth Corps' 168th Division were behind in support.

Degoutte and Berthelot were both doing their utmost to break the German Seventh Army flanks. Berthelot, however, trying to pierce the point where the German Seventh and First Army lines joined west of Reims, had no fresh reserves, and neither was able to give more artillery support to the British in the Ardre valley where they were meeting strong resistance in the Bois de Coutron and in front of Marfaux village. There, the 51st's objective was to force the Germans back through the Bois des Eclisses, while on their right, the 62nd division was trying to encircle Marfaux. To the Highlanders' left, the 9th French Division was making yet another attempt to capture the hamlet of Paradis. The German positions were so close to the 51st Division's jumping off line, that attempts to send strong patrols into the undergrowth were immediately met by ferocious machine-gun fire, and they had to withdraw, in danger of being surrounded. In spite of French efforts, Paradis remained uncaptured.

However, the French attacks further north did gain some of the heights west of Reims in spite of repeated counter-attacks, and the planned German First Army attack by Group Borne had to be postponed, as the whole area round the city from Vrigny to Fort de la Pompelle on the east was now strongly held by the Allies.

Although Berthelot had no reserves, Degoutte had two fresh divisions, (the 63rd – kept back the previous evening to guard against counter-attack – and the 52nd) and rushed them to reinforce the IInd and VIIth Corps' attack at 3pm, cutting the roads leading from Château-Thierry while the 39th Division continued a fierce attack round the town itself. By mid-afternoon the XXXVIIIth Corps, transferred to his command, was told to set up positions round Gland and Mont St Père on the north bank, and its heavy artillery was told to shell the Corps' objectives of the Bois de Barbillon and the plateau between Verdilly and Épieds before leaving to help de Mitry's coming attack. Everything was now ready for Degoutte's forces to outflank and isolate Château-Thierry.

In spite of this chance to cut off the southern tip of the salient, Foch always had in mind his ultimate objective of breaking the entire German line from Château-Thierry to the Aisne and Vesle thus trapping the entire enemy force below it.

Visiting the front with von Böhn that afternoon, von Lossberg spoke of the German Seventh and Ninth Armies' 'unshaken resolve'. 'No praise' he added, 'could be too high'. All the same, he realised the troops were under extreme pressure, and ordered preparations for their withdrawal to new defensive positions. Von Eben made plans for his badly mauled Group Staabs to be first to pull out to the Aisne's north bank late that afternoon, warning Headquarters not only that Group Staabs, but also that the right wing of von Böhn's Seventh Army were both exhausted, and recommending a move to better defensive positions in the Saconin ravine; this was a proposal for a longer line that would need six fresh divisions to defend it. The High Command could provide only four.

Amazingly, during his evening staff meeting, von Böhn expressed satisfaction at the day's results:

> '. . . all our units have caused heavy losses to the enemy. Many of his tanks lie destroyed in front of our lines.... reports from prisoners speak of their increased casualties. While our losses, too, have been considerable, the attitude of our troops – particularly in view of their reduced numbers - cannot be praised too highly'.

By nightfall Hunter-Liggett ordered his Americans to push forward 'at all costs', establishing a new front along the railway from Nanteuil to Château-Thierry. Each division in the sector (including the French) would send one regiment forward to make a speedy advance. Cavalry again was brought up in anticipation of a breakthrough.

Liggett told Edwards, commanding the 26th New Englanders, 'every human effort must be made to accomplish the action as soon as possible'. Round the destroyed bridge at Château-Thierry, the attack-front was very narrow. On the right, the US 3rd Division was ready to cross in boats. Edwards was to attack in the gap between them and the French, while more French troops protected the far flank. Edwards, certainly in mental and emotional turmoil because his brother had been killed, not only made no move; he actually broke contact with the enemy. Schmidt waited until 8am the next morning, then sent his French 167th Division into the gap, but knowing Château-Thierry would soon be surrounded, the Germans wisely abandoned its ruins during the night. They had escaped the trap.

Degoutte dispatched the Pennsylvanians' 56th brigade to stiffen the New Englanders, and Liggett descended on the staff of the 26th in fury. Officers above the rank of Colonel were sacked, and the men responded. Even with Pennsylvanian support, another six days were to go by before Épieds was taken, equalling what the Soissons attack had accomplished in two.

Sunday 21 July

More reinforcements were coming to join Mangin and Degoutte's attacks. The 69th, 15th British, 87th and British 34th Divisions moved up to relieve the 153rd, 1st American, Moroccan and 38th Divisions which were the most battle-weary of the Tenth Army.

Round Soissons troops of von Eben's Ninth Army had somehow succeeded in hanging on to their positions between the neighbouring Eighteenth and Seventh Armies. This gave rise to Allied fears that the Germans might mount a new offensive across the Oise, if, as French Intelligence predicted, more troops were likely to come into line west of the Seventh Army, between the plateau north of the Ourcq and the river Oise. Von Böhn's troops would probably then man a line from that plateau to where von Below's First Army had positions in the Ardre valley and round Reims to the Suippe.

The Tenth and Sixth Armies moved three divisions across to guard against the possibility, for if that happened the troops attacking towards Fismes would be at risk. As a result of this move, only local attacks were made against the German Ninth Army that Sunday, the French Ist Corps making a further slight advance towards Soissons, while the German line south of the Aisne was mainly held.

Von Böhn's Seventh Army, on the other hand, particularly Group Watter, suffered far more seriously. Below Soissons, Mangin's XXth Corps met fierce resistance west of Berzy le Sec and Villemontoire, although the Allies increased their grip on Berzy le Sec itself. More fierce fighting was going on west of Buzancy, Villemontoire and the Bois de Plessier, and both the XXth and XXXth Corps suffered heavy casualties. From Villemontoire north to Noyant, the German 20th and 5th Infantry Divisions were taken by surprise in a sudden strike across the main Soissons/Château-Thierry road, and the Allied capture of Plessier-Huleu forced Group Etzel to pull back. Group Winckler's front line was driven out of the woods in an all-day attack, and its second line was held only after fierce hand-to-hand fighting. Group Schoeler's new positions were under constant pressure.

Mangin was told he could bring up the two British divisions, provided (and this also applied to the exhausted French 12th and 25th) he obtained further authorisation before using them in battle. However, even before the British 34th had reached the front line, permission came to use it in an attack on 23 July. Both British divisions came into the line that night, the 15th behind the French and Americans attacking the heights between Tigny and Belleu where losses had been heavy and fresh troops were needed to continued the attack; the 34th relieving the French 38th Division opposite Hartennes. The 15th had had a difficult move. Dust thrown up by their march in the light of a full moon attracted German bombers with inevitable results.

At 5am Degoutte's Sixth Army quickly started to gain ground along its whole front. His IInd and VIIth Corps and the Americans bypassed Latilly, Bonnes, and Etrépilly, while the 39th Division entered Château-Thierry. The Marne's north bank was cleared as far as Brasles and Gland with the help of the 3rd American Division, Dickman's men crossing in pontoon boats and over the railway bridge they had defended on 1 June. Their target was Ronchères 17 kilometres north-east. Flanked by French divisions, the next three days became almost a race between them. Dickman's troops captured Mont St Père and Chartèves the first day, and made a frontal attack against von Conta's troops at Jaulgonne.

Fayolle again hoping to use cavalry to exploit the situation, asked Pétain to send the Ist Cavalry corps 'with despatch', and to move the 6th Cavalry to Longpont and Troënes for orders. These were for a speedy advance towards Hautevesnes, by-passing Bonnes and Brécy, with the aim of reaching the woods between Fresnes and Fère-en-Tardenois. 'They should then', Degoutte ordered, ' together with the Infantry, capture this zone, and move in the general direction of Fismes, with a view to throwing the enemy rearguard into confusion and cutting the main route of troops retreating from the south making towards Cierges, Coulonges and Courville.'

Once again, they arrived after the Germans had strengthened their defences to deny any possible cavalry breakthrough .

By that evening the Sixth Army was west of Mont St Père, Bézu St Germain and Brény, its IInd and VIIth Corps having been heavily engaged all day. The VIIth Corps made most of its headway on the right. The heights of St. Gervaise, Billy-sur-Ourcq and the Bois de Latilly were occupied by the XXXth, XIth and IInd Corps, and the Americans were beyond Etrépilly. The XIth corps had reached a line between Oulchy la Ville and Oulchy-le-Château.

After von Lossberg's visit to the Ninth and Seventh Army fronts the previous day, he realised the Allied advance could not be stemmed much longer. By now the reserves were used up, the men exhausted; some companies, fighting in dense undergrowth open to infiltration, were down to a strength of 20 or 30. 'My exhausted replacements', he reported to the Crown Prince, 'have struggled forward only to find themselves facing the fiercest of attacks. My artillery is worn out, needing replacements of men, guns and horses.'

In the few places where de Mitry's troops had not yet crossed the Marne, and in the Montagne de Reims, where Berthelot's Vth Corps, and the British, Colonial and Italian divisions had sustained heavy losses in their attacks against Groups Schmettow and Borne, Maistre ordered the advance 'to be renewed with utmost energy, using the 166th and 77th Divisions on the flanks to give it new impetus'. A creeping barrage started at 10.30 am . By the end of the day, both the 103rd and 123rd German Divisions opposite the British 62nd had to be replaced by units from the 50th German Division after furious attacks by the Durhams and Yorks and Lancs. Nevertheless, German resistance remained fierce, and all the objectives were not reached. In spite of his enemy's lack of progress, Ludendorff had decided by noon that if Group Borne's four divisions lost the important heights south of Vrigny, the whole position would have to be evacuated next day, and consequently attacks on the far side of Reims against Fort de la Pompelle were broken off.

By lunch-time Foch was again that urging the attacks be made 'with all possible vigour'. He told Mangin to reorganise the left of the French Front, ' ready for the battle that will maintain our pressure by eventually moving above the Oise and below the British sector.' Already he was looking beyond the Marne battle itself to future campaigns. A letter to Haig that evening explained his plans in greater detail; not only for the current battle, but for ones still to come. Again pointing out that Ludendorff would have to bring his reserves south and must eventually give up his aim of attacking the British, he said that once those reserves were on the move, there would be 'a fabulous chance' of mounting a series of offensives on more thinly held parts of the German Front. With this in mind, he urged Haig to plan the recapture of Mount Kemmel and to continue the attack round Festubert towards Estaire, knowing it would further delay Rupprecht's offensive. Also he asked for Haig's views about a combined offensive by Rawlinson's 4th and Debeney's 1st Armies that would recapture the Amiens area. By asking Haig to prepare his own attacks, Foch opened the opportunity for a counter-offensive in the centre and on the left of Fayolle's group, or by the British 12th and 18th Divisions taking over French positions south of the Somme.

The most battle-weary French divisions now began to move between St Just-en-Chausseé and the Oise to regroup and reform. That evening Fayolle ordered the Moroccan Division to Breteuil to be the first division of a new Corps to be established on the left wing of his Reserve Army Group. Mangin, naturally enough, did not want to lose one of his best divisions, but realised the need for it to refit before being used again.

The offensive was to continue, aiming for the previous day's objectives. Degoutte, moving his headquarters forward to Marigny-en-Orxois, wanted 'an ardent pursuit of the enemy, without which the enemy retreat could not be changed into a rout' and ordered his commanders to keep in touch both with him and with each other. Second-line troops were to be ready to follow up, the advance to be supported by the minimum of artillery but provided with ample ammunition.

So Sunday saw the completion of two very important stages of the battle; Château-Thierry was recaptured, and the Marne's south bank had been cleared.

That evening, after a daylong step by step retreat by their troops, made under constant artillery fire, it seemed to the German Command that if the battle were to be fought out on the Aisne's north bank, their weakened divisions would be in grave peril. They were faced with another stage of the long retreat that had started at the Marne. More attacks that night further threatened their main artery of supply; Missy aux Bois was under fire and the railway to Fère-en-Tardenois increasingly endangered, and both areas were vital if the Germans were to hold the salient.

It was at this point Ludendorff decided to suspend 'Hagen' 'for the time being', and commit his reserves to the Marne battle, for the idea of pulling out completely from the salient was anathema; he refused even to consider the possibility.

CHAPTER 19

MONDAY 22 AND TUESDAY 23 JULY 1918

– The Germans bring up more reinforcements to defend the flanks
– by now all four British divisions are in action – some Allied
progress made at the base of the salient – Château-Thierry and the
Marne's south bank recaptured –

'Its dogged as does it. It ain't thinking about it'.
(Anthony Trollope)

*   *   *

Monday 22 July

Within months American Generals were saying openly that if an all-
American force had been used, and if they had been in charge of
planning and directing the Soissons attack, the Germans would have
collapsed and the war would have ended. Von Böhn strongly disagreed.
Once enough forces had arrived to stiffen the line, any order from
Avesnes to retire could be ignored and planning could begin for an
orderly retreat to the Vesle.

He and the Crown Prince were in complete agreement that if the
flanks could be held, the front could be held, and if exhausted divisions
– such as Staabs, Watter and Etzel – could be replaced, the Allies would
'pay dearly for any further attempted gains.' The defence could be
rebuilt; Rupprecht's offensive could still be mounted; Haig's exposed
army smashed, and final victory still achieved. Because of the scale and
violence of the Marne attacks, Foch surely, they argued, must soon run
out of fresh reserves.

By now both sides had brought up more troops, particularly to the
area between Soissons and Château-Thierry, for both sides knew the key
to the battle's outcome lay in controlling the flanks. Foch wanted a
quick breakthrough and a tightening of the noose; a note to Mangin
that Monday said that the fresh divisions given him should lead to 'a
strong unified action'. Ludendorff's determination in holding the
plateaux below Soissons, the heights around Vrigny near Reims, and
halting the Allied advance up the Ardre valley, showed in the fierce

127

defence made throughout 22/23 July. The positions were hinges on which any effective German counter-attack must pivot, and had to be held. As long as the line north of the Ourcq (especially between Fère-en-Tardenois and Marfaux) was held by the Germans, there would be no need for a further retreat to the Aisne and Vesle. Following from that, time would be won to prepare stronger defensive positions, and so only the centre of the Seventh Army could be allowed to withdraw to a line between the Ourcq and Dormans as Degoutte advanced. The wings of the army would have to hold on to their positions at least until the night of 23/24 July. Von Böhn could only exhort the troops manning those wings to 'fight on to the utmost limits of their ability'.

Von Eben's Ninth Army now had eleven divisions in the line, with seven more either in reserve or moving towards the Aisne's north bank. Hans von Böhn's Seventh had sixteen divisions divided between six Army groups, while Fritz von Below's First Army above, and to either side of Reims, though having to pull out three Bavarian divisions because of casualties, was replacing them with Jägers.

The lie of the land allowed a strong defence to be made on each flank. To the west, the main road to Soissons, rising steeply from Château-Thierry, runs more or less northwards along a ridge flanked by spurs and ravines, giving extremely good cover for strongpoints and interlocking lines of defence. On the eastern flank, the route from Épernay to Reims also climbs steeply to the Montagne de Reims and the Tardenois plateau. There again, forests covering the region, and the heights round Vrigny west of Reims presented formidable obstacles, and during the coming days all four British divisions were to be involved in trying to break the defences on both these flanks.

German Intelligence that morning listed the French XXth Corps still opposite Group Watter on the heights between Tigny and Belleu below Soissons. The part of the line held by Watter's Jägers overlapped with the three Jäger divisions of Group Etzel facing the French XXXth Corps. Because of the Allied reliefs and reorganisations that were taking place, the two German groups enjoyed a much quieter day. Mangin, having lost his Moroccan Division, now found that Pétain's Headquarters intended taking away his 153rd Division to become the second of the new left-wing group. The 47th Division was taken from Degoutte to join the Moroccans and 153rd two days later. All three were extremely exhausted, and needed time to rest and re-equip.

That day the 15th (Scottish) Division started to relieve the Americans and the French between Buzancy and Noyant below Soissons. Three kilometres behind the front, a plateau, sloping gradually south-east from the Villers-Cotterêts road and crossed by sunken roads, leads to gentler country about eight kilometres away. The forward slope, facing north-east, is far more difficult; steeper, split by two valleys, and broken into several very steep spurs. Facing the ridge another similar one, the Buzancy plateau, falls sharply at the northern end overlooking the valley containing Noyant and Septmonts. Buzancy itself is in a side glen. The front had no natural feature to divide brigade attacks. On the right, the boundary between the 15th Scottish Division and the French 87th was marked by a railway cutting and ran from Visigneux to about 200yds north of Buzancy, with the front line running parallel to Buzancy ridge. To the left, where the line joined the 69th French Division's sector, there was a gentler slope taking the line towards Noyant as it followed the course of the Crise river from Berzy le Sec to south of Septmonts. An officer of the 15th Division taking over south of Berzy was pointed vaguely in various directions by the departing French officer, told, 'Mitrailleuse là, et là. Boche là . . . Moi, je vais' . . . and was left in charge. His men saw even less of the French, and their first task of burying the American dead left them little, if any, time to reconnoitre. The relief was completed by evening, and at 9.20pm General Reed received orders that his Division's attack between Berzy and the north-west corner of Buzancy would start at 5am the following morning.

That same day the 34th British Division was also taking over from the French 38th opposite Hartennes-et-Taux, with two of its brigades moving immediately into the front line to relieve French Divisional Tirailleurs and the 4th Infantry Regiment. The 34th Division, one of those disbanded by Haig and only reformed in June, had already received orders to attack on the 23rd. None of its Infantry had yet seen action in France, and this, coming at the end of an exhausting move, was bound to be a difficult introduction to warfare on the Western Front.

Over on the Reims flank, Groups Gontard and Lindquist near the city were already being attacked by the Ist Colonial Corps, and the Germans were rushing up two Jäger divisions to meet the threat. The 62nd and 51st Divisions were still trying to advance along the banks of the river Ardre against Group Borne's 53rd and 86th Divisions, their progress slowed by conditions that were totally unlike any that either the West Ridings or the Highlanders had come across in France. The Ardre valley – only two to three kilometres wide – is hemmed in by steep hills whose high ridges and spurs, covered and crested by thick woods and tangled undergrowth, provided perfect country for hidden German defences and machine-gun nests, and that turned any attempt to advance into a continuous series of guerilla actions.

On the Ardre's east bank are the Bois de Rouvroy, of Pourcy, of the Petit Champ and of Courtagnon. On the west, the Bois de Coutron and the Bois des Eclisses lead to more woods – the extensive Bois de St Quentin, de Courton and du Roi – all part of the large Forêt de Reims that stretches west to Châtillon sur Marne.

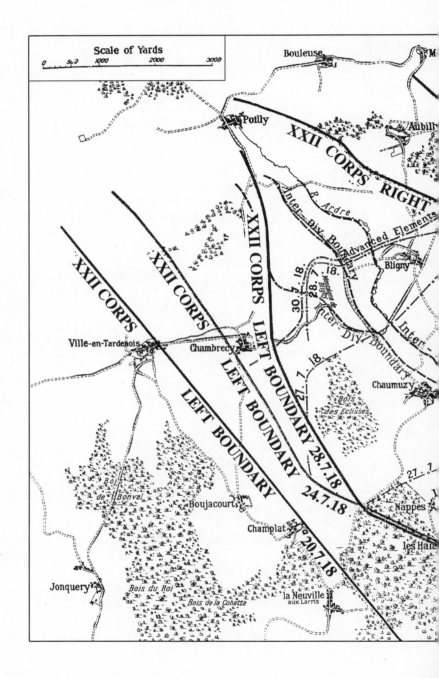

Figure 14 62nd and 51st Divisional Operations – Ardre Valley

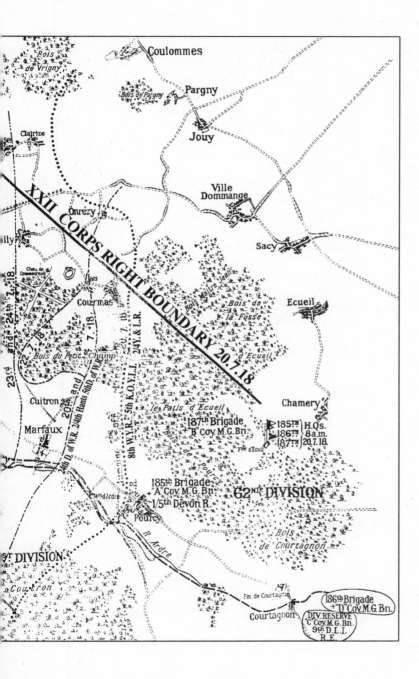

The Germans were able to give support to their strongpoints at Marfaux and Chaumuzy in the valley bottom by enfilade fire both from the woods and from the hamlets on the slopes, as well as from the Montagne de Bligny – the British final objective. The steep slopes and marshy ground made the use of tanks impractical, and the Germans used the cover provided by crops round the villages and the thick undergrowth of the woods to full advantage. Many sunken roads and high banks also ran at right angles to the Allied line of attack, giving further strong lines of defence.

The 51st Division was on the left bank trying to reach Espilly and set up positions on the south-west edge of the Bois de Coutron to support another French attack on Paradis. Attacks went on all day against increased numbers of German machine-guns. The French attack on Paradis again ground to a halt with heavy losses after an advance of only a few steps that afternoon.

On the right, the West Ridings had to clear some 1,800 Prussian Infantry and machine-gunners from the woods and spurs before Marfaux and Cuitron could be attacked. Strongpoints were difficult to pinpoint and had to be surrounded before they could be wiped out with bomb and bayonet in hand to hand struggles. The 2/5th Battalion of the Duke of Wellington's Regiment forced its way through the undergrowth with severe loss, but captured more than 80 prisoners and 15 machine guns. By mid-afternoon one company finally reached the edge of the wood, only to be immediately bombed, counter-attacked and driven back at bayonet point. The survivors used a Lewis gun to fight their way to a shell hole south of the wood, where they came under increased fire both from the wood and from the hamlet of Cuitron. Eight men, making a fighting retreat, eventually reached 'B' company's posts and safety.

The battalion as a whole took more than 200 prisoners and 40 machine-guns from the élite 53rd Prussian Infantry that day.

Meanwhile, the defences of Marfaux were being probed (with 50% casualties) and a line consolidated on the Courmas-Bouilly road. This action too was carried out under severe difficulties. The high ground on the corner of Bois du Petit Champ was lost, and had to be retaken before Marfaux could be attacked. Two companies of the 8th West Yorkshires (in actual fact the whole battalion, casualties having been so heavy) were told to capture the ground from Marfaux to Cuitron, and the spur down to the river about 400 metres north of the villages, and that evening the New Zealand Cycle Corps battalion provided additional troops.

Along the base of the salient, Allied operations on 22/23 July made more progress, and the very last pockets held by the Germans along the river had now been given up, even though Hindenburg considered using fanatically loyal storm troopers to re-establish a bridgehead.

Group Winckler again was forced back, giving German Headquarters more cause for concern. In fact, Ludendorff's problems increased as the day wore on. The IIIrd Corps of de Mitry's Ninth Army was now across the Marne near Passy-sur-Marne and Courcelle, ready to extend its bridgehead, and by evening the Sixth Army had reached a line from Brény, just below Oulchy-le-Château on the main road from Château-Thierry to Soissons, through Bézu St Germain, to Jaulgonne, from where the Grenadiers' initial attack had been launched across the Marne on 15 July.

Tuesday 23 July

A letter from Foch to Pétain proposing cavalry attacks along the Ourcq towards Fère-en-Tardenois , and more in the Ardre valley, showed that the Supreme Commander still hoped to strangle the German salient by mounting converging offensives against the Tardenois plateau. During the afternoon Foch again went in person to Provins to give Pétain his written comments about the battle's progress, wanting more pressure to be made against the strong German resistance, but stressing the need to be flexible.

> 'Everything hangs from this . . . that we do not focus all our attention on the Tenth and Fifth Armies: between them is another one that needs to be involved . . .
>
> 'The German tactics', he went on, 'have consisted in making a solid defence of their flanks. To do this, fresh units supported by artillery and provided with numerous machine guns, have been brought up to slow our advance with a rearguard action. It is therefore necessary to rupture the enemy front, so, at the least, one of his flanks is pushed back as quickly as possible. The obvious one is that in front of the right wing of the Tenth Army and the left of the Sixth. It is there we must concentrate all our efforts, mounting a powerful attack in a direction that offers unusual potential . . . to the north of Fère-en-Tardenois.'

So all that day, Mangin's XXth and XXXth Corps tried to advance from the positions reached by the American 1st and French 38th Divisions, but in spite of almost 100 tanks being used in the XXXth Corps' attack, little was achieved. The general scheme was for the XXth Corps on the left to capture Tigny, Villemontoire and Taux, outflanking the German positions in the wood north of Hartennes-et-Taux, while the right wing of the XXXth, advancing through Le Plessier-Huleu on the Orme of the Grand Rozoy, would make the German positions in the woods of Bois du Plessier and Bois de St Jean untenable.

The British 34th, flanked by the other Divisions of the XXXth Corps, (the French 25th and 58th) was to link these northern and southern advances by capturing high ground east of the Soissons/Château-Thierry road. The division was told to remain in position until the XXth Corps had crossed that road.

Rushed to the area, the British troops had not had time for reconnaissance during the previous day, and found the German positions by walking into them. Indeed, General Nicholson had only taken over command of the sector at 7am. – fifteen minutes before the order came to advance. His men moved almost a kilometre through chest high corn before being caught in a deadly crossfire from the Bois de Reugny and Tigny village. The first wave of the right-hand brigade was almost wiped out, and as the French on the flanks had not even begun to move, the troops dug in and formed a defensive line facing the village.

In spite of the 34th Division having advanced, the XXth Corps had still not managed to cross the Château-Thierry road; indeed, it probably was not crossed that day, for the XXth Corps had its own problems. The 15th Scottish, like the 34th division, had discovered the German positions opposite through its patrols walking into them during the night and bringing down fierce retributory shelling along the entire front. Even so, the relief was completed by 3am.

The objectives for the 15th's attack were the village of Rozières and the high ground leading to Buzancy on the right, and le Sucrerie southwest of Noyant and crossing points on the river Crise to its east and north on the other flank. American, French and British artillery acted together to provide the supporting barrage. Unfortunately, the maps were inaccurate, and the barrage overshot the German advanced positions, so the assault was at once held up by fierce machine gun fire, the Scots suffering heavy casualties. The barrage itself was far from satisfactory as some sections of the front were untouched. The problem again was faulty maps, placing the French/American line half a kilometre from its true position, so that most of the shells landed behind the Germans.

'Open warfare' like this was completely new to the troops, and though they attacked Groups Staabs and Watter fiercely, they suffered heavily. There was a slight advance on the right, but losses and the lack of artillery support brought it to a halt. Le Sucrerie on the left was captured, but the line had to be extended to the railway bridge over the Crise to protect the flank – an objective that should have been gained by the right-hand brigade. At the far end of the sector the remnants of two companies held the outskirts of Berzy together with French troops.

Realising the attack was in trouble, General Reed asked for another artillery barrage, and when it could not be given, broke off the action.

The French divisions on either side still had made no advance by midmorning, and so the Scottish flanks were vulnerable. Along with trench mortar troops, a defensive right flank was somehow cobbled together.

The centre was held in spite of a determined German counter-attack in the early evening, but on the left le Sucrerie was given up and the line pulled back to the railway embankment .

Although gains were small, for the Scots to have won ground at all under these conditions was an achievement, despite later dismissive remarks from the departed, twice as large, American division that described them as 'under strength and not able to succeed in their attack'.

Foch, already starting to plan another offensive round Amiens, and seeing the lack of progress in Tenth and Sixth Army efforts to advance towards Fismes and Fère-en-Tardenois, had changed his tactics, and had ordered Berthelot to increase the pressure north-westwards along either side of the Ardre and to try to cut off the Germans still in the salient. New Allied attacks therefore were made along the Marne and up into the Forêt de Reims, both against the south-east sector of von Böhn's Seventh Army and Group Borne's sector in von Below's First. Some gains were made both against Group Schmettow, and also south-west of Vrigny where some important ground was wrested from Group Borne, but the advance was patchy.

As his Fifth Army was still unable to break through to the Ourcq, Berthelot decided to concentrate on the attack towards Fismes, narrowing it so that only the two British divisions were involved. They were told to continue their attack along the river, supported on their flanks by the 14th division (Vth Corps) and the Mordrelle group. The day's objective given to the Highland Division was a line from the Bois de l'Aulnay to Espilly, and for the West Ridings to capture Marfaux and Cuitron after they had cleared the woods.

The French barrage supporting the Highlanders opened on time at 6.10am, but many shells fell short, causing casualties among the attackers. The only progress was at the extreme left of the flank, and the troops were soon pulled back from there because of lack of support. The right flank all day made repeated but unsuccessful attempts to reach Espilly.

The 62nd's advance began at 6am, but within a half-hour all the officers in the leading section had become casualties. The troops were rallied by a sergeant and established a post on the outer edge of the wood. A second section worked along the heights overlooking the valley. The Divisional narrative for the day reads almost like a Fenimore Cooper 'Cowboys and Indians' saga. Thick undergrowth caused sections to charge each other, scouts to stalk each other, while machine gun and sniper fire came from unexpected places.

> 'The woods were certainly held in strength. The nervous excitement of scrambling through undergrowth, sometimes meeting a terrified Hun popping up out of a hole, or sometimes finding oneself in the centre of an amazed group of attacking Germans was rather wearying.'

135

However the edge of the woods was cleared, and troops of the Durhams and the New Zealand Cycle Corps attached to the Division were able to capture and consolidate the villages of Cuitron and Marfaux. (A Demarcation Stone was later set up south-east of Marfaux to mark the limit of the German 1918 advance). During the afternoon combined attacks by the French 77th and the West Riding Divisions cleared the southern part of the woods and the grounds of the Château de Commetreuil, (German machine guns there had been a perpetual thorn in the flesh for the past days), and that night the German strongpoint on the spur was eliminated. Divisional Headquarters moved forward to the tiny village of Hautvillers (famous for Dom Pérignon's 'invention' of Champagne) on the steep slopes north of the Marne opposite Épernay.

The previous day's Sixth Army's successes along the Marne led to hopes that more advances could be made; the VIIth Corps was brought back into line, and 23 July saw positions set up west of Rocourt-St-Martin and north of Jaulgonne. Degoutte ordered a new attack to start on the 24th at 4.55am. The Ninth Army had reached a general line from Marcilly to Trélou that day, and pontoon bridges across the Marne were to be used to bring up reinforcements during the night. In the evening, de Mitry ordered a 73rd Divisional advance through the forest of Ris, helping the Sixth Army's right wing and reinforcing the 18th Division on the left wing of the Fifth Army in an assault north of Dormans.

Detailed timings and precise objectives were allocated to integrate the attacks and gain more ground. The Fifth and Tenth Armies on the flanks were now able to come into line with the rest of the front because of the Sixth and Ninth Army successes. The Tenth Army's XIth Corps reached Oulchy-le-Chateau, while the Fifth Army was able to put more troops across the Marne north of Troissy and Port-à- Binson.

The German High Command ordered the ground that had been lost by Groups Etzel, Winckler and Schoeler to be retaken in a night attack. Once it was recovered, the Germans set about repelling further Allied attacks, knocking out tanks and forcing infantry to retire under a hail of bullets.

Fayolle ordered up more reserves to smash the front opposite the Sixth Army. Pétain approved his Army Group Commander's orders to place the 12th and 25th Divisions under Tenth Army control, and to send the French 62nd Division, the American 32nd Division and the Ist Cavalry Corps to Degoutte.

It was obvious that if more progress were to be made, a further general reorganisation and regrouping would be needed. Pétain tried to hurry the necessary moves by taking personal control of the Central Army Group. The 16th, 10th Colonial and 120th Divisions, together with troops from the XIVth Corps and the IInd Italian Corps, were to be taken from Berthelot (who was to receive suitable replacements) and units from the XIIIth Corps moved into the general reserve together with the 36th and 35th Divisions . Interestingly, Pétain's orders to Fayolle and Maistre also contained a secret personal note. Where Foch on 20 July had given Fayolle the main objective of Bazoches, Pétain had instead ordered an intermediate objective of the Plateau de Lesges, near Arcy Sainte Restitue, before 'making towards Fère-en-Tardenois, covering that advance by a second one south of the Ourcq also towards Fère-en-Tardenois past Villeneuve s. Fère'. His order to the two Groups now complied with Foch's instructions, ending with the words: 'Make certain in all cases that the main attack on any front is carried out with the maximum of force and determination, and that pressure is kept up along the entire front with all possible means . . .'

Maistre was to continue his Central Army Group's advance on Fismes, with its main thrust along the right bank of the Ardre towards the plateau of Germiny. If that plateau were captured, the entire enemy defence in the region would fall. Both Groups were warned to be constantly on guard against counter-attacks, anticipating and preventing them by their own attacks towards the Aisne and Vesle.

Also as part of this general reorganisation, the 58th Division was moved by car behind the front to allow the 12th Division into the XXth Corps' line, and to give Fayolle opportunity to order an immediate start for the Tenth Army to plan operations to capture the Butte Chalmont, the Orme of the Grand Rozoy and Arcy Sainte Restitue, while the Sixth advanced as quickly as possible on Fère-en-Tardenois, keeping in touch with the Tenth Army's Butte Chalmont attack. 'Every effort being made by all units of the Tenth and Sixth Armies to gain the prize of Fère-en-Tardenois.'

Mangin was told yet again to keep two divisions behind his left wing to guard the flank: one round Attichy, protecting the Aisne corridor, the other round Dommiers ready to move on Soissons.

Foch not only had his sights on making reorganisations within the salient. That day he started moves that would send his forces round Amiens, ready for the offensive there. The 47th division, detached from the IInd Corps, was ordered south of Amiens by rail, allowing the two British divisions there to pass back into Haig's control.

CHAPTER 20

WEDNESDAY 24 JULY 1918

– An important day for future plans.–

'Un joli fleuve, la Marne . . .'
(Marshal Joseph Joffre)

Encouraged by the way the battle had started, Foch told his Government he expected victory to be won in 1919. 'The Americans,' he wrote in a memorandum, 'will be making their greatest efforts in the Spring. If the war is to be shortened, we must redouble our efforts and provide every available resource to our armies from now on.' Not only did he forecast an end to the war the following year, but he had begun to think that victory might possibly come earlier if every effort were made. 'What am I risking, after all? I asked myself,' he was to write later. 'You can prepare for the worst and another year of fighting, but there is no crime in hoping for the best – victory within a few months.'

'In the main interests of France', his memorandum to the Government went on, 'measures must be taken at the opening of 1919, to apply our utmost force to bring about victory', and, 'recognising the consequences', he asked the Minister of War to call up the 1920 class of conscripts in October, to be trained and ready in time to take part in a huge Spring offensive.

On three occasions between the 18th and 22nd the President of the French War Council had visited Bombon to discuss Foch's request in detail, and on the 20th, General Alby (Chef d'État Major-Général) also went there to discuss how the communications and supply systems behind the front might best be organised.

Only a few hours after Mangin's counter-offensive had started, the German High Command realised the threat to the Crown Prince's troops in the salient, and the urgent need to bring up fresh reserves. These they took from Rupprecht, so delaying the Flanders attack that was planned to open on the 20th. Haig's fears – although Rupprecht's threat was real enough – were eventually to prove groundless, and Foch proved correct in deducing that the Lys offensive would have to be postponed. Certainly , Allied intelligence reported some of Rupprecht's divisions already on the move as early as the 19th, then others joining them during the next two days, and prisoners admitted that the northern offensive had had to be delayed because of the failure of the Reims attack.

This was confirmed by the German daily situation report of 22 July. At their meeting that morning, Ludendorff's staff described the military situation between Soissons and Reims as 'extremely grave'. . . 'Our far-reaching attack in Flanders should be delayed while a possible retreat to the Aisne existed'; ordered the present positions in the Marne salient to be held, fresh artillery to be brought up, and a new counter-offensive prepared. Some of Rupprecht's divisions were to be used for this. Foch had come to the same conclusion a couple of days earlier. The Germans would not only have to resist his attacks, but must also reorganise their forces before they could mount any major counter-stroke between the Aisne and Marne. To do this, some of Rupprecht's divisions would certainly be needed . . . And now the Germans were weaker; the average fighting strength of a German battalion had declined by a hundred from the 980 norm at the start of the March offensive.

By contrast, Allied strength was now so quickly on the increase that Foch was planning to return the British XXIInd Corps to Haig. The two British divisions under French control south of Amiens had already been given back. The last of the three French divisions sent to the left sector of the Reserve Army Group was moving west that very day, and two American divisions were almost ready to enter the line round Château-Thierry. This increase of Allied force was taking place along the entire war-front. The rôles were reversed at last. While German troops were scurrying south from Flanders, Foch was able to match the overall estimated enemy strength with 2 Belgian, 18 British and 25 French divisions. 10 American divisions (most of them now with their own artillery) brought the total to 55, not counting the 9 Allied cavalry divisions available.

West of the Avre the First French Army had already carried out a brilliant attack the previous day. General Debeney, using the IXth Corps with the 3rd French and 15th Colonial Divisions against the plateaux of Mailly-Raineval, Sauvillers and Aubvillers, had recaptured three villages, a large number of guns and almost 2000 prisoners, opening the way for further advances towards the Santerre area below Amiens. De Mitry's Ninth Army was extending its bridgehead above the Marne. Degoutte's Sixth was advancing from the previous night's positions round Rocourt-Saint-Martin, and Fayolle was bringing up more reserves to smash the German front.

Four days back, Pétain's orders to Mangin had been for the Tenth Army's main thrust to be towards the plateaux of Ambrief and Lesges, while Degoutte aimed for Villeneuve s. Fère. Up to now Foch's designated objectives of Bazoches and Fère-en-Tardenois had not been reached. Now there was a different emphasis. On the 23rd, Pétain had at last conformed to Foch's directives, and ordered Mangin to use his right flank and make his main attack further south. This meant that the general reserve had to be reorganised. Already the 68th and 27th Divisions were replacing two sent to the left wing, and planned exploratory attacks by the Reserve and Central Army Groups would mean the Ninth Army being squeezed out of the line and its units available for use elsewhere. Ever since the 20th, the Ninth Army front had been gradually reduced until there was only a single Corps in the line, and now Provins told its Chief of Staff to pull out the entire force during the afternoon of the 25th, and transfer headquarters to Méru as part of the general reserve. Its air squadrons had been ordered to fly west during the 23rd and 24th to Jouarre, Sézanne and Ermenonville, to be ready for action again by midday of the 25th.

Its IIIrd Corps was allocated to Berthelot, whose Fifth Army line now ran from Connigis, through Parcy, Mézy, Le Charmel and Ronchères to Cierges. Now the promised reinforcements of the 4th, 18th and 73rd Divisions were on their way, together with the Ninth Army's artillery, Berthelot started to dispatch the troops earmarked by Pétain for the general reserve (the IInd Italian Corps together with the 120th, the 10th Colonial and all the non-divisional units of the XIVth Corps).

Passing on the High Command's orders, Maistre urged his Fifth Army Commander to use all available force in attacking limited objectives, harassing and breaking the entire German defence along the Ardre towards Germigny and Romilly. By the 24th, the two British divisions central to the advance had been heavily engaged for five full days and needed time to regroup and rest. The West Ridings consolidated Marfaux and Cuitron in spite of heavy shelling, and shortened their front to allow units to be rotated and given a brief period of rest. Even then, there was no respite behind the lines. The Germans, amply supplied with artillery for the original advance, used it not only to defend their front but to disrupt Allied supplies and reinforcements in the rear. This constant shelling and machine gunning was compared by veterans of the Highland Division to that experienced at High Wood on the Somme in 1916, and young replacements in both the Highland and West Riding Divisions found it particularly unnerving. That night, Épernay was bombed, causing dislocation to arrangements for the evacuation of wounded, and German 'planes discovered and attacked the West Riding's ammunition column parked by the Reims-Épernay road, producing a nightmare scene of losses among the gunners and their teams of shire horses.

The Highlanders had planned to capture the Haies-Neuville road on the 24th, but delayed the move until Espilly was captured. Posts were established in front of the village against stiff opposition, but by now the battalions were very much weakened . . . the 6th battalion of Seaforths had only enough men left to form a single company. Each unit replaced 100 of its most exhausted troops with reinforcements that had arrived the previous night. A regiment of the French 14th division relieved more of the Scots, who pulled back to the woods near St. Imoges to rest. They had lost a third of their strength through casualties up to the 24th, yet after a full day's rest, returned to carry on the attack for a further four days.

Mangin could not change the deployment of his forces to any great extent. The only fresh division immediately available to him, the 12th, was ordered into the line on the right of the XXth Corps. Precise objectives were allocated. The Ist Corps was to attack the Mountain of Paris and the plateau south of Vauxbuin; the XXth to make for Villemontoire and Tigny; the XXXth to aim for the Orme of the Grand Rozoy and the plateau north of Beugneux, while the XIth was to take the Butte Chalmont. The High Command made every effort to concentrate the available forces to produce the maximum possible effort. The French 12th Division captured Villemontoire (the third time it had changed hands), but the Germans held out at Tigny. On the extreme right of the XXXth Corps and the left of the Sixth Army, much better progress was made, and there were signs that the enemy was making ready for a further retreat.

South of the Ourcq, the centre of the Sixth Army followed up the retreating enemy all morning without meeting too much opposition; Group Schoeler was pushed back north-east of Château-Thierry to Coincy, where an Allied air raid on the rail yards destroyed ammunition and prevented a successful German counter-attack. On the left below Beugneux however, the French Infantry were halted by concentrated enemy fire from the Butte Chalmont. Degoutte therefore started to exploit the centre's success. Again cavalry was ordered up to spearhead the attack, and this time the 6th Cavalry, moving up through the VIIth Corps, broke the German line and threw it into disarray. Three divisions of the Ist Cavalry Corps joined them, their commander ordering them to make for the plateaux of Branges, Lesges and Serches in the hopes of forcing a German retreat both on the right of and in front of the Tenth Army's centre, and of retaking the area between the Vesle and the Aisne. To build on this success, the Sixth Army's centre, together with the VIIth Corps, was ordered to mount an attack towards Villers-sur-Fère (a little south of Fère-en-Tardenois) the next day. The Americans pushed on to Sergy, their flanks defended by the IInd and XXXVIIIth Corps.

The Germans were hard-pressed by this Franco-American advance around and north-east of Château-Thierry, and their salient at that point was becoming dangerously narrowed. McAlexander's 38th Infantry (US 3rd Division) were at Le Charmel, 4km above Jaulgonne, linking with the Fifth Army. The New Englanders, divided from their countrymen by a French division and once more lacking decisive leadership, were able to gain only a few metres, von Böhn's numerous machine gun posts 8km inside the salient's perimeter saw to that, but the 3rd Division advanced 5 valuable kilometres.

That evening Fayolle urged the Tenth, Sixth and Fifth Armies to continue their pressure on the German flanks. In spite of utter weariness, it was not the time, he said, to call a halt to the pursuit.

On this – the seventh day of the counter-offensive – far-reaching decisions were being taken well behind the battle lines at the Headquarters of both combatants.

The German 18th Division that had been moving up on 22 July to join the battle, within the short space of joining the conflict had been so badly cut up that von Böhn was forced to pull out its few survivors. When this news reached the Crown Prince's Headquarters, it at once precipitated a staff meeting, which after much heart-searching, decided that the entire ground south of the Aisne and Vesle would have to be evacuated. Losses were now so great that the weakened divisions defending the front could make only limited counter-attacks. The First Army, as well as the Seventh, would have to be pulled back and reformed. 'It is obvious that much material will have to be abandoned, and must be replaced. This particularly applies to heavy artillery. Precise losses cannot be ascertained, but the state of the 18th Division gives some indication. The enemy is now certain to resume the battle in strength.'

The new Aisne-Vesle line would need at least 14 divisions to defend it. The Crown Prince and his staff next had to decide whether setting up a series of advanced defence positions was worth the risk. Any counter-stroke would need to use the positions in the Reims area as a hinge, and those would certainly have to be strengthened. A reconnoitring force was put on standby.

It was obvious that as soon as they knew what was happening, the Allies would mount more attacks to disrupt the retreat. The Germans planned to prevent this by making their own assaults. Once the Crown Prince's staff had agreed that the line must be reformed behind the Aisne and Vesle, Supreme Headquarters was contacted strongly recommending this course of action. Ludendorff was far from ready to agree. Hoping that an attack by the First Army round Marfaux and Vrigny the next day would halt the breakthrough, he was also working on plans suggested by Hindenburg a few days previously for a Ninth Army attack, and sent the following answer:

'1- It is intended that the First Army should resume its attack from Marfaux to Ormes (4km west of Reims) to capture that position and, if possible, to advance from it.

'2- North of the Aisne, the Ninth Army has an imminent possibility of attacking on the sector held by the 15th and 20th Divisions, and certainly across that of the 53rd Reserve Division *(ie. a front of about 13km from Nampcel to Fontenoy)*. Reinforcements will provide for this. Along with the 14th Infantry Division they must explore a possible advance westwards across the Aisne above Soissons. It is imperative these intentions are limited on a 'need to know' basis to those planning, and those carrying out the attack.

'3- No decision has yet been taken with regard to the Seventh Army's retreat. However, tonight Corps Conta and Schmettow will re-align their wings to maintain a defensive arc between Chattillon and La Neuville. Before any further withdrawal is contemplated, the result of tomorrow's First Army counter-attack must be awaited. As long as there is hope of the situation being improved the important Marne front will be held.'

That same day, Foch had arranged to meet Haig, Pershing and Pétain at Bombon to confirm the overall plan of campaign. The numbers of fully-trained American troops meant Pershing was at last able to demand an 'All-American Front' with full control of the First American Army, formed from the two Army Corps and the six American Divisions in the Marne area (ie the 3rd, 4th, 26th, 28th, 32nd and 42nd). All were initially to take over a quiet sector such as St. Mihiel.

Foch approved the move, and thanked him for placing his troops under French Army Headquarters' control during the Marne operations. Pétain and Pershing were authorised to plan the move together, and by the next day it had started. Degoutte's Sixth Army began to relieve the Americans at La Ferté-sous-Jouarre, while over in Lorraine, the Commander of the Eastern Army Group was told to prepare for their arrival around Woëvre – the sector the US 1st and 2nd Divisions were to take over -along with the US 82nd and 89th Divisions that also were being sent to to Lorraine.

During the previous days Foch and Weygand, walking together in the grounds of Bombon, had discussed the future, not only of the Marne battle, but of the campaigns to follow it. Foch admitted Weygand had urged him to put these thoughts on paper, but he had delegated the task. This resulted in Weygand's production of a memoir that reviewed the general situation and summed up their joint thoughts on future policy. This, read out by Weygand at the meeting, started by stating that Ludendorff's fifth offensive had now been turned into a defeat, and went on:

'The Allied Armies have therefore reached the turning point of the road. For the first time, because of the number of divisions the Germans have been forced to commit, we have a superiority of reserves; and, because of the number of battle-worn divisions the Germans have had to pull out of the line, we also have more fresh reserves . . . and more than this, we have superiority in equipment: in aeroplanes . . . in tanks . . . and now behind us stands a powerful force of Americans, increasing at the rate of 250,000 men each month.

'We know the exceptional measures the enemy has taken to make good his losses, and the difficulties he has in maintaining the numbers of his front line troops. A further crisis would cause him grave problems.

'In our favour we have material superiority and much better morale due to the fact that the enemy has not, in spite of unprecedented efforts, produced the decisive result that is vital to him . . . '

It was impossible for the Marne offensive itself, it was conceded, to produce outright victory, but its progress gave hope of further developments that would enable France to play a full part in the war. The programme proposed was to be undertaken quickly, and the enemy 'struck again and again' across a wide front.

Operations must be undertaken to free the rail network which was vital to moving troops quickly; in the Marne area the rail link from Paris to Avricourt (Avricourt is on the Lorraine border) by developing the present offensive, and the Paris to Amiens line by a combined Franco-British operation; a second section of the the the Paris-Avricourt line to be freed round Commercy, and the St Mihiel salient to be reduced – this task to be mainly undertaken by the Americans; an offensive to re-capture the northern mines, and to outflank enemy positions between Calais and Dunkerque.

All these operations were to be fierce, successive surprise attacks, causing the enemy maximum trouble in organising his reserves, and preventing him consolidating his forces.

It was impossible to tell how far they would succeed, but 'if their aims were to be realised before the year was too far gone, there would be every reason for a major offensive at the end of summer or beginning of autumn that would build on any gains, and offer the enemy no respite.'

Finally it was foreseen that 'the enemy, to escape from our grip, or to conserve his resources, would have to attempt, by mounting a series of counter-attacks from a shortened line, to regain the initiative.'

The Allies should therefore constantly watch for movement behind enemy lines and along the front, so that any counter-attack is prevented or repulsed.

After this had been read, Foch asked for observations. Haig's immediate comment was that the British Army was still in process of being reformed: Pétain's, that the French Army had been bled white; Pershing's, that the Americans were willing to fight, but that their Army had not yet been formed. 'Study it,' Foch urged, ' for twenty-four hours, then give me your considered opinions as soon as possible.' Then a questionnaire was given out asking for two lists – the first of forces the Commanders in Chief would be able to put in the field on 1 January 1919, and a second similar estimate for 1 April, 1919. Projected numbers of troops, field batteries, aeroplanes, and heavy artillery were all to be given. Foch also particularly wanted estimates for mechanical transport and especially of tracked vehicles to cope with the problem of crossing country that had been devastated by battle.

According to Foch, these proposals completely staggered the various Commanders in Chief. 'They thought I had gone mad!' he said, describing events later. 'It is to be understood', the questionnaire ended, ' that this study is made with an unalterable principle in view – to end the war at the earliest possible moment in 1919 – an objective towards which each Allied nation must prepare to make its maximum effort from the beginning of the year. To this end:

'The British and French armies must increase the number of their divisions; the American army augment its numbers as quickly as possible, ammunition must be more than sufficient to sustain a long-lasting battle. The air-arm and the artillery must be enlarged as much as possible.'

It was emphasised that 'The Allied Armies have therefore reached the turning point of the road: they have the initiative. Their force allows them to keep it, the principles of war command them to keep it.

'The moment has come to abandon the attitude of general defence brought about by numerical inferiority, and move over to the offensive.'

CHAPTER 21

THURSDAY 25 TO SATURDAY 27 JULY 1918

–The Paris railway freed – the German First Army's counter-attack
at Reims fails – Ludendorff has to order a retreat – the Allies follow
up – Pétain tries to modify Foch's plans –

'I know death hath ten thousand several doors
For men to take their exits.'
(John Webster – 'The Duchess of Malfi')

Throughout the battle, Foch's aim, if the flanks could not be pierced
and the salient strangled, was to keep up pressure all round the
perimeter, constantly worrying the Germans so that the need for retreat
would be at the forefront of their minds. Therefore, that Thursday,
more attacks towards the Vesle started along the entire line between
Aisne and Marne. From early in the morning, the intention was to drive
the Germans still further into withdrawal towards that river, but as soon
as Degoutte's divisions to the west of Maistre's bridgeheads on the
Marne's north bank started to attack the enemy in the forests of Fère
and Ris, they came up against such a fierce resistance that all thoughts
of using cavalry in the attacks had to be abandoned. The rest of the Sixth
Army, strengthened by Pershing's American units (Pershing hoped
eventually to make it an all-American operation), continued to push
strongly towards Bazoches, and after some progress had been made, the
attack swung left to involve the massed reserves placed there some days
back, as the quickest way to reach Foch's objectives was by advancing
along the line of the Ourcq towards Fère-en-Tardenois.

Fayolle planned to increase the pressure by transferring Mangin's
XIth Corps (5th and 41st Divisions and their artillery) to Sixth Army
control that afternoon. This, added to the constant attacks already using
American strength, would force the enemy into an even quicker retreat.
Indeed, those American attacks were so fierce and decisive it seemed
Pershing's hopes might soon be realised, for the results encouraged
plans for the doughboys to take over the entire Sixth Army Front by 15
August.

But even as Fayolle sat down to draft orders for the XIth Corps' transfer, its 41st Division started a brilliant pincer attack round Oulchy-le-Château. By midday the town had been taken, and the Division's right flank was almost at Cugny. The IInd Corps, advancing alongside, was advancing on Nanteuil-Notre-Dame, while further north the 5th Division had bypassed Oulchy la Ville by mid-morning, and had started to clear the Bois de la Baillette. The verve and the dash shown by these two divisions caused the German loss of important positions on either side of the Ourcq.

Round Soissons, von Böhn was again under severe pressure. A long, heavy barrage preceded a series of strong attacks against the sector held by Group Endres (the former Group Watter, now under a new commander, General Ritter von Endres) that resulted in the Germans losing Villemontoire, because the fresh French 12th Division, at the centre of Mangin's Tenth Army, was leading an advance in force towards the plateaux of Buzancy, Villemontoire and Parcy-Tigny, and had captured the entire area from Oulchy la Ville up to Kleinbarn, hill 180, and beyond to the round-topped hill 200, east of Coincy.

Even though the main railway line along the south bank of the Marne from Paris to Nancy was being hastily repaired, and the first stage of Foch's overall plan was very nearly completed, there was neither time nor opportunity to pause, rest and regroup. In spite of the fact that the attackers were now near to utter exhaustion, another attempt had to be made to break the salient's flanks.

During the afternoon, the XXXth Corps continued its advance to the western edge of the Bois de Plessier, while the XXth Corps round Villemontoire reached the edge of Buzancy Château grounds. The road from Soissons to Oulchy was crossed at several points, and the desperate struggle to reach the objectives set by Mangin some days back was finally over. This allowed Mangin breathing space to plan the reorganising of his right flank (he intended to send the fresh 68th Division there, along with the 25th as reinforcements, and soon the 127th Division would be available as well). The 38th Division, after a period of comparative rest spent reconnoitring the approaches to Soissons, was moved to the left flank.

Because the situation had changed so much, there was no need to transfer Mangin's XIth Corps to Degoutte. Fayolle cancelled the move, and sent back not only the Corps, but added the 68th Division to it the following day. The promised 127th Division also moved to replace the American units ordered south to join Pershing's First Army. Other American divisions remained to help drive back the Germans. The 42nd Division (Rainbows) relieved the 26th in typical Champagne country, chalkland with many small streams, and dotted with woods and hills (the woods filled with German machine-gunners and 2½cm canon). Muir's Pennsylvanians also came into the front line, sending a brigade to support the 3rd Division's advance on Ronchères, while another of his brigades joined up with the 'Rainbows'. Their uniforms now powdered by chalk, the men looked very much like the original 'doughboys', originally given the nickname because of their uniforms whitened by 'adobe' dust during the Mexican campaign.

The troops of the US 32nd Division were also moving towards the Vesle during the last week of July, after less than a month's battle training, ready to relieve Dickman's 3rd Division. This was to be their first experience of war conditions. Many of the men from the Michigan and Wisconsin areas came from German families so recently arrived in America as to be still speaking German and living a German lifestyle. This had caused doubts about sending the Division into the front line to fight the German Army, and up to then it had been used in the supply section, but now the attack, needing the impetus of increased American strength and known ferocity, caused Degoutte to order its troops into battle to help throw the Germans back to the Vesle.

That afternoon Pétain's situation report arrived at Bombon. So far he had given the Tenth Army six fresh Divisions; the 15th and 34th British, and the 12th, 25th, 68th and 127th French. Two more – the 17th and 56th – were on their way from the Eastern Army Group, Their tanks had been brought back up to strength, but they were still absorbing replacements and needed time to move their heavy artillery across the salient.

Nearer Reims, in the thick woods round Marfaux, and towards the Marne in the Bois de Coutron, the British, flanked by the Mordrelle Group and Vth Corps, were still fighting hard but making little progress. The commanding ground west of the Ardre had to be captured before the advance could make further headway. The Highlanders were to make the attack, but needed a whole day's preparation and additional help from a battalion of the West Ridings. The fact that troops from another division could be inserted between the Scottish battalions – planning and operating successfully together – shows how close the co-operation now was between the two Divisions. But the rising number of casualties was giving cause for concern throughout the entire Fifth Army. Berthelot discussed his own, and his Divisional Commanders' worries with Maistre, and in turn, Maistre asked Provins for two Divisions (preferably the 10th and 16th, who were under orders to go to Gouraud) to remain in his reserve. Provins agreed, on the understanding that this was the limit of help they could provide. So all that day and the next, the men of the Fifth Army attacking in the Montagne struggled against a hardening defence, and became more and more exhausted in the process.

However, attacks along the north bank of the Marne were causing the salient to contract. In the sector held to the left of the Vth and XIVth Corps, as far as that held by its IIIrd Corps, the Central Army Group started to see progress after its long, constant, and bitter struggle against the Seventh German Army. The spearheading divisions on the Marne's north bank were able to set up positions towards the Ferme des Savarts (in the southern part of the Bois du Roi north of Port-à-Binson) and Vandières-sous-Châtillon (north of Dormans and Trélou.) Maistre now was able to implement GQG's instructions to reorganise his Central Army Group reserves. The 120th Division and the two Divisions of the Italian Corps began to move towards Épernay behind the Fourth Army Front.

Even if German Supreme Headquarters, looking back on the difficulties of the past week, could glean some satisfaction from the stubborn defence their troops were making, Avesnes was plunged into turmoil when by midday it became clear that the First Army counterattack west of Reims, on which Ludendorff had pinned such hopes, after having made a promising start, was first brought to a standstill then driven back. Far worse, during the struggle, the strategic heights round Vrigny – so important to the defence of the salient – were lost in a third fierce French counter-attack. Group Borne's attack had failed completely.

This resulted in an immediate flurry of discussions at Headquarters whether to try to continue holding the Marne front, or whether to confirm the preliminary instructions of 22 July (for the Seventh Army to prepare to withdraw to the new 'Beugneux' line from Oulchy-le-Château north-west to Fère-en-Tardenois and forward to Bligny above Marfaux). Options were eventually left open; orders were sent to hold the present positions until midday of the 26th, but at the same time to make preparations for a retreat during the night of the 26th/27th. The west flank from Soissons to Condé was of vital importance, and could not possibly be given up, so orders went out that afternoon to strengthen defences along the north bank of the Aisne.

Even now, Ludendorff could not bring himself to issue the order that would actually start the withdrawal. However, that day he was visited by Graf von Schwerin, head of the Herresgruppe Scholz in Macedonia, who had been faced with a similar situation when the withdrawal of German forces from Sofia was discussed.

> 'What' Schwerin asked him, 'would be the impression on our Austrian and Turkish allies, and what would people say at home, if the wrong decision . . . or worse still, the correct decision should be made too late, and troops lost needlessly?'

All day Ludendorff wrestled with increasing problems that put him under greater and greater stress as the situation deteriorated. By evening things were becoming desperate. On the east flank where his First Army attack had been driven back, the Allies were consolidating the gains they had made since the 21st. On the west, the position was deteriorating rapidly. Late in the evening a staff meeting was called, and Ludendorff announced his decision. An order (even though it was a provisional one) went out at midnight for the new Aisne-Vesle line to be made ready, and for the troops in front of that line to be evacuated.

Not only the Marne battle, but the entire war, was at its turning point.

Friday 26 July

Ludendorff delayed confirming his provisional order until the last possible moment. His consent was not given until midday. Furious, not only that he had been out-generalled and outfought, he was enraged that the whole world would know it as soon as the retreat started. However, more reports coming from the Seventh Army the previous evening had finally convinced him there was nothing for it but to act on von Schwerin's unpleasant advice.

> 'The First and Seventh Armies', his order read, ' are to withdraw tonight to strong bridgehead positions which are to be held.' Another message to the Kaiser informed the Emperor that 'now the conclusion of this long, testing battle is at hand, a withdrawal of the Ninth, Seventh and First Armies to positions behind the River Aisne can be allowed: they are to retire by sections and submit their new positions for approval.'

Because of the difficulties round Villementoire on the west flank, and the failure of Group Borne's attack the previous day on the east, the front held by Groups Schoeler, Wichura, Conta and Schmettow had to be abandoned, and the troops withdrew, harassed all the way by repeated attacks.

Foch's orders of the 24th had not altered the Marne battle's objectives to any extent. During the 22nd and 23rd he had ordered increased pressure on the German Seventh Army flanks and for the Paris-Avricourt railway to be freed in the Marne area. These orders had been carried out by his Army Group Commanders. Now, on the morning of the 26th, a second report arriving from Pétain told him that, discussing the situation with Fayolle and Mangin the previous night, both had seen the need for a powerful attack, and the necessary orders had been sent to them.

Mangin received the details that afternoon. His Tenth Army was to continue the advance by making a three-phase attack on the Buzancy, Droizy, Saponay line; the 68th Division (allocated to the XIth Corps and supported by every available gun in the XXXth Corps' artillery) would first capture the Butte Chalmont. The XXXth Corps (with the 25th Division on the left and the British 34th on the right) would then take the area from the Crete de l'Orme to the Grand Rozoy. This meant that the 34th Division would have to pull out of the line to move closer to its objective, so the 12th Division (now on the right of the XXth Corps) and the 19th Division holding the central sector of the XXth Corps, were ordered to extend their fronts to cover the 34th Division's departure. The XXth Corps would help by taking over the XXXth Corps' line as far as Coutremain. Six groups of their artillery were allocated to the XXXth Corps. In this second phase of the attack, the XIth Corps would cover and reinforce the XXXth in an advance against the heights of Beugneux and Wallée further south.

When the southern attack had gained these objectives (ie the XXXth and XIth had reached a line from Plessier-Huleu through the Orme du Grand-Rozoy and Beugneux to Wallée) the final stage could start, and the XXth Corps attack would drive towards Droizy. Briefly, this meant the Army's left had taken over more of the line, and the right's main attack as a result was able to use greater force against a shortened front. As part of the preparations, Berdoulat ordered the British 15th Division to extend its front southwards and take over the section of the XXth Corps' line held by the 91st Regiment of Dehers' 87th Division immediately west of Buzancy. This was an occasion when none of the previous difficulties were experienced, and General Reed wrote, thanking General Dehers for his Division's assistance. When completed, the relief meant that the Divisional boundary on the south ran east to west just below La Foulerie to just north of Bois l'Éveque, and the inter-brigade boundary from Aconin Farm to Écuiry. The 44th Brigade on the right was situated behind a wood opposite Buzancy.

The new objectives were to be captured on the morning of the 27th, but in attacking, all Army Corps were to be ready to support cavalry attacks under the command of the General in charge of the 1st Cavalry Corps, and were to place their forces so that they could quickly move north towards the Ourcq given the opportunity.

Degoutte, meanwhile, had reorganised his troops with the twofold aim of keeping the IInd Corps' attack alive, while preparations further south went on for the Americans to take over the entire Sixth Army Front. This was now considerably shortened because of the progress that had been made, and Degoutte made ready to pull back more of his troops, knowing that their sector would soon be taken over by the Americans.

In the Forêt de Reims, the British attack along the Ardre had needed a full day's preparation, and units of the 62nd Division not involved had been allowed 24 hours rest. Even then, most had no sleep because of an all night downpour.

By now the Germans held only a small sector on the north bank of the Marne between Belval-sous-Châtillon and the Forest de Riz, and there too, they were starting to disengage.

That day Pétain's reply to Foch's questionnaire of the 24th was delivered at Bombon. The French First Army, he agreed, should exploit its previous day's success, and be ready by 10 August to attack east of Amiens together with the British. The mass of French resources, however, he argued – particularly the heavy artillery – should be sent east to use against the St Mihiel salient. Operations north of the Somme should be the last major engagement of 1918 in which French troops would be involved. In that way, the 1919 conscripts could be kept back and not mobilised until the following Spring. (Foch, of course had already asked for the class of 1920 to be called up during October, to be ready for battle six months later). Pétain, ever cautious, was obviously trying to modify the timetable of Foch's plan with its insistence on attack, already approved by the other Commanders in Chief.

The recapture of ground between the Marne and Aisne continued, with American and French divisions side by side following up the withdrawal of the German centre. There were more French divisions than American, but the size of the US divisions meant they were often able to help neutralise troublesome strongpoints.

Saturday 27 July

In spite of all the achievements of the last two days, Foch complained that morning that the Tenth and Sixth Army attacks were far from producing a uniform advance on Fère-en-Tardenois. Writing to Pétain, he insisted that the tank battalions should be brought back to strength and more artillery be sent to the Tenth Army. The stalemate must not continue: new attacks must take place next day, not only by the Tenth and Sixth Armies, but also a 'well-organised attack by the Fifth that would bring about a strategic advantage'.

But now the Germans, realising their lines of communication and supply were increasingly in danger, had started a general retreat between the Ardre and Ourcq soon after midnight. The deadline for taking up the 'Blücher' position had still to be fixed, but could not possibly be before 1 August. Once the evacuation to the Aisne's north bank as far as Missy had begun, the small pockets of resistance, between four and five kilometres south of the Vesle on the eastern front, also began to pull back during the next night to new positions between the Aisne and Vesle. At least two days would be needed between the start of any further retirement and the fixing of 'X' day to occupy the Blücher position.

The overall plan was bedevilled by problems of logistics. The supply areas back near the Rhein could not move the amount of material needed in the time available because of the poor road and rail network to the battlefield, so Ludendorff decided the operation was to begin on

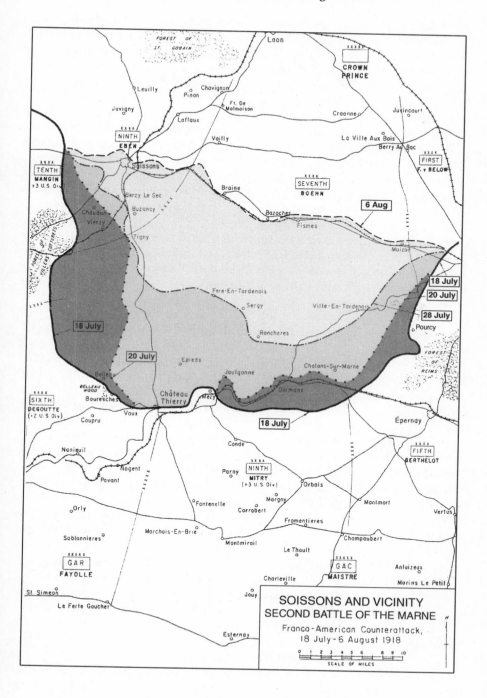

Figure 15

the night of 2 August. Success depended on sufficient ground being held to allow the retreating troops to move freely. In the meantime he ordered that the 'battle positions taken up from 27 July onwards are, for the Seventh Army, and the right wing of the First, to withdraw completely behind the river Vesle. As a result of this, the troops acting as rearguard may well be asked to take on further bloody fighting, and inflict more heavy casualties on the enemy.'

The Seventh Army made its retreat to the new positions as planned. Only Group Endres (the former Group Watter) remained in line, while Groups Winkler and Wichura, acting as rearguard to prevent the enemy following up too quickly, continued to hold the commanding heights of hills 180 (Butte Chalmont) east of Oulchy-le-Château and 231 near Ronchères. There were local engagements there all day, and heavier fighting round Fère-en-Tardenois.

Berthelot's Fifth Army had already begun to follow up the retreating Germans just as Maistre's urgings for 'a determined advance' arrived. Both it, and Degoutte's Sixth, were hard on the heels of the enemy rearguard, keeping up the pressure by maintaining contact. In the Ardre valley, Espilly and the Bois de Coutron were given up at last. The British reached Nappes by 10am, just in time to see the last Germans leaving Chaumuzy. Compared with previous attempts, the advance met almost no opposition, and by mid-afternoon patrols were scouting the old French trench lines round the side of the Montagne de Bligny. The neighbouring Vth French Corps' 14th and 9th Divisions, having stormed, and at last conquered the Paradis defences, were moving through the Bois de Courton, reaching Neuville-aux-Larris before 10 o'clock. The XIVth Corps entered Châtillon-sur-Marne and Vandières-sous-Châtillon; the IIIrd Corps made good gains above the Marne, while the XXXVIIIth, 1st American, and VIIth and IInd Corps advanced towards Fresnes through the Forêt de Fère towards Villeneuve-sur-Fère. After midday, cavalry moved up along both army fronts to join the infantry, and in several places spearheaded the advance.

The Germans were in retreat along a line running about 12 kilometres above the Marne, almost due west from the left of the British line in the Ardre.

North of the Ourcq, the Tenth Army's right flank made significant gains west of the Butte Chalmont, where the 41st Division succeeded in gaining a foothold. Mangin ordered his XIth Corps to continue its advance, and the XXXth Corps to be ready to attack on the 29th. Fayolle urged Degoutte to help these Tenth Army operations by capturing more ground along the Ourcq towards Fère-en-Tardenois. The message ended, 'the moment has come to gather the fruits of our ten days' bitter counter offensive. Advance!! even if the troops are weary!!' Seeing the main objective given by Fayolle almost within reach, Degoutte ordered redoubled efforts to prevent the enemy digging in on the plateaux north of the Ourcq, so that massed cavalry could break out towards Fismes. The morning was to be spent in reaching the new objectives, but everyone was to be ready to join the attack along with the cavalry and exploit the possibility of a quick advance north towards the Ourcq.

The 27th was a quiet day for the 15th Scottish Division until orders arrived at 7pm from General Berdoulat (commanding the XXth Corps) for them to attack Buzancy the next day. The 87th French Division had now taken over the much fought-over village of Villemontoire. Next Buzancy itself, and the high ground to its east had to be captured before another advance could begin. Five companies of the 91st French regiment were to co-operate on the right, while two more of the 87th Division advanced from Villemontoire to occupy the ground south of Buzancy to where the road leads from the village to Bois l'Éveque. Another was to clear the wood south-west of the village and a fourth, to the immediate right of the Scots, was to capture the 'Grenade Work' there and clear the ground back to the village. A further company of the 87th was to stay in Villemontoire as reserve. If these arrangements had been kept, the following day might have gone differently.

Groups Winkler and Wichura were still holding the Butte Chalmont and Hill 231 near Ronchères, and at Fère-en-Tardenois the US 42nd (Rainbows), after making progress through two days and 5km of machine gun nests, were engaging the Germans east of the strategically important railway centre, the Americans fighting on the high ground above the town; the French taking the town itself. Douglas MacArthur, Chief of Staff to the 42nd Division, later to win greater fame during the Second World War, had previously issued a situation report based on information given by captured German officers. In it he concluded the Germans had not enough artillery to support fighting on both sides of Reims, and that the ravages of influenza, the heavy losses suffered in the Spring Offensives, and a shortage of rations (caused by the blockade) were all affecting morale. He also confirmed that the German Quartermaster General had mounted sentries in every captured village between Reims and Chalons to guard loot that was to be shared after the battle, but that booty from Chalons itself would become the property of the state.

Second generation German-American doughboys also talked freely with captured rank and file. German second-line troops, treated less well than the élite shock-troops, were ravenously hungry and their morale was very low. Comments such as 'the game is up', and, 'we must hope for peace on reasonable terms', were widespread. They also told of troops made to stand by their machine-guns and artillery pieces by officers with drawn pistols.

In spite of this, MacArthur concluded that, given time to reorganise, the Germans still could put up a strong resistance.

Because of its very success, the Sixth Army Front was becoming increasingly restricted as the salient lessened. The VIIth Corps, along with the 2nd, 164th, 167th and 39th Divisions, was pulled out of the line during the evening of the 27th. The French sector was now manned by the IInd Corps (33rd, 62nd, 52nd and 63rd Divisions), and the front to be taken over by the Americans was to be in the hands of their Ist Corps (26th, 42nd, 4th Divisions), and the XXXVIIIth Corps (including the 3rd US Division and a brigade of their 28th).

Although Villemontoire had fallen on the 25th, Tigny still remained uncaptured. Where the French Tenth Army sector joined that of the Sixth, there were signs that the enemy was making ready for a further retreat, and so, relieved during the night by the French 25th Division, the British 34th Division was told to move ready to take part in the XXXth Corps' attack against the Grand Rozoy ridge on 30 July. Because the imminent capture of Fère-en-Tardenois by the French on the 28th would make a German retreat even more certain, the XXXth and XIth Corps' attacks were brought forward to the 29th.

CHAPTER 22

SUNDAY 28 AND
MONDAY 29 JULY 1918

–The Kaiser is concerned – British fortunes vary at Buzancy and
Bligny – Fère-en-Tardenois captured – German outposts begin their
withdrawal –

> *'Tis not in mortals to command success,*
> *But we'll do more, Sempronious, we'll deserve it.'*
>   *(Addison)*

That Sunday the Kaiser and Field Marshal Hindenburg met at Spa in
the Ardennes to discuss the situation, the Kaiser deeply concerned that
if a stubborn defence were to be made south of the Vesle:

> 'It could well result in producing casualty lists similar to those of the
> Somme or Passchendaele. The number of casualties resulting from such
> a course of action would be difficult to justify, and I would ask that we
> hold a line north, rather than south of the Vesle... Before I embark on
> any difficult meeting with the politicians, I must have clear indication as
> to how the new defence will be directed.'

When Hindenburg told him of this, Ludendorff wrote to the
Emperor at once, confirming that:

> '. . . enemy attacks will be met from the Blücher Stellung. The position is
> sufficiently strong to meet all the weight of enemy attacks experienced so
> far. From there we can win the operational freedom to mount further
> attacks.'

The German line, now running from above Villemontoire through
Buzancy down to Fère-en-Tardenois and Ronchères, was under heavy
attack all day. At Buzancy, the 15th Division's 44th Brigade (Brigadier
General Thomson), reinforced by men of the Scottish Rifles, some
Royal Engineers from the 91st Field Company and French flame-
thrower troops (who were determined to show the Germans how the
invention they were responsible for introducing into warfare ought to

157

be used) was to carry out the main attack. Their orders were to clear the Château and its grounds, take the village and link up with French troops of the 87th Division advancing from Villemontoire. Both the short preparatory barrage, increased by guns from the 87th French division, and the attack itself, were timed to disrupt the Germans' lunch-hour.

It was agreed after consultation with the French Corps Commander, General Berdoulat, who wanted to arrange air observation , that it should start at 12.30pm. During the morning short-lived barrages, known in British slang as 'stonks', took place from time to time, making the Germans expect attacks which never came, and produced a situation of 'Wolf!' being cried so often that they were disinclined to 'stand to' yet again when the actual attack came after the final three minute burst of shelling.

The attack started on time, prisoners soon started to arrive, and Scottish troops were seen on the plateau below the village. The Château and its grounds were cleared in spite of heavy machine-gun fire, then the sappers, moving on to the village, blew up a cellar near the church silencing more machine-guns while more strong points were wiped out by the flame-throwers. The village was in Allied hands by 1pm, and the high ground to its east was being cleared, when a fierce counter-attack drove the French on the right flank back to their starting line, and placed the Scottish positions in grave danger.

A message dropped from a French 'plane giving warning of the changed situation was brought by a French officer to the dugout General Reed was using as his Divisional Headquarters. The superstitious messenger immediately plunged the place into darkness by blowing out all three candles, expostulating that any attack directed from a HQ lit by three candles had no chance whatever of success. Two being relit, the message was found on the back of a photograph of an attractive young lady, together with an apology that the pilot had lost his notebook, and could the photograph please be returned? A second message coming soon afterwards from the same source was on the back of another photograph – of a different, even more attractive young lady. Both photographs were returned without comment by General Reed next day . . .

By 3.45pm the German counter-attack had swung the battle back in their favour. It would have been fruitless for the French to attack again as by that time the Scots, outflanked, had abandoned both the village and Buzancy Château. It must be said that the French troops had been in battle for a considerable time and were strained almost to breaking point. Their task was not only difficult; it had to be performed in extremely difficult country.

So, though the ground was lost again, the Division, even if suffering heavy casualties in the process, caused severe losses to the enemy who, besides killed and wounded, had half a dozen officers and more than two hundred other ranks taken prisoner.

Lieutenant Lamb, in charge of the men from the 91st Field Company of the Royal Engineers, gave a first-hand account of the day's struggle:

'The first wave of the Seaforths captured the Château, and the second passed through the Château grounds. The sappers got mixed up with the infantry . . . Sergeant Coleman then told the party to stop in the grounds until he got in touch with the Officer commanding the company clearing the village. At this point the section came under machine-gun fire from the vicinity of the Château, which had not been properly 'mopped up' and got split up. Each party separately engaged the enemy and Lance-corporal Brazier with four sappers got in touch with OC 'A' Co., 8th Seaforths – I think Captain McElderney – who told him to report to Lt. Thomson. Lance-Corporal Brazier then blew up a cellar near to the church which contained enemy machine guns, silenced them, and killed several of the enemy. He and his men then returned to the Château and with Lt. Thomson and one platoon of the Seaforths, rushed a cellar,and captured between 100 and 120 Germans. At this point the enemy counter attacked on our exposed right flank and practically the whole of the sappers fought their way back to our old front line, as they were nearly surrounded . . .'

Those divisions of Berthelot's Fifth Army facing the Ourcq reached the river that morning and started to consolidate, with their flank protected by Mangin's XIth Corps' attack on, and, by mid-morning, its capture of the Butte Chalmont. This in turn allowed the IInd Corps' 52nd Division to reach Fère-en-Tardenois, but the American 1st Corps further south made no progress in spite of attacking the heights round Sergy all day.

With Fère-en-Tardenois taken at last, Mangin's staff began to prepare for more attacks next morning. The reinforced XXXth Corps' objective was the high point north of the Grand Rozoy between Servenay and the Bois de Plessier. While the 19th and 25th Divisions held the line, the 34th British, moving nearer to its objective overnight, was to join the attack on the 25th Division's right. The IXth Corps, now the Butte Chalmont was recaptured, and in line from the Station of the Grand Rozoy to the Ourcq, would guard and reinforce the XXXth's right flank advance towards Cramaille and the Bois d'Arcy, with the rested 68th Division and the 41st who were again ready to join in the attack in spite of having been constantly in action since 18 July.

Berdoulat, too, spent much of the day working on the details of his XXth Corps' planned advance towards Droizy on 30 July. Now that the French 38th Division had been relieved by the 15th British, the Corps' battle-order was, from north to south, the 87th, the 15th British and the

THE SECOND BATTLE OF THE MARNE 1918

French 12th Divisions, so that the freshest division would be the one to force its way forward to Taux and Hartennes-et-Taux.

Over in the Ardre valley, a battalion of the 62nd Division, reinforced by 200 men (many without battle experience) arriving the previous day, with its hastily reorganised platoons led by young lance corporals, and trained gunners for the Lewis guns redistributed as best it could, was to attack one of the main strongpoints on the eastern flank. The 8th West Yorkshires set out at 4am in heavy mist.

'Our section followed not far behind 'D' Company as they wound their way through corn pasture. It was now growing light enough to see something of our surroundings. On our left there loomed a spur topped by occasional trees; across the road on our right was a miniature prairie, yellow with ripened corn which ceased only when it reached the Bois de Bligny on higher ground, while far away in the distance was a dim incline of some prominent hill. This far off knoll, then, and its encircling trenches, formed our goal this morning. We were getting along in great style, and not a sight of the enemy was to be seen. We then reached the Bligny-Chambrecy road which cut across our front. In the crossing we had to climb over a rather high bank, but we were soon over this obstacle and into the cornfields. The Montagne grew more and more distinct with such details as a small wood halfway up its steep slopes and isolated trees became easily distinguishable. It was now broad daylight, the and the mists were clearing. There were no enemy to be seen and the battle was progressing well.

'The sharp report of a Mauser rifle rang out. Then rifles and machine guns spluttered and cracked from scores of hidden emplacements in the hillside. Two guns were spurting destruction from the high ground on our left. Were we going to be caught in some deadly machine gun cross fire? Our advance received a decided check. The delay did not last long for each section changed its steady marching programme to one of quick rushes and short rests . . . Forgetting fatigue, section after section darted up in the corn, rushed a few yards, dropped down and opened fire . . . we were making headway, though slowly, against this strong resistance.

Then up the road, where we joined up with the Devons, a cavalry patrol galloped towards us and, to the cheers of the men, dashed past us... Snipers and machine guns began to thin our ranks. Some sections lost heavily . . . One gun section consisted of a gunner, his gun and a pannier of ammunition which he hauled along when not firing at the Boches to keep them down until his pals made their rush forward . . . The line crept forward . . . the German fire became less certain, and finally wavered. Fixing bayonets the West Yorkshires charged the enemy who eventually broke and fled . . . helped on by fire from their own captured machine guns. The usual clearing operations had to be carried out, but finally the hillside was cleared, the crest was reached and the position consolidated.' (Lieutenant Burroughs, 'B' company.)

160

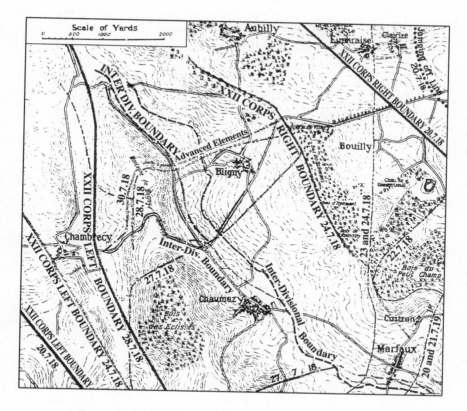

Figure 16 The Capture of Bligny and Montagne de Bligny

This action against the Montagne de Bligny won the battalion the Croix de Guerre.

The 62nd having gained the Montagne, the Scots were able to occupy the old French trenches and make contact with the right wing of the neighbouring French division. A report that Chambrecy had fallen to the French proved false, so the Highlanders were held up. Instead, they were ordered to support a French attack on Ville-en-Tardenois, providing artillery fire from the high ground north of Chambrecy. This meant the guns racing full tilt across open ground under heavy fire.

The French attack failed, and the Scots had to pull back. Chambrecy was now in no-man's-land, but any attempt to occupy it brought down heavy shelling.

At the day's end, Allied advanced units, reading from west to east, had reached points west of Buzancy (the village again in German hands), of Tigny and of the Bois de Plessier. The station of the Grand Rozoy was reached, the Ourcq as far as Ronchères, the areas south of the Bois

161

Meunière (the wood itself strongly held by the enemy), the southern outskirts of Sainte-Gemme, of Romigny, of Ville-en-Tardenois, Chambrecy, then a line from Bligny, through Sainte Euphraise to Vrigny.

That evening Fayolle ordered his army commanders to 'continue the advance, no matter how tired the troops'. The plateaux of Tardenois had to be retaken, and the enemy retreat towards the Aisne and Vesle constantly harassed.

During the night, German outposts on the heights east of Oulchy-le-Château were pulled back, and Group Winkler was also withdrawn as the defence front was now shorter.

At the end of the Scots' difficult day at Buzancy, orders arrived at 11pm for them to relieve sections of the French 87th and 12th Divisions by 3am on the 30th. Somehow or other it was done, under extremely difficult conditions, as an almost constant bombardment of gas shells forced the wearing of respirators throughout the move.

Monday 29 July

In describing the Allied operations exploiting the counter-attack's success, it must be remembered that preparations for further offensives both to the north and the east were going on at the same time. Foch was determined to ask Pershing to mount his American offensive against the St Mihiel salient before August was over, and behind the Marne battle-front troops were already gathering for the Amiens offensive. The 56th Division, already on the move to Lorraine, was rerouted to Crèvecoeur behind the left of Fayolle's Army Group, joining the 153rd, 47th and the Moroccan divisions previously sent there, while another three divisions – the 126th, 1st and 5th – were regrouping behind Fayolle's centre.

These moves, all being organised and operated while troop movements to meet the demands of the Marne battle were going on, made it vital that nothing should alert the Germans. Even the High Command Staff became involved in deception. General Weygand, Foch's Chief of Staff, was told on no account to go to a conference at Sarcus where the Franco-British offensive east of Amiens was being planned, in case his mere presence was reported and aroused German suspicions. The meeting was attended only by the army commanders involved, and paperwork was kept to an absolute minimum. A few staff officers were briefed, but only on a 'need to know' basis.

Weygand personally had taken Foch's letter placing Haig in charge of the new offensive to British Headquarters at Montreuil the previous day, while General Destiker, (his Assistant Chief of Staff) went to Pétain at Provins with copies. In these letters Foch argued that the Germans, now in serious difficulties above the Marne, 'would certainly establish defensive positions behind a river, safe from immediate attack, and win time to reorganise, re-equip and replace his losses.'

Given Debeney's First Army to add to Rawlinson's Fourth, and with the prospect of his XXIInd Corps coming back into the British Zone, Haig pressed forward his plans for the new offensive. He would have adequate resources: Rawlinson's Army had 12 Infantry and 3 Cavalry divisions; Debeney's was similar in size. The aims set for him were to throw back the German forces threatening Amiens, reopen the Paris/Amiens railway and force the enemy between the Somme and the Avre into retreat.

And so on 29 July – the date on which the first phase of Foch's 24 July plan had been completed – the next phase had started. Already his plans to mount a further massive offensive in the very area where Ludendorff was short of reserves, and his armies struggling to rebuild both strength and morale, were under way. This new Haig offensive would also prevent the Germans recovering from the Marne retreat. Ludendorff's withdrawal from the salient was in itself to become a prelude to the war's last great battle.

As the British were gathering men and material for the Amiens offensive, the American Army also was preparing to play its part in Foch's overall plan, Pershing asking for his forces on the Marne to be hurried across to Lorraine as soon as possible to help destroy the St Mihiel salient.

Realising the Allies were bringing more artillery into the salient, the Germans prepared to resist heavier attacks there, while secretly, hour by hour, behind the lines, Pétain was moving troops west behind Fayolle's centre, and Haig's reserves were being sent into the Amiens-Montdidier area. These plans for fuelling an ongoing battle and a coming offensive were extremely complicated, and it was to be more than a week before Haig's attack opened on 8 August – a day that Ludendorff later described as 'the black day of the German army' – but to ensure Ludendorff's attention remained focused on the Marne and his retreat there continued, more assaults were made against the Grand Rozoy and the Tardenois plateau.

The XXXth Corps' attack started at 4am, followed by the XIth Corps' two hours later. The British 34th Division, having moved overnight to its new position (and being heavily shelled on the way) arrived in the nick of time to advance through thick fog behind the rolling barrage. Before long important gains had been made. The Grand Rozoy was taken by 8am and the 34th Division had bypassed Beugneux; but then a lively counter-attack by the Guards Ersatz Division saved the German line by throwing back the French on the right flank, and the entire attack had to retreat and reform under the cover of an artillery barrage, while the Fifth and Sixth Armies advanced to relieve the pressure. By the end of the day, the troops, completely exhausted, could not push the Grand Rozoy line forward beyond the south of Saponay, Seringes-et-Nesles and Cierges.

During the 29th, when heavier Allied attacks were also going on south east of Fère-en-Tardenois and the Germans were being forced back between Forzy and Romigny, the Kaiser's permission arrived for further withdrawals. Even now, Ludendorff hoped to hold the bridgehead, but Crown Prince Wilhelm's experience of the battle (he had now only 13 divisions fit for battle out of 23) made him argue against it. Allied attacks were sucking more and more replacements into the salient. The Blücher Stellung needed only 17 divisions, and if the enemy attempted to attack the new, extremely strong position, they would, he said 'be welcomed with open arms.' He would agree to holding the present line only if OHL 'at the cost of providing far more men and resources, wanted to force the enemy to commit his reserves, and then strike elsewhere.'

In the Tenth Army, Mangin's Ist Corps, spearheaded by the 69th Division, was making another attempt to capture ground round Soissons, advancing towards Les Pentes and Vauxbuin. The 72nd and 162nd Divisions guarded the northern flank while the 38th Division defended the Aisne crossings. Mangin was keeping Fayolle's repeated warnings of the last ten days to protect the General Reserve by guarding the river very much in mind. Fayolle also reinforced the Aisne-Ourcq sector, replacing the 1st Division with the 128th.

Mangin now moved the 48th Division (so battle-worn it had to be almost completely rebuilt) into reserve, knowing that the 127th and the 17th divisions would arrive at the end of the day and could attack if there should be an opportunity.

During the morning XXth Corps Headquarters ordered the British 15th and French 12th Divisions to attack the Buzancy ridge next day, the 15th Division working round the north side of the Bois d'Hartennes while the French came round its south.

Degoutte's Sixth Army was now along the Ourcq from Corbeny to Ronchères. As the front narrowed, there was room for only three Corps in the front line . . . the IInd French (the 63rd and 62nd Divisions), the Ist Americans (the 4th US Division relieving the 42nd) and the XXXVIIIth Corps (with the 3rd US Division and a brigade of the 28th). The VIIth Corps (the 164th, 2nd, 167th and 39th Divisions together with the American 26th) was to the rear reorganising, and Cavalry units on the plateau between Château-Thierry and Beuvardes were ready to break out above the Ourcq.

Degoutte ordered the advance to start again that morning, 'the minimum objective by the end of the day to be a line from Chéry-Chartreuve to Bruys, with advanced units established on Mont-Notre-Dame, and Mont-Saint-Martin'.

West of Reims, Berthelot had the IIIrd Corps (4th and 18th divisions), the XIVth Corps (20th Division), the Vth Corps (9th and 14th Divisions), the Mordrelle Group (77th, 2nd Colonial and 168th Divisions) in line. The 134th, 3rd Colonial and 45th Divisions held the right flank. The 10th and 16th Divisions were brought out of line into the reserve, and the two British divisions, clearing the last few pockets of resistance from the Montagne de Bligny, were told to be ready to return north to Haig. It was vital that pressure continued on the German rearguard. 'Give that rearguard time to reform,' Berthelot warned his troops, 'and you will have to use all your strength to throw it back along the Ardre in the direction of Lagery and Crugny.'

Meanwhile, the Americans mainly still occupied the positions they had reached between 21/25 July, but Foch intended their period of rest and regrouping to be brief. He asked Pershing to hurry the transfer of those divisions that were to go to Lorraine and, with regard to the American units in the Marne salient, it was 'imperative they should be fully involved in the battle and pursuit of the enemy. Their *re-organisation* should not slow the *action*, and I ask you that all should be dictated to by the circumstances of the moment – an uninterrupted pursuit that demands a good deal from your Corps commanders.'

The French High Command having plotted the gains made by the Tenth Army's right flank, and realising the difficult task facing the Sixth, and the impossible one of the depleted Fifth Army to mount further attacks, altered tactics, Pétain sending his Army Group Commanders these instructions:-

'The enemy appears to be strongly entrenched on the plateaux south of Soissons and on the heights between the Vesle and the Ardre. If we hope to destroy his forces south of the Aisne, from now on we must aim at forcing the kind of withdrawal that prevents an orderly retreat with time to lay waste the country, and that brings the time nearer when we can use the Marne railway to exploit the situation.

'The Sixth Army, which has the best means at its disposal, must aim for a quick and constant advance along its entire front in the general direction of Fismes and of Bazoches, its left gaining a foothold round Saponay to help the Tenth Army's right wing break out towards Cramaille'. His orders continued for it 'to take over the IIIrd Corps' sector by midnight of the 30th, so that the Army of the Reserve's line takes in Verneuil, Sainte-Gemme, Vezilly, Arcis-le-Ponsart and Courville.'

The Tenth Army, 'which cannot be reinforced', was 'to continue using its right flank, advancing towards Arcy-Sainte-Restitue and Braine together with the Sixth Army'. The centre was to manoeuvre 'in such a way that the heights on the left bank of the Crise are occupied', but action at Soissons was to be limited to 'mopping up' captured territory for the time being, and providing cover for the operations on the right.'

Mangin immediately allocated the 127th Division (relieved at Montgobert by the 17th) to join the attack on his right flank. In order to cover and reinforce his left, he moved the non-divisional elements of the VIIth Corps (from the Sixth Army) under their own commander into the 128th Division's sector between the Oise and the Aisne. He ordered that next morning be spent in reorganising and re-equipping, while the 127th Division completed its move towards Louâtre and Blanzy.

Pétain's orders went on,

> 'The Fifth Army, again which cannot be reinforced, must make plans to release the two divisions of the British XXIInd Corps by the end of July. It will continue to press the enemy south of the Ardre from Romigny to Lagery and Crugny, to help the 6th army's right wing.
>
> 'The Army Group Commanders must employ their forces methodically, making an advance that leaves their reserves intact, and ensure the enemy is not able to make sudden counter-attacks between the Oise and the Aisne or on the Reims sector.'

Degoutte had finished reorganising his forces by evening, pulling back the Ist Cavalry Corps. Next day's advance was to aim towards La Veille.

The reasoning behind these orders was as follows. Pétain was already sending his reserve of two Cavalry Corps away from the Marne, the second towards Beauvais and the first towards Vitry-le-François, admitting that by doing so he considered 'the progress of the battle excludes the possibility of using cavalry'. Also, in a second telegram he informed Fayolle that the non-divisional units of the XXXVIth Corps, were to move to the Crèvecoeur area to join the four divisions in the general reserve behind Fayolle's Army Group. Pétain now obviously was intending to spare the French more casualties by easing the ferocity of operations north of the Marne while his armies were being prepared for an offensive on another sector. Foch's objective of completely freeing the Paris-Avricourt line was still in mind, but he was determined to cause minimum casualties and fatigue to his men in carrying it out. The advance was still to be towards the two objectives of Bazoches and Fismes that had been given on 20 July, but now the task was given to the Sixth Army. The Fifth and Tenth, because of the impending departure of the British troops, and the ultimate loss of the American troops Pershing was pressing to be moved to Lorraine, were now too weak.

Pétain stuck to these decisions during the next few days. On the 31st he was telegraphing Fayolle that 'the situation, because of our resources, forces us to adopt a new style . . . regulate your efforts to your means. The aim is gradually to push back the enemy on the Vesle by successive attacks, in accordance with my orders of 29 July, but giving more and more of the main thrust to the Americans still with the Sixth Army.' At the same time another letter to Foch gave a résumé of the general situation and the available men and material, so that Supreme Commander was able to decide what part the French Army would be able to play in the coming operations. The letter concluded, '58 French divisions have been engaged in the Marne battle to date, and I am now only able to provide one single fresh reserve division. Our losses in infantry alone are already 120,000 men: I have only 19,000 reinforcements to mobilise and can count on only 29,000 more after a two or three months' delay. The front line troops are admittedly in excellent spirits, but extremely weary. We are at the limit of our effort.'

However, as it happened, the Army Group and various Army Commanders were already directing the battle in accordance with Pétain's orders even before they were sent out. Fayolle, on the evening of the 29th, had ordered the Sixth Army to continue pressing the enemy along the whole front, working in conjunction with the Fifth Army on its right, and regaining the Ourcq on the left, bypassing Saponay on the west and advancing through the passage between the Bois d'Arcy and the Bois of the Old Château of Fère.'

CHAPTER 23

TUESDAY 30 AND WEDNESDAY 31 JULY

– The Sixth Army attacks against the Tardenois plateau – the Grand Rozoy retaken – German preparations for the retreat to the Blücher Stellung –

'The three o'clock in the morning courage, which Bonaparte thought was the rarest.'
(Thoreau)

Early morning attacks by the Sixth Army started again along the whole front, but there was fierce resistance from the Ourcq to the west of the Bois Meunière, and little progress was made. The action was broken off, and the morning used by the entire Reserve Army Group to prepare more attacks to start next day before dawn, organising the resources available so that strength was allocated according to the importance of the objectives.

Degoutte again warned his commanders to watch for possible counter-attacks, and in their own attacks to deal with machine-gun nests and strongpoints by outflanking them, rather than taking them by storm. This made clear, he ordered next day's IIIrd and XXXVIIIth Corps' advance either side of the Bois Meunière to start before dawn, while the Ist American and the IInd French Corps took more territory north of the Ourcq.

The Tenth Army's XXXth Corps had retaken the Grand Rozoy without opposition and the flank was secured by 6am. The line now ran from the Bois de la Terre d'Or, round the northern edge of Grand Rozoy village to south of the Beugneux-Cramaille road. The Corps then spent the remainder of the day preparing an attack for the 31st, but Foch, visiting Mangin and discussing the situation, decided to delay the attacks of both the Corps until 1 August. The XXXth Corps was then to take the section of the Grand Rozoy from the Allont crest to Servenay, and, passing between the 25th and 127th Divisions, make for Launoy. The XIth Corps, in support, was to advance towards the Bois d'Arcy with the 68th and 41st Divisions, while the other flank kept contact with Degoutte's troops. To the north, left of the XXXth Corps, the 19th Division and the whole of the XXth Corps were to advance on Droizy as soon as the southern success allowed. Mangin then would expect ' a rupture of the enemy front from them that would carry, treading on the heels of his rearguard, as far as Launoy and Bucy-le-Bras.'

The Scottish Division's sector of the XXth Corps' line ran north from the Bois de Tigny, in full view of the enemy. On the right was a ridge with three hillocks – 'Les Trois Mamelons' – the words soon translated into a form more easily understood by the average private, and north of those strongpoints, as it followed the road east of Villemontoire, the line faced open ground sloping up to Buzancy ridge. The Germans opposite had the advantage of two ravines giving shelter to, and a hidden route for, their reinforcements.

The attack against the Bois d'Hartennes depended very much on success further south. The 15th Division was to take the wooded hills between Tigny and Villemontoire, then go on to reach the main objective of the Soissons road, but it was decided after discussion that the attack should be linked with the southern attack, and it was therefore delayed to 1 August.

That morning, German Supreme Headquarters ordered the move to the Blücher Stellung to start during the night of 1–2 August. It was to be completed as quickly as possible, as the rearguard would not be able to hold back the enemy longer than one more day. Headquarters' staff, however, agreed first to discuss arrangements with the First and Seventh Army staffs. After that, responsibility for the move would be in the hands of Crown Prince Wilhelm's headquarters.

Berthelot, in his order of the day, paid handsome tribute to the work of his two British Divisions. Translated, it read:

'Now that the XXIInd British Corps has received orders to leave the Fifth Army, the Army Commander expresses to all the thanks and admiration which its great deeds, just accomplished, deserve.

'On the very day of its arrival, the XXIInd Corps, feeling in honour bound to take part in the victorious counter-attack, which had just stopped the enemy's furious onslaught on the Marne, and which had begun to hurl him back in disorder towards the north, by forced marches, and with minimum opportunity for reconnaissance, threw itself with ardour into the battle.

'By constant efforts, by harrying and driving back the enemy for ten successive days, it has made itself master of the valley of the Ardre, which it has so freely watered with its blood.

'Twenty one officers, and more than one thousand three hundred other ranks taken prisoner, one hundred and forty machine guns and forty artillery pieces captured from an enemy, four of whose Divisions were successively broken and repulsed; the upper valley of the Ardre, with its surrounding heights to the north and south recaptured: such is the record of the British share in the operations of the Fifth Army.

'Highlanders, under the direction of General Carter-Campbell, commanding the 51st Division, Yorkshire lads under the command of General Braithwaite, commanding the 62nd Division; Australian and New Zealand Mounted Troops; all officers and men of the XXIInd Army Corps, so brilliantly commanded by General Sir A. Godley – you have added a glorious page to your history.

'Marfaux, Chaumuzy, Montagne de Bligny – these famous names may be inscribed in letters of gold in the annals of your regiments.

'Your French comrades will always remember with emotion your splendid valour and perfect fellowship as fighters.'

The Americans by now had arrived at Grimpettes Woods, slightly north-east of Fresnes en Tardenois. Wheatfields in front of the position, stiff with concealed machine-guns, had first to be negotiated. The task of clearing the woods themselves proved almost as formidable as the task faced by the Marines at Belleau, and the fighting, although shorter-lived, was almost as fierce.

After helping with house-to-house fighting at Ronchères, the Pennsylvanian 55th Infantry Brigade attacked the position twice that morning without artillery support, in spite of heavy losses. Even when the guns arrived in the early afternoon, the Pennsylvanians refused to wait for them to register their target, but rushed the woods with the bayonet.

The key to the whole position was the village church at Courmont. German snipers were hidden behind the altar, and cannoneers controlling 2½cm weapons, were among the defenders. The Pennsylvanians fought their way step by step through the building and up the belfry stairs. The only survivor from that part of the attack was a sergeant who killed three gunners and reported that the German officer in charge had jumped to his death rather than surrender.

Two of the Pennsylvanians' chaplains had the most unclerical of talents: one, an amazing facility for spotting hidden snipers; the other taking command of a company when all the officers became casualties. General Muir also personally led an attack, saying he 'just couldn't miss the opportunity.'

After their experiences at Courmont, Grimpettes and Hill 192 behind the woods, the Pennsylvanians were pulled back for seven days rest.

The untried 32nd Division had moved up the salient to relieve the US 3rd, a new-found patriotism overriding any feelings the men had about their German origins. When a slightly wounded German officer, insisting he was a stretcher case, started to harangue his bearers that America was not going to win the war, he was tipped off, and told in polite German that he, personally, was not going to win anything. The Division arrived on the right of the Pennsylvanians at Grimpettes, advancing against heavy machine-gun fire to the village of Cièrges. After a night of hand-to-hand fighting, German troops, confused by orders shouted in German from in front and behind, lost the village next morning and were driven back across the Ourcq with the Americans in hot pursuit.

The 32nd and 42nd Divisions now held a line along the river.

During these last days of July the politicians, in Paris to discuss munitions supply, were invited to take a holiday from their labours and view the scenes of the victory. Winston Churchill was among them.

> 'Passing through Château-Thierry and along the pulverised front, we repaired to Mangin's headquarters at Versigny. We approached the General's house through a long avenue of captured German cannon and trench mortars. Mangin received us with cordiality. His modest bearing did not conceal his joy. After luncheon I found myself alone with him, and knowing the ups and downs which he had survived, I offered some few words of admiration upon his signal victory. I record his reply exactly as he gave it: 'Le Maréchal Foch l'a conçue. Le Genéral Gouraud l'a rendue possible. Moi, je l'ai faite.' Some years afterwards when I repeated these words to General Gouraud, he considered them for an appreciable moment, then said 'That is quite true'.'

Wednesday 31 July

Before the German retreat to the Blücher Stellung had even started, more quick Sixth Army advances up the valleys destabilised the situation. In the face of these attacks, and no longer able to hold back the IIIrd and XXXVIIIth Corps (who had by now taken almost all the Meunière and Cièrges woods) the Germans seemed about to give up the struggle. German officers taken prisoner admitted their 'Seventh Army would shortly withdraw to a fortified position', due to difficulties of communication and supply and 'to the lack of rail links.' But it seemed this would be limited to the plateau between Fère and Ville-en-Tardenois, for other prisoners spoke of 'orders to hold the position of the Orme of the Grand Rozoy to the last man'.

These reports did not change Pétain's tactics ordered two days back. A telegram to Fayolle stated that 'the situation, because of our resources, forces us to adopt a new style . . . regulate your efforts to your means. The aim is gradually to push back the enemy on the Vesle by successive attacks, in accordance with my orders of July 29th, but giving more and more of the main thrust to the Americans still with the Sixth Army'.

His letter to Foch on the same day had already given a résumé of the general situation, the numbers of troops and quantities of material available, to help estimate what part the French army would be able to play in the coming operations. It had ended with ominous words. 'We are at the limit of our effort.' This feeling that France had contributed more than her fair share to the struggle, and it was time for the British and the Americans to take up the burden was shared by many in the French Army. Foch himself told the story of his old friend, Fayolle, saying to him after each stage of the advance, 'Perhaps now you'll allow us a breathing space!', to which Foch had always replied, 'On the contrary – we shall push forward harder than ever! Yes, I know your troops are dropping with fatigue. The Germans are dropping with fatigue even more!'

That night the troops of the XXXth and XIth Corps moved into position for the 1 August attack; the objectives were those set out on the 29th.

General Reed met his brigade commanders to plan the 15th Division's capture of the two wooded hills west of Soissons and its advance to Taux. When Taux was taken, the left flank would then start to move on the final objective – the north end of the Bois d'Hartennes – and link with the French coming from the south. The greatest danger would be the move to assembly points which were in full view from the woods between Buzancy and the Bois d'Hartennes. It was decided to move by night, using the cornfields as cover. As soon as the southern attack had achieved success a message to that effect would be dropped from an aeroplane. Half an hour later, the troops would go into action.

By dusk the 51st Highland Division, like the 62nd Division the previous evening, was starting back down the Ardre valley away from the fighting – most of the troops having somehow acquired a few bottles of the region's speciality en route. Berthelot planned a march past for both British divisions.

The Central Army Group had made some progress between Sainte-Gemme and Ville-en-Tardenois between the 29th and 31st, but further north stiff resistance – even counter-attacks – were being met west of Vrigny, also west of Sainte-Euphraise and between Bligny and Chambrecy.

In passing on Pétain's orders, Maistre reminded Berthelot that 'in spite having reorganised his army so the British divisions could leave, he must allow time to rest the troops and let them sleep and eat so they could come back fresh to the battle. By doing this, 'the Army Group will be able to mount further attacks using rested infantry.'

To relieve the British Corps quickly, Berthelot ordered the 77th Infantry Division (Mordrelle group) and the Vth Corps' 14th Division to extend the line during the 30th and 31st and take over the British sector. The General commanding the XIVth Corps also sent two divisions in between the Vth and the Ist Colonial Corps.

In spite of these complex reliefs, Berthelot told his troops to continue the offensive; 'The task of the army remains the same – to follow up the enemy and throw him back beyond the Ardre and the Vesle. All Army Corps must therefore continue to claw at his rearguard . . . '

But by 1 August it was obvious that the Fifth Army would be forced to reorganise, and would not be able to make any significant contribution to the Sixth and Tenth Army offensives.

CHAPTER 24

THURSDAY 1 AND FRIDAY 2 AUGUST 1918

– Preparations for the Amiens offensive – more actions on the Orme of the Grand Rozoy – the Germans pushed towards the Vesle – Soissons retaken –

'The lads that will die in their glory and never be old.'
(A.E. Housman)

General Debeney started preparations for his First Army's joint attack with Rawlinson's Fourth, secretly moving his troops towards Conty, Froissy and Beauvais by night to avoid air observation. The German High Command, as it happened, had already decided to evacuate the left bank of the Avre on 3 August – the date which Debeney intended to start pinching out the German positions west of a line from Moreuil to Montdidier. This German withdrawal was caused by the constant attacks going on below the Aisne and Vesle rather than because of Debeney's threatened attack. Finding replacements for losses in the Marne battle meant taking troops from other sectors, and that in turn meant the lines on those other sectors had to be shortened. Indeed, between 21 July and the beginning of August, 12 full divisions had been taken from Rupprecht to try to stem the Allied advance.

Although further south in the salient, Maistre's Central Army Group had taken more ground between Sainte-Gemme and Ville-en-Tardenois. During the past three days, German resistance remained stiff – in spite of Berthelot's desire to continue the advance, it was becoming more and more obvious that, lacking his British troops, he would be unable to help the Sixth and Tenth Army offensives that Thursday. He had no option but to use all day reorganising the Fifth Army front.

During the previous night, the right flank of the Tenth Army had been making ready for its morning attacks on the Grand Rozoy and Servenay. These were both vital to the enemy defence, and German Headquarters ordered that they had to be held. (Information from prisoners was that the orders to the troops there included the words 'to the last man'.)

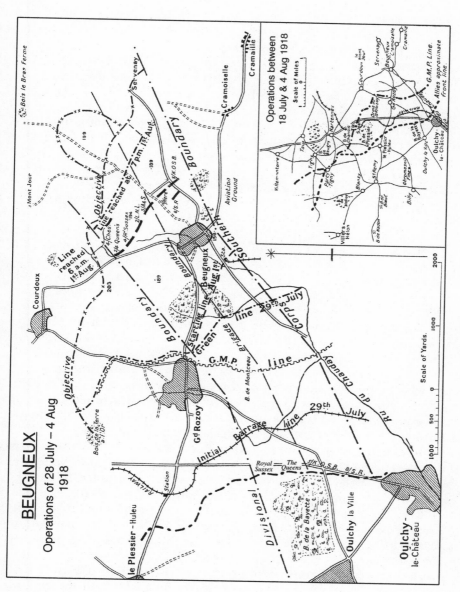

Figure 17

The Tenth Army's XXXth and XIth Corps' first attack started at 4.45am. This time, more than a hundred and fifty howitzers and field guns opened up to plaster the German line, and the infantry following up the barrage had more success. The 34th British Division took Hill 158, and advanced through the airfield east of Beugneux before being held up by heavy fire coming from Saponay.

Degoutte ordered his IInd Corps to help drive back the Germans by 'making an approach to Saponay from the east, and advancing west of the woods north of Fère'. Meanwhile other men of the 34th had cleared the woods north of the road from Grand Rozoy to Beugneux in a fixed bayonet charge. The crest was reached by 6am. Two hours later the neighbouring 25th Division had taken the peak south of Courdoux, and the 34th British and French 68th Divisions had arrived together in front of Servenay. This success meant Mangin could send the order to his XXth Corps further north to start its attack towards Droizy.

By now, the 34th British Division, advancing still further forward towards Le Mont Jour (a move to cover the 127th French Division's advance to take over the crest line by late morning) was suffering severe casualties from an exploding German ammunition dump, and from corn set on fire by tracer. When the French Division did arrive in position, it was immediately subjected to a violent barrage, and badly mauled.

Mangin had no more troops to send into the attack. Early that morning he had used the VIIth Corps, with its 128th division in the front line, to go between the XVIIIth and Ist Corps, reinforcing his left flank.

The Tenth and Sixth Army assaults made in thick morning mist, had again been spearheaded by large numbers of tanks, and before long aircraft from both sides were heavily involved in almost non-stop dogfights. In spite of this activity, reconnaissance aircraft, both from the Central Army Group and the Aerial Division, came back saying that extensive fires had been started by air-raids on Fismes, Soissons, Loupeigne, Arcy-Sainte-Restitue, Branges, Lhuys and Orton. More patrols in the early afternoon also reported that the Germans seemed to be moving their supplies to the Vesle valley.

This encouraged Mangin to order a major attempt to disrupt the retreat by breaking the line at Severnay and on the Orme of the Grand Rozoy. The Orme of the Grand Rozoy, the main strongpoint guarding the retreat, was particularly important, and as the Germans were equally determined to hold both strongpoints to cover their withdrawal, it meant that, apart from the taking of Cramaille by the 68th division, no more progress was made that day despite extremely fierce fighting.

The XXth Corps had been in position since well before dawn, waiting to join the combined operation while the XXXth and XIth Corps' attack was going on. Its move to the attack line had been easier than expected, as French fighter 'planes had succeeded in keeping the enemy spotter aircraft away from the area. Now the success of the XXXth and XIth Corps further south meant the XXth Corps' advance could start at 9am.

Within the first few minutes the Scottish Division's right flank came under heavy shelling and fierce machine-gun fire from derelict tanks in front of the 'Mamelon' knolls which caused heavy casualties. A counter-barrage seemed to make no impression, and the attack ground to a halt. The left flank, however, was able to reach the main road and to consolidate positions at two points. Realising that his right flank was stalled, General Reed ordered another bombardment of the tanks and the knolls north of Tigny to cover a second assault – again with little result.

The French attack on Tigny and Taux started well, but by mid-afternoon SOS flares were going up from the village and the poilus were retreating under a hail of fire from the same knolls that had halted the British advance. Again the German positions were shelled, again with no apparent effect, then an extremely fierce German counter-attack drove the entire French line back. By 5pm the 15th Division's left flank had to pull back to conform. By now the average strength of the Scottish battalions was down to no more than 250, and Berdoulat ordered the Division to pull back, telling it simply to keep in touch with the French on either side. The very last available reserves were shared out between the battalions during the night.

Although the XXth Corps' attack seemed to have made little impression on its own account, it was certainly a factor which, when taken in conjunction with the success further south, led to the Germans' decision to straighten their line by a retreat in thick fog during the night.

The operation continued as the XIth corps consolidated the positions it had won, making the Sixth Army's task easier by capturing Saponay and covering the flank, while the left of the XXXth Corps and the XXth Corps started a manoeuvre to force the enemy out of the Bois de Plessier.

At the end of the afternoon Fayolle ordered his Army Commanders to take up the attack again next day 'and throw the Germans back to the Vesle', but that they were 'not to overextend their resources'. In particular, he warned the impetuous Mangin that the Tenth Army must cut its coat according to its cloth, 'regulating its means, and releasing the British divisions with the least possible delay'. Mangin started to do this at once, and the 127th Division (XXXth Corps), now on the Crête east of the French 25th, relieved the 34th British, while next day the 17th Division was told to take over from the 15th Scottish Division during the next two nights, as the Scots were severely strained from eight days of almost continuous fighting.

Early in the evening, it was obvious a further advance on the Grand Rozoy was needed to cover the valleys either side of Hill 199 and to relieve pressure on the French troops in Servenay. An advance of some 300 metres was carried out under a creeping barrage by men of the British 34th and the French 68th Division (who had by now taken Cramaille).

At last the Sixth Army had gained Degoutte's objectives of 31 July. Saponay was taken, the flank was covered, and the combined actions of the XXXth and XXth Corps had forced an enemy retreat from the Bois de Plessier. Strong night patrols sent out by the XXXth Corps continued to probe the German rearguard. The US 42nd Division had cleared all the high ground east of Fère-en-Tardenois by nightfall, and the French Commander was using the house that had previously been von Conta's headquarters. Further east, Degoutte's XXXVIIIth and IIIrd Corps had now outflanked the Bois Meunière and made good progress towards Goussancourt.

Friday 2 August

The reorganised Fifth Army was again cautioned by Maistre to conserve its strength, using only limited, short-lived attacks until reserves arrived, but before Berthelot could pass the instructions to his Army Corps and Divisional Commanders, messages arrived from the front that the enemy rearguard had joined the general retreat that had taken place overnight.

At Tenth Army Headquarters, reports from the XIth Corps started to arrive as early as 6am that areas south of the Bois d'Arcy had been found unoccupied. Within a short time the IIIrd Corps was also reporting a German retreat, and its troops following up had already bypassed Courdoux and were advancing on Launoy. The XXth Corps reported Tigny and Hartennes in their hands. Mangin immediately passed the information to French Headquarters, where similar messages from Berthelot and Degoutte were also arriving.

The long fought for general advance had started at last.

The 12th French Division, spearheaded by cavalry, was pushing east, driving the enemy helter-skelter before them. All thoughts of its relief abandoned, the 15th Scottish Division immediately sent out strong patrols to keep contact with the German rearguard. The French 25th Division moved up through the 34th British to join the general advance and when, a little before noon, Mangin knew that his advanced parties were beyond a line from Arcy -Sainte-Restitue, Droizy, Buzancy and the lower part of the Crise valley, he ordered them not to wait until cavalry arrived, but to push ahead as quickly as possible. Divisional commanders were ordered to ensure enough officers were with the troops to encourage and lead a speedy advance. Soon orders were going to field artillery; to communication and signals units; indeed to the whole support system – to join the pursuit. 'We must', Mangin telegraphed, 'be on the Aisne and the Vesle by evening.'

The 15th Division ordered a brigade to advance through Taux, contacting the French to the east. After that, the next objective was the River Crise. By 3.30pm Divisional troops were reported at the edge of the Bois de Concrois. Headquarters at once moved up to Vierzy, and another brigade advanced to Villemontoire.

The front-line units in both the Fifth and Sixth Armies were using the situation to the greatest possible advantage; keeping casualties to a minimum, infiltrating weak points, using cavalry to harry the retreat, and giving no opportunity for counter-attack by making over-rash advances. Progress was monitored carefully by Army Group headquarters, as the Germans were now moving behind what effectively would become a moat formed by the Aisne and Vesle. Once there, not only could they lick their wounds and set up a strong defence, but could deal severely with any over-hasty advance. Fayolle wisely ordered the offensive 'to continue under control, the reserves ready to set up a defence line if needed, and the advance units to be fully supported by massed artillery'.

The Sixth Army reached Loupeigne, Mareuil-en-Dôle (a hill town where the Germans were strongly entrenched) and Cohan: its advance parties were even reported at Dravegny. Degoutte ordered his advanced units to keep up their pressure on the enemy rearguard, while the main body of the Army was to keep in close support. In the middle of the fast-dwindling salient, Cameron's 4th Division (The Ivy Leafs) joined the US 32nd, relieving the 42nd (Rainbows) on a line facing the Bois de Dôle, running towards the Vesle below Bazoches. This was difficult country as no roads ran through the valleys. On the left, the French were still trying to take Mareuil-en-Dôle, so the Americans joined the attack, left their Allies in occupation, then went on forcing their way through the forest towards the Vesle with the 32nd Division on its right flank. The troops of the 32nd were to advance another 18 kilometres to the Vesle during the next two days, then attack Fismes, where the Germans were again firmly entrenched.

The advance guard of Berthelot's reorganised Fifth Army, now beyond Lagery, Tramery and Gueux, had orders similar to those of the Sixth and the Tenth.

'The main body must be preceded by assault parties and cavalry; the advance should be protected by artillery, some sections working alongside front line battalions, providing immediate support when needed. The enemy rearguard must be under constant pressure and finally be thrown back across the Vesle.'

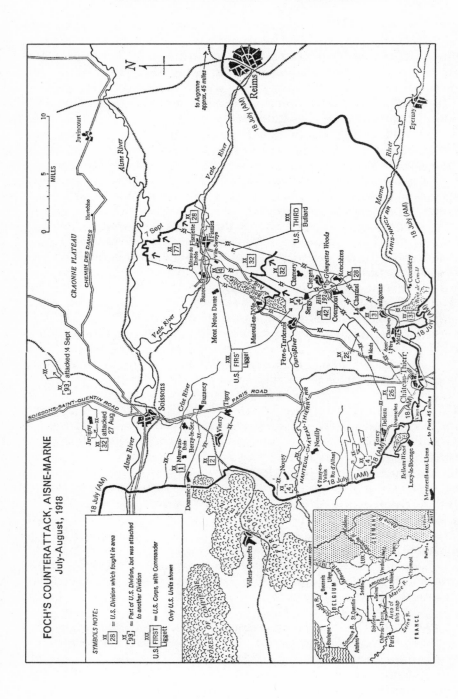

Figure 18 American involvement in Foch's counter-attack

With Pétain's agreement, the most battle-weary divisions began to pull back to rest and re-equip. The 2nd, 33rd and 18th Divisions moved to Pierrefonds, Coulommiers and to the Eastern Army Group respectively. Mangin was told to send the 15th and 34th British Divisions to Clermont and Nanteuil-le-Haudouin.

By nightfall the results far exceeded all expectations. Brigadier General Thomson summed up his 44th Brigade's involvement:

'It was certainly a dramatic moment when orders for the advance reached my brigade . . . the men formed up in groups on the parapet, seemingly dazed at these new conditions of warfare. Fortunately a few old hands remembered training at Aldershot and on Salisbury Plain and the dash forward quickly became general. Never have I seen men press forward with such eagerness, and when the first mounted officer's horse was brought up, the pace was hot indeed. We were out of touch with the French on our right and did not know what the woods might contain. There was, however, no time for delay. One platoon was told to deal with the right flank, and the remainder of the brigade pushed across the Crise to a line Amberif-Chacrise where we regained touch with the French and dug in, in full view of the enemy, in open fields on the high ground east of the road between the two villages. Torrents of rain fell during the evening, but neither this nor the intermittent shelling by the enemy, both during the advance and the occupation of the new position, could damp the ardour of all ranks.'

The retreating Germans drenched the whole area with gas; cornfields, woods, caves and dugouts were all affected and several men were gassed as a result.

Mangin again repeated his instructions by telegraph. 'The Vesle must be reached during the night, and artillery established on the plateaux to support a crossing of the river.' The Scots were told to prepare for a further move forward, but then the order was countermanded: the relief, originally planned to take place over two nights, was now to be done in one. Scottish guides went to meet the French 17th Division at the cross roads south of Villemontoire. The Division's machine-gunners stayed with the relieving division until the afternoon of 3 August then rejoined the rest of the battalion at Vierzy.

The 17th Division's men from the Nancy area were like British Guardsmen in both build and in appearance. Even after being rushed across from Verdun prior to starting a long forced march, they were immaculate. Their commander obviously expected – and obtained – high standards.

The Scots marched back to Liancourt to return north by train, but the move was delayed until artillery and transport could rejoin the division.

By nightfall, advanced parties of the French XLth Division were at Soissons: the entire German Ninth Army had retreated to its new positions across the Aisne, while their Seventh Army prepared to evacuate its last bridgeheads below the Vesle around Fismes. Allied infantry of the XXth, XXXth and XIth Corps were setting up their positions on the plateaux of Ambrief and Branges, and making preparations for units to cross the river and capture positions on the north bank.

But at last the Seventh, Ninth and First German Armies were occupying a solid front from Fontenoy to positions north of Reims, with 20 divisions holding the line. The 'Blücher Stellung' was a far more formidable proposition than the line occupied by 33 divisions on the Marne on 20 July; so formidable, in fact, that the Allies did not even attempt to bring forward tanks to join the assault.

CHAPTER 25

SATURDAY 3 TO WEDNESDAY 7 AUGUST 1918

– The Tenth, Fifth and Sixth Army advances halted at the Aisne and Vesle – the Picardy attacks by the First and Third French Armies –

'The Prussian sang his Hymn of Hate
Doughboys "drummed everywhere".
While weary Tommies trod
Their Long, long Trail, that wound its weary way
Far from the Land of their Dreams.
And yet, it seems
Poilus could cock a cheeky snook at all war's horrors.
(How Muses on Parnassus must have chuckled
To hear their marching song flung in the face of doom)–
"Il est Cocu – le Chef de Gare!
The Station Master is a cuckold!"'

(Paul Barry)

As the Germans moved into defence, the Allied Armies, particularly the units along the Aisne and Vesle, were told merely to reconnoitre, find out German intentions by taking prisoners, and avoid any sudden surprise counter-attacks by interrogation and assessing information. Fayolle had issued explicit orders about this the previous day, and that morning, when pressed by his staff to make a strong reconnaissance of the river crossings, he simply restated his orders to reorganise, reconstitute the reserves and bring up the artillery.

At Central Group Army Headquarters Maistre took the same approach. Telling Berthelot: 'certainly, patrols should be employed on the right bank. If possible, cavalry should make contact with the enemy, and small units should defend the construction of bridges and rafts. Certainly, plans must be made to cross the river and to increase the number of crossing points,' . . . 'but the freeing of the river and the establishing of footholds on the heights to its north must not be put into operation until our artillery is in position between the Ardre and the Vesle, and plans for a supporting barrage are worked out with the infantry.'

Towards midday, the Aisne and the Vesle had been reached at several points between Soissons and south of Fismes. The Sixth and Fifth Armies' main force could not move up because a violent enemy barrage during the afternoon plastered the plateaux south of Fismes, Jonchery and Muizon.

Degoutte had ordered the front-line units of his Sixth Army to probe the Vesle crossings during the night, but if they found resistance, the artillery would lay down a heavier barrage before the main body tried next day. That evening he ordered the advance guard to stay in line, but the main body to spread out in the rear; any further move forward was to be 'by bounds'. Like Degoutte, Berthelot ordered his advance units to try to cross the Vesle during the night, but they were subjected to such a heavy barrage that evening, they had to spread out on the plateaux south of the river, take cover and abandon the idea.

Having no orders to cross the river, Mangin started to pull out divisions from areas where Fayolle thought fewer were needed on the narrowing front. Those with most casualties; the 87th Division (XXth Corps) 19th (XXXth Corps) and 41st (XIth Corps) all moved back to reform and and re-equip. Tenth Army Headquarters moved to Coyolle, and Mangin obeyed Fayolle's orders by setting up defences, supported by artillery, on the crossing points of the Aisne and Vesle.

And now Debeney's troops were also in a position to take advantage of the enemy retreat. Like the Tenth, Fifth and Sixth Armies, his First Army Commanders were reminded not to rush headlong into a reckless pursuit. The ground was always to be reconnoitred and preparations made against sudden counter-attacks:

'. . . divisional advanced posts should be manned by a single battalion holding several strongpoints, and backed up by more strongpoints to the rear. Individual gun batteries and small cavalry units should work with them. Further back, the main body should prepare for further advances, reorganise and rest . . .'

In all the Armies, Corps Commanders were particularly warned to keep contact with the rear, keep open the supply routes for food and ammunition, and prepare to advance again at the first opportunity.

Late that night, the British 34th division made ready to return to Haig's sector. Captured German documents later confirmed Mangin's view that the capture of Beugneux and of the ridge above the Grand Rozoy by the French 68th, 25th and 127th Divisions and the British 34th, had finally forced the German retreat to the Vesle. The attack by the 34th had taken the position that formed the key to the entire ridge.

Saturday 3 August

On the morning of 3 August, Pétain confirmed Fayolle's and Maistre's orders. The Allied objective was still to throw the enemy back across the Aisne and Vesle, but 'without incurring needless casualties, or, in the event of an attack failing, the troops finding a river at their backs.' No premature attack must give the enemy a chance to 'ring down the curtain' on the Aisne and Vesle operations. Contact must be kept, and the German rearguard harassed, but always harassed by limited attacks. A major assault would need troops to be brought from other sectors, and that would be a decision for Foch himself.

Degoutte moved his headquarters to Château Thierry, while Fayolle, as well as congratulating his troops, saying 'the Second Battle of the Marne, like the First, has achieved a victory', sent detailed instructions about reconnaissance and thinning the line. He asked Mangin to assess the chances of a Tenth Army attack round Braine, and Degoutte to do the same for the Fismes area, where the 4th and 32nd American Divisions were still forging their way through the forest towards the river Vesle.

The Americans arrived at the river that night, the 32nd Division at Fismes, and the 4th in front of Bazoches. At Fismes, the Milwaukee brigade was replaced by men from Detroit. Mondésir, the Corps Commander, saw them attack, capture the town and establish bridge-heads across the river in hand-to-hand fighting, and praised 'Les Terribles' so highly that Mangin asked for them.

After they had enjoyed a fortnight's rest, Mangin was to give them a hard two days fighting 32 kilometres north-west of Fismes, moving them all the way round the edge of the salient to do it. Since 18 July his troops had been able to advance only 8 kilometres above Soissons, held up by the steep wooded hills at Juvigny. Two days of heavy fighting in the middle of August saw the 32nd capture the town. Mangin expressed his gratitude to 'Les Terribles' and brought them out of the line. That attack cost 1,100 out of the 15,000 casualties suffered during the 32nd's war service.

Sunday 4 August to Monday 5 August

Fayolle's orders regarding probing, rather than attacking the German positions opposite the Tenth and Sixth Armies were carried out. The 19th Division (XXXth Corps) pushed several units forward west of Braine; the 68th Division (XIth Corps) established a small bridgehead across the Vesle east of the town, but in each case progress was stopped by heavy artillery and machine-gun fire. The Ist and IIIrd American Corps consolidated their positions on the Vesle in the Sixth Army sector but only managed to put across a few patrols.

Several small groups of Berthelot's Army crossed the river between Magneux and Champigny. By late afternoon of 5 August he had again reorganised his Army, ordering the XIVth Corps to take over Group Mordrelle's sector by 9am next day. During the evening, he again reminded his Corps Commanders of the importance of reconnaissance, and this reconnaissance by their advanced units, together with air observation, revealed the enemy now solidly established behind both rivers.

Maistre asked the reconnoitring parties to find out what Ludendorff had done about regrouping his forces and reorganising his reserves, but then, without waiting for reports to come in, told the French High Command the conclusions he had reached.

'Obviously the main enemy force is covered by his rearguard, and equally obviously, his front has been completely reformed. It follows that a full-scale attack supported by artillery will be needed to dislodge him. The valley across which we must advance forms a very serious obstacle: it is boggy, and can only be crossed by road, any general advance would be open to enfilade fire from massed machine guns coming from the right bank as well as from an artillery barrage. To mount our attack we would first have to take the plateaux from north of Fismes to Romain (i.e. 7 kilometres north east of Fismes). This seems to be a task for the Sixth Army working in conjunction with the left group of the Central Army.'

Pétain had arrived at the same conclusion, writing on the morning of the 5th, 'We should hold our positions south of the Vesle, but give the enemy the impression that a fierce attack is to come there on the 8th of August' (the date fixed for the Franco-British offensive).

His detailed report to Foch confirmed that the enemy was installed in force in its positions on the Vesle; that a strong attack by a powerful force would be needed to capture the new line, and that present resources did not allow the French Army to engage in battles on the Avre and on the Vesle at the same time.

Tuesday 6 August to Wednesday 7 August

By 6 August the 15th Division had arrived back round Arras. The French were obviously more than satisfied with the Division's performance as members of General Berdoulat's XXth Corps ('Corps de fer'); 11 Legions d'Honneur, 20 Medaille Militaire, 60 Croix de Guerre avec Palme and 120 of that award (avec Etoile) were awarded for work 'on the field of battle'.

The Commander of the relieving French Division was equally impressed.

From General Gassoins to General Reed:

Mon Général . . . After relieving your division in the pursuit on the Vesle, I established my Headquarters at Buzancy. I found there the traces still fresh of the exploits of your Scottish soldiers, and the officers of my staff were able to see clearly what hard fighting you had to gain possession of the village and, above all, the park.

Wishing to leave on the spot some lasting tribute to the bravery of your soldiers, I entrusted to one of my officers, Lieutenant Réné Puaux, the task of erecting there, with the material at hand, a small monument, emblematic of the homage and admiration of my Division for yours.

The monument has on it a medallion, on which are inscribed thistles and roses, and beneath the words -

HERE THE NOBLE THISTLE OF SCOTLAND WILL FLOURISH
FOR EVER AMONG THE ROSES OF FRANCE

and beneath -

17TH (FRENCH) DIVISION
TO
15TH (SCOTTISH) DIVISION

The monument was erected on the highest point of the plateau, where we found the body of the Scottish soldier who had advanced the farthest (on July 28th, 1918 – Buzancy).

The photograph of this monument has appeared in the last number of the journal 'L'Illustration'. I thought you would be glad to have a few copies of the photograph, which I send you herewith. They convey to you, together with the memories I have kept of our short meeting at Vierzy, the expression of my esteem and my admiration for your valiant Division.

Will you please accept, my dear General, the expression of my sincere regards?

(Signed) C. Gassoins
Commanding 17th (French) Division.

The total casualties during the 15th Division's involvement in the Marne Battle were 3516.

The reorganisation of the Allied front line continued. During the morning of the 6th the Ist Americans took over the French IInd Corps' sector, the IIIrd Americans replaced the 38th Division and the IIIrd French Corps.

During the 6th and 7th, messages were read out congratulating the troops, but warning of new efforts to come. Further attacks on the German positions were only postponed while a new, major offensive was being planned. Mangin thought his left sector offered the best possibility, 'because we already occupy a large bridgehead there north of the Aisne.' The Vl1th Corps' staff was ordered to plan operations that would 'improve our front-line position, enlarge our hold on ground north of the Aisne, and keep our offensive spirit alive by mounting raids on the enemy positions.' Supplies and ammunition were to be gathered as quickly as possible ready for a powerful surprise attack.

By proposing this to the High Command, Mangin considerably helped their overall plan, for any offensive north of the Oise logically demanded another, mounted east of the river to act in conjunction with it.

Approving the plan, Fayolle and Pétain decided the XIth Corps' sector should be extended by 9 August. This would also help the Americans take over the Sixth Army sector.

Degoutte ordered the 3rd American Division to cross the Vesle wherever footholds could be gained 'without meeting too much resistance, and where counter-attacks could be repelled and pontoon bridge-building, to establish still more bridgeheads, could be protected.' The American Ist Corps was to improve its positions by limited actions, and establish strong communications across the river while the XIth Corps consolidated.

While waiting for the order to retake the plateau between the Aisne and the Vesle, scouts were to cross the river (protected by strong artillery barrages) map the enemy's front line and identify units by taking prisoners, so that possible counter-attacks could be anticipated and repulsed at once. The front was to be strengthened so that a powerful surprise attack could be mounted as soon as possible.

Pétain, summing up the situation on 7 August, spoke of the the invader withdrawing with diminished strength and tottering morale, ending with the words 'My message is 'be firm...have patience . . . our comrades are coming. I say to you today . . . tenacity . . . audacity . . . and force a victory!'

And so the Marne battle ended at last, apart from a few mopping up operations; 2 August had seen the new German position established, their retreat ended, and the Allies on the south banks of the Aisne and Vesle making preparations to cross. Within two days Pétain was telling his forces to try to throw the enemy back from the north bank only if it could be done 'without causing needless loss of life, or risking being thrown back across the river'.

The battle might well be said to have ended in stalemate rather than outright victory, but the following morning – the opening of Haig's 'final offensive' round Amiens – saw, almost unbelievably, the first of what has become known as 'The Last Hundred Days' to the war's end.

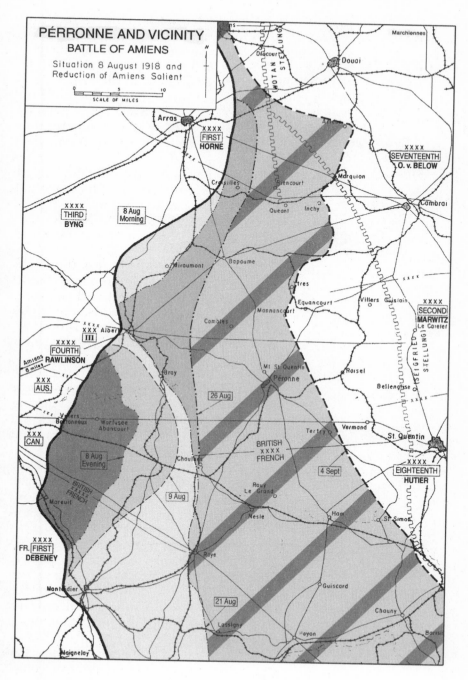

Figure 19 Dispositions of Rawlinson's and Debeney's troops.
8 August 1918

Amiens was freed from threat that first day, and the situation changed so quickly that a few days later Ludendorff offered to resign. Within six days Germany had appointed a new Chancellor and given him the task of starting negotiations for 'peace with honour'.

August and September saw the Germans driven back beyond the Somme and retreating from the Ypres salient. In the first days of October the main defences of the Siegfried Stellung were smashed, and by the middle of the month, Ostend and Cambrai were both liberated.

November saw more advances, and by the 9th, the Germans were in full retreat.

On Martinmas day – 11 November 1918 – the Canadians reached Mons, where the British Expeditionary Force had been blooded in 1914. Where, as the wheel came full circle after four years, the last Canadian casualty was to fall to a sniper's bullet two minutes before the Armistice came into effect, and where, just one year before, members of the German High Command had made their various ways, in a coincidence of place as well as date, to discuss German policy and the coming attacks of 1918 . . .

CHAPTER 26

EPILOGUE

'But what good came of it at last?'
Quoth little Peterkin.
'Why, that I cannot tell,' said he,
'But 'twas a famous victory.'
(Robert Southey – 'After Blenheim')

Foch was created a Marshal of France immediately after the Marne battle.

His unalterable determination to wait and mount his own counter-attack on 18 July was vital in making Ludendorff withdraw from the salient. With one hand fending off Pétain's preoccupation over Paris, and the other calming Haig's worries about the Flanders front, he gave the battle time to develop before mounting a devastating blow on the German flank. Mangin's bombardment of the enemy communications was also extremely important, but, because he was able to forestall any likely German counter-offensive by his constant pressure, Foch forced not only the evacuation of the salient, but the halting of Rupprecht's intended offensive against Haig, and so was able to plan the devastating attacks that opened the final phase of the war.

Ludendorff, writing later about the Second Battle of the Marne, admitted, 'This offensive by Foch on July 18th towards Soissons interfered with my operations . . . Because of it, the army had to be pulled back beyond the Vesle to a line Soissons-Reims . . . The whole Marne salient captured in May had to be given up.'

'This,' he added significantly, 'was the first great set-back for Germany.'

Army War Diaries assessed the 'set-back' caused by the attack in greater detail:

War Diary – German Seventh Army

'On July 18th the enemy started a carefully planned and prepared double offensive with enormous fighting means against the salient, Ambleny, Chateau Thierry to Reims. The weaker attack struck the east front of the Seventh Army, and was in general defeated. The main attack, however, almost shattered the divisions of the Ninth Army from the Aisne to the

Clignon brook where these divisions had been very shaken by limited attacks from July 13th.

'The enemy was, in a certain sense, fortunate in achieving practical surprise. Although the concentration of his attacking Army in the woods round Villers-Cotterêts had been hidden, it appears we did not appreciate the number of troops hidden there. In addition we expected our successful advance on Reims would compel French General headquarters immediately to use the forces it had intended to use against the west front of the Seventh Army and the south part of the Ninth Army against the arc, Épernay, Reims, Chalons to prevent annihilation there. This calculation was based first on the assumption that our offensive would overrun a weak and surprised enemy without interruption, or, in other words, that a catastrophe would develop in the Reims arc, into which the available hostile reserves would be drawn.

'This first assumption was based on a second, which presumed that the number of divisions opposed to the Army Groups of the Crown Prince was so low that a simultaneous concentration in the Villers-Cotterêts woods and a strong occupation of the Reims front was out of the question. We believed that the remainder of the hostile reserves would be held down by threatening Amiens. Both assumptions were wrong.

'The enemy had early information of our preparations for the attack against Reims and Chalons and had been able to arrange his defence. He adopted our system of defence, with a deep foreground in front of a rear zone strongly supported by artillery and infantry. The enemy, by thus following our methods, accomplished a complete defensive success. In addition the number of the available battle reserves opposite the forces of the German Crown Prince was far larger than we supposed. He had sufficient reserves for a main attack after equipping his defensive front with enough divisions.

'Finally, we underestimated the offensive value of tanks. The November 1917 battle at Cambrai ought to have furnished us with some indications of what success might be obtained by surprise use of a mass of tanks. We know now that our enemies grasped the fact and improved their tanks technically and augmented the numbers. We on our part paid little attention to this auxiliary arm, and didn't believe the enemy had done so.

'During our offensives of March and May tanks appeared but rarely, as they are principally an offensive arm, and could find little employment at that time. July 18th for the first time taught us differently. Tanks employed in mass hitherto unknown and technically highly developed came in front of the infantry with their lumbering gait in long connected lines. Our defence had not been prepared for the mass employment like that, and we could work only through gaps. Our infantry felt helpless opposite the fire disgorging, rapidly moving machines and lost their nerve. This later on was overcome but the mobile artillery of the divisions

192

in the rear soon countered this method of fighting and from their positions in the open destroyed many of the tanks. Deprived of their protection, hostile infantry very soon lost offensive spirit and being densely formed behind the tanks in thick columns which the enemy had risked because of tank protection, they suffered heavy loss. But in any case this regular defence against tanks by our rear echelons started too late as we mentioned above the enemy's offensive didn't surprise us strategically, but rather proved our assumptions to have been incorrect, tactically achieving surprise.

'The enemy had improved on his tactics, as applied in November at Cambrai. His concentration in the woods found very favourable conditions for screening. The enemy didn't care for a lengthy fire preparation and brought forward his infantry after a short, heavy fire. What his infantry lacked in fighting values essential to such a procedure was made up by tank squadrons. So on the very first day the enemy on a broad front gained ground and captured supplies. He didn't understand how to take advantage of it on the same day.

'When our defence coming from the rear became effective and his tanks started to suffer, the advance the next day tended to halt, and his objective which, without doubt, was to cut off the German forces between the Aisne and the Marne could not on the 18th be accomplished.

'But nevertheless the effort to recover ourselves and support the front between the Aisne and the Marne cost us so heavily that the Army Group of the German Crown Prince was forced to give up all intentions of continuing our offensive for some time to come, and here we undoubtedly see a great strategic success for Marshal Foch, and based on his viewpoint, July the 18th, 1918 marked a turning point in the history of the World War.'

During their four-day advance down the Ardre valley and the crossing of the Marne, the Germans took more than 20,000 prisoners. Foch, however, had more reserves and greater resources than the German High Command realised.

War Diary – German Crown Prince's Army Headquarters:

'We had expected our advance on Reims to overwhelm a weak and surprised enemy, and make French General headquarters immediately commit its reserves there to prevent a disaster.

'This was based on the assumption that the number of opposing Allied divisions was so low that a concentration both round Soissons and on the Reims front was out of the question. We believed that the remaining hostile reserves would be held down by threatening Amiens. We were wrong.'

In all, 59 divisions, including 7 American, 4 British and 2 making up the Italian IInd Corps, joined the French attack, defeated 65 German divisions, and drove the invaders back up the spine of the salient. Five French Armies (the Tenth, Fifth, Sixth, Ninth and Fourth) between them captured 609 officers and 26,413 other ranks, according to army records. The Americans took around 8,000 prisoners; the British some 1,600. German losses of equipment and weapons were severe. 612 guns, 221 mortars and 3,330 machine-guns were taken; 181 Allied canon and 393 machine-guns lost between 15–17 July were recaptured. Other war material was taken in such quantities that German Supreme Headquarters reported it 'could not be estimated'. The Front was eventually shortened by 48km, and the Paris to Chalons railway was repaired and put to use.

Compared with other major battles of World War One, this Second Battle of the Marne was amazingly short-lived. Within a period of twenty-eight days a complete reversal of fortunes had taken place, and the Germans never advanced again. Their attempts to defend the salient and the forced retreat cost them almost as many casualties as in their initial attack of 15 July. The battle was, literally, the turning point of the war. From that time the initiative stayed firmly in Allied hands. On the other hand, without Ludendorff's leadership, and in particular without the devotion and tenacity of his troops holding the flanks, the retreat might have turned into a rout. Still, if Ludendorff had seen the danger, and at once had moved the Bavarian Crown Prince's divisions to stiffen the line, the salient probably could have been held.

> 'The successful execution of this most difficult retreat demonstrated the valour and ability of our troops. But the losses were great. Many divisions were used up. Fresh forces were required to rehabilitate the situation . . .' (Ludendorff – War Memoirs).

On the day before Foch's counter-stroke, the Germans had 62 reserve divisions – 52 of them being fresh or reformed. More than half were behind Rupprecht, ready for his coming Flanders offensive. By 6 August there were 67 reserve divisions, but only 39 of them fresh, and about 40 of the 67 were now behind the German Crown Prince's sector. Some had been pulled back to rebuild behind the shortened Marne Front, while Rupprecht, in Flanders, had now no more than 25 in reserve. Several of his divisions having been sent to the Marne, the Flanders offensive was impossible.

Estimates of available reserves on Rupprecht's sector were only made at the end of July, so Ludendorff must have committed about 26 divisions from his general reserve, and about 75 in all to the Marne Battle. Rupprecht's offensive first was postponed, and then finally:

'With heavy heart, I had to give up the Flanders offensive. The situation I had tried to prevent now came about. The initiative passed to the enemy. It was no longer possible for us to win the war in a military sense. Politics must bring the war to a conclusion.'

In his account, Ludendorff then complains of being accused that he took charge of politics as well as the direction of the war. This he firmly refutes. Any political involvement was solely from a feeling of responsibility for so many thousand German lives. He had no thought of personal ambition. It was merely his duty to check the weak, unfruitful policy of Chancellor Bethmann-Hollweg, responsible for the development and the outcome of the entire war.

'Field Marshal Hindenburg felt as I did. No thought of self entered our minds. The national honour: the safety of the armies entrusted to our charge were not only uppermost . . . they were our only thought.'

According to Ludendorff, Germany lost 'because of politicians and American intervention. The French, British and Belgians were all inferior fighters . . .'

'Inferior' they may have been in Ludendorff's view, but they were certainly no longer inferior in numbers. By 7 August, the Allies, having used fewer divisions, could match the Germans' 67 divisions with 10 American, 4 Belgian, 21 British, 38 French, 2 Italian and 2 Portuguese . . . not counting 10 divisions of cavalry.

If only the French had not been so certain there would be no attack on the Chemin des Dames...! if only Duchêne had used a system of elastic defence with reserves hidden in the caves between the Aisne and the Vesle . . . ! if only . . . ! . . . if only! . . . But that kind of speculation is fruitless . . . a defeat of the German attack on 27 May might have caused the war to drag on well into 1919, instead of coming to an end within a matter of months.

CHAPTER 27

THE COST

*'The king hath a heavy reckoning to make when all those legs and arms and heads,
chopp'd off in battle, shall join together at the latter day, and cry all. "We died at
such and such a place" . . '*

(Shakespeare – 'Henry V')

The battle might have been relatively brief, but German casualties
between 15 July and 2 August were reckoned to be around 110,000. The
Allies' were estimated at 160,000 . . . again far less than those experienced on the Somme, at Verdun and at Passchendaele, but should these
numbers have little impact, *it means that for every word in this narrative,
between three and four soldiers of the German and Allied armies involved were
killed, wounded or went missing.*

The French Armies lost 499 officers and 11,542 other ranks killed,
1,870 officers and 68,396 men wounded, and 170 officers and 4,688
men missing from 15 July to 5 August. Casualties suffered by the other
Allies, listed in the French Official History, are 83 officers and 2,291
men killed, 339 officers and 13,898 men wounded, and 2,656 missing
(a total of 19,184). This is probably an underestimate: casualties from
the two British divisions fighting with Mangin's Tenth Army totalled
7,286, and bearing this in mind, the total of Allied battle casualties is
probably nearer the 160,000 mark than the 114,000 reckoned by the
French Government.

The agony was experienced not only on the battlefield. Back at home,
families waited anxiously for news, dreading the ring of the bell or the
knock on the door that would herald the telegram telling of a death or
a wounding. Soldiers of every nationality had their own ways of circum-
venting the censor, and most of their loved ones knew, from a
predetermined innocent phrase, or from pin-pricks under letters
spelling out a message, that the soldier was expecting to go into action.

The wounded would apply field dressings, or be helped by their pals
if the stress of battle allowed. Then would come shouts for 'Stretcher
Bearers!', or walking wounded would help each other. Back at the
Regimental Aid Post (the members of the 51st and 62nd Divisions who
were fighting their way through the woods, tied bandages round the
trees to mark the way there) the Medical Officer redressed wounds,
injected morphia, amputated limbs past saving, and regimental details

would be noted. Soldiers acting as orderlies both there and at the next stage, the Casualty Clearing Station further back manned by the Royal Army Medical Corps, unfortunately had more than the odd 'opportunist' among their numbers. Edward Brittain, writing to his sister, Vera, and quoted in her moving account of of the war, 'Testament of Youth', described what happened when he was wounded on the Somme. '. . . .At the C.C.S. I found crowds of officers and men that I knew; I'd quite lost count of the time, but after a while I was put to bed and was just dropping off to sleep when a damned orderly, thinking that I was worse hit than I was, tried to make off with my watch; I cursed him pretty thoroughly, as you can imagine.' Such episodes were all too common throughout the war, unjustifiably branding the Corps as a whole with the unfortunate soubriquet of the 'Rob All My Comrades'.

After that, a journey to the rear by ambulance – then possibly by train or barge if the wound was serious enough to demand it – had to be faced before hospital attention could be given in the rear areas, and then, for some, months or even years of treatment back in 'Blighty'. Some of the extremely disabled from World War One were still hospitalised after the Second World War had ended. As well as having to come to terms with handicap, many had an additional fight against addiction to drugs given to kill the pain.

Even those who came through battle physically unscathed were often troubled for years by recurring nightmares . One old soldier who died at Montdidier in 1965 had never taken part in a bayonet attack, but dreamed night after night of finding himself in one, and would waken screaming. In those days there were no such thing as counsellors offering help at the drop of a hat! Men walked the streets in the small hours rather than face the horrors brought by the night.

Little remains in the area to remind the visitor of what took place during those twenty-eight days. There are no memorial parks with preserved trenches as on Vimy Ridge or grassed-over mine craters like that at La Boisselle. Here and there monuments have been set up such as that to the 15th Scottish Division and one commemorating the efforts of the 'Big Red One' American Division near Buzancy. The memorials that make the greatest impression are the number of Military Cemeteries scattered across the battle area. Some have graves from the 1914 Marne battle; others from the battles on the Chemin des Dames. In others, like the American one at Belleau, or the Italian cemetery between Bligny and Chambrecy, the dead, almost without exception, are from the late Spring and early Summer of 1918.

British Cemeteries were often set up in the area where engagements had taken place, and show the units involved and the degree of ferocity. The headstones at Marfaux, for example, carry the badges of men from the 51st and 62nd Divisions and a memorial to the missing from a unit of New Zealanders attached to the West Ridings. The number of graves there, and the size of the German cemetery alongside, show the struggle for Marfaux was exceedingly bitter.

American policy was to make 'communal' cemeteries. Bodies in the Aisne-Marne cemetery were brought from the immediate vicinity and from the Marne area itself; 6,000 more from later stages of the battle are buried at the Oise-Aisne cemetery near Fère-en-Tardenois. Of 310,000 Americans who took part in the battle, 67,000 were reported killed, wounded or missing. The names of the missing, and those buried as 'unknown' are listed.

The Italians also have two cemeteries in the area. One, situated where the road climbs up from Chambrecy, lies just below the highest point of the Montagne de Bligny; 3,453 soldiers from the IInd Italian Army Corps lie there in order of rank. Their commander's, grave is at the rear of the cemetery.

Like the Americans and Italians, the French, too, tended to bury their dead in larger cemeteries. One such is on the road from Ville-en-Tardenois to Reims, only a few kilometres away from that of the Italians near Chambrecy.

German cemeteries contain more mass graves. Double burials seem also to be the rule, but each grave – German, British, Italian, French, American or Colonial – carries its own tragic story.

To take but one from the many thousands; Captain Norman Muller (West Yorkshire Regiment) was killed by a sniper on 28 July while reconnoitring prior to the capture of the last German trenches on the crest of the Montagne de Bligny, leaving a small daughter to be brought up by his wife Doris, whom he married in 1915. Doris had earlier lost a brother in the Gallipoli campaign. Captain Muller is buried in the British Chambrecy Military Cemetery at the foot of the Montagne.

And what of the survivors? Private Alf Thompson, from the same village as Norman Muller's wife, was wounded for the second time during his two years of army service – this time very severely in the body and the arm. He was still in Gosforth hospital in October, 'progressing as favourably as can be expected.' He lived as full a life as possible until 1946.

81781 Sapper Greenwood of the Royal Engineers received shrapnel wounds to arm and leg, living with pain until 1951.

American Laurence Stallings – his wooden leg a momento of the battle – went back to visit the Marne after the war and found himself confronted by a French woman who berated him for not picking up his spent copper cartridge cases, and poisoning her land . Most of the words quoted by American defenders, particularly during the German attack on 15 July, are taken from his excellent book 'The Doughboys'. He was also co-author of a novel, drawing on experiences of the war, which became the basis of the highly-acclaimed silent film of 1926, 'What Price Glory?'

The politicians and generals responsible for these events, on the whole lived easier lives and died easier deaths than those they had commanded, though military leaders who turned their hands to politics seemed to be less fortunate.

The last weeks of the war found Ludendorff sitting impotently at his headquarters staring blankly in front of him. Dismissed, he fled to Sweden disguised in tinted spectacles and false whiskers. On his eventual return to Germany, he fiercely denounced those he considered had betrayed the German Army, singling out Jews, Communists, Freemasons, Gypsies and Jesuits. He saw Hitler as the saviour of the nation and became an ardent Nazi, marching unarmed (and amazingly, unscathed) through a hail of bullets during the 1933 Munich Putsch. Hitler did not purify Germany sufficiently of its subversive elements for him and, leaving the Nazi Party, Ludendorff took refuge in occultism and astrology. His funeral in 1937 was almost like a scene from 'Götterdämmerung' with adherents, wearing winged helmets, giving him a good send-off to a Valhalla specially prepared for the Master-race.

Paul von Hindenburg supported the founding of a Republic at the end of the 1918 revolution, and in 1925 became its President. He staunchly supported the new Weimar constitution and the move to apply for membership of the League of Nations, and by 1930 had negotiated the withdrawal of French troops from the Rhineland five years ahead of schedule. His opponent in the next election was Adolf Hitler, whom he appointed Chancellor. He died in August 1934.

Ferdinand Foch was loaded with honours. As well as being created Marshal by Clémenceau (in spite of their bitter disagreements), Oxford honoured him with a degree; he was elected member of the Académie Française and the Académie des Sciences. His last years were soured by continuing controversy with Clémenceau over the latter's failure at Versailles to take the Rhineland as a buffer state. The posthumous publication in 1929 of his 'Mémorial de Foch' stirred Clémenceau into a stinging reply 'Grandeurs et Misère d'une Victoire' that appeared after the 'Tiger's' own death later that year, so their quarrel continued beyond the grave. Today there is scarcely a town in France without its 'Avenue Foch'.

Haig, despite an Earldom and being decorated by nations as diverse as Serbia, France and China, found himself snubbed by Lloyd George. Not for him an army command, or the governorship of a colony. He died unexpectedly of a heart attack early in 1928. Foch, in spite of declining health, at once left Nice, where he was to unveil a war memorial, for the long journey north, a bad Channel crossing and all the stress of official engagements attendant on his presence at the funeral. It was the beginning of his own decline, and he died only five months after the annual visit to Gorcy to kneel at the grave of his son, Germain, who had been killed in the very first month of the war.

Lloyd George won the 1918 election and tried to water down Clémenceau's demands at Versailles for German reparations. He was defeated in the 1922 election and as the Labour Party's popularity increased through the 'twenties, the Liberals' fortunes declined, and Lloyd George's influence along with it. He approved appeasement towards Hitler until World War Two changed his mind. In the second war, he had no governmental post, and had to be content with sniping at Churchill. At the age of 80 he married his long-time secretary (and mistress) Frances Stevenson, and to the glee of his opponents, the 'Great Commoner' was offered, and 'gratefully accepted' a seat in the Lords. The once lively, devious mind deteriorated during his last months, and he died in 1945.

Georges Clémenceau, hailed as 'Père de la Victoire' at the time of the Armistice, chaired the Paris Peace Conference, arguing that Germany should pay reparations for the entire cost of the war, cede the Saar basin to France and give up all land on the west bank of the Rhine. He was forced to give way on all these issues, and France never forgave him. His party lost heavily in the 1919 election, and he was defeated in the following year's Presidential election. His last years were spent in giving lecture tours, writing and travel. He died in 1929, eight months after Foch.

The Kaiser of All Germany followed Hindenburg's advice and Ludendorff's example when the war was in its last days, and fled to Holland. In spite of calls to 'Hang the Kaiser' and a request from the Allies that he be extradited to face charges at Versailles of having brought about the war, Holland allowed him sanctuary, and he lived quietly at the little village of Doorn until his death in June 1941.

John Joseph Pershing argued that the Allies should have taken the fight to Berlin and that Germany ought to have been occupied to prevent any further upsurge of militarism.. Back in America in 1919, he was made 'General of the Armies' – the highest military rank since the time of George Washington. Retiring from active service , he spent the next years writing 'My Experience in the War' which brought him the Pulitzer Prize for History in 1932. He acted as a consultant from time to time during the second World War. His burial at Arlington Cemetery took place in July 1948.

Sir Henry Wilson went into politics in 1921 as the Member of Parliament for North Down. His strongly-voiced opposition to Sinn Fein led to his assassination on the front doorstep of his London home in June the following year.

Perhaps the saddest end was Pétain's – also created a Marshal of France in 1918. Between 1925 and '26 he put down a Moroccan rebellion, and was elected to the Académie Française in 1929. Later, entering politics, he became Minister of War and acted as Ambassador to Spain in 1939. When France collapsed in 1940, he became President and signed the Armistice with Germany (in the same railway carriage used for Germany to sign the 1918 document, and he must have been a spectator during Hitler's famous 'Jig for Joy'). His government moved to Vichy and he was made Chief of State with power to draft a new French Constitution. A further meeting with Hitler started his four-year collaboration with the Nazis. When the Allies invaded he fled first to Germany, and when Germany surrendered, to Switzerland. He returned voluntarily to France, was arrested at the border, tried for 'Intelligence with the Enemy' found guilty and condemned to death in 1945. This being commuted to life imprisonment, he spent his last six years on an island off the coast of Brittany.

In 1923 two old soldiers were discussing the war's last stages. One was 'Black Jack' Pershing: the other, a former aide, Thomason.

> 'But General,' said Thomason, 'those Germans might have been tough hombres once we neared the Rhine. They still had a lot of good soldiers. I know they weren't using blank ammunition the morning of the Armistice when I scampered across those fire-raked pontoons on the Meuse.'
> 'Some might have fought on, ' Pershing conceded, 'until we came down the Linden in Berlin as an army with banners.'
> 'There'd have been a lot of sniping from the rooftops of the Linden. I've seen some who would have mounted machine guns on the Brandenburg Gate!'
> 'Yes, and we'd have flushed 'em out and hanged 'em on the lamp-posts of the Linden to let the Germans know who won the war. The Germans are being told the people let the armies down. In Berlin, they never knew they were beaten.
> 'It will,' Pershing prophesied, 'all be to do again . . . '

BIBLIOGRAPHY

It is impossible to list all sources of material used in research; some have been recollections of conversations with old soldiers or their children in France and Germany, as well as in this country. However, the following list may be of help if further study is needed.

American Army in France (The). Harbord. Little Brown – Boston. 1936.
Armées Françaises dans la Grande Guerre (Les). État-major de l'Armée p.1929.
Armageddon 1918. Falls. Weidenfeld and Nicholson 1964.
Atlas for the Great War (West Point Military History series) Avery Publishing group. Wayne. New Jersey. 1986.
Australian Official History of the War. Bean. p Angus and Robertson. Sydney.
Battlefields of the Somme. Middlebrook. Viking 1991.
Before Endeavours Fade. Coombs. Battle of Britain Press 1976.
British Campaign in France and Flanders (The), Jan-Jly 1918. A Conan-Doyle. Hodder and Stoughton 1919.
British Official History of the War. Edmonds. p H M Stationery Office 1948.
Doughboys (The). L Stallings. Harper and Row. N Y 1963.
Experience of World War 1 (The). Winter. p. Macmillan.
Field Marshal Sir Henry Wilson.His life and diaries. Callwell. p Cassell 1927.
Fields of Death. P Stowe and R Woods. Robert Hale. 1986.
Fifteenth Scottish Division (The) Stewart and Buchan. Blackwood. 1926.
Fifth Army (The). Gough. Hodder and Stoughton 1931.
French Army (The). P M de la Gorce. Weidenfeld and Nicholson 1963.
German Offensive. Jly 15th 1918 (The) (Marne Source book). General Service Schools Press, Fort Leavensworth, Kansas 1923.
Haig. Duff-Cooper. Faber and Faber 1936.
Haig. Despatches (ed Boraston). Dent. 1919.
Haig. Private Papers (ed Blake). Eyre & Spottiswoode 1952.
History of the Duke of Wellington's Regiment (The), Brereton and Savory. p by the regiment- Halifax. 1993.
History of the Great War (A). C R M F Crutwell. p 1934.
History of the 51st (Highland) Div. 1914-1918 Bewsher. p Blackwood 1921.
History of the 62nd (West Riding) Division (The). Wyrall. p John Lane: The Bodley Head.
Lloyd George. Jones. p Oxford 1951.
Ludendorff's Own Story. Ludendorff. Hutchinson 1919.
Prelude to Victory .Major-General E L Spears 1939.P Jonathan Cape.
I was there. ed J Hammerton , Amalgamated Press 1938.
König (Der). Karl Rösner.
Last Four Months (The). The end of the War in the West. Major-General Sir F Maurice. Cassell 1919.

Marshal Foch. Aston. p. Hutchinson.1929.
Memoirs. Foch. p Heinemann 1931.
Military Atlas of the 1st W W (A) Banks. Heinemann 1975.
My Experiences in the W W . Pershing. Hodder and Stoughton 1921.
Nelson's History of the War. John Buchan (24 volumes!).
No Man's Land: the story of 1918. J Toland. p Methuen 1982.
On the Western Front. John Laffin. p.Alan Sutton 1985.
Open Warfare: the way to Victory. Gibbs. Heinemann 1919.
Seizing the Enigma. David Kahn. Souvenir Press.
Smoke and the Fire (The). John Terraine. p. Sidgwick and Jackson 1980.
Soldiers and Statesmen. Robertson. Cassell 1926.
Stories of Famous Regiments. Philip Warner. p. Arthur Barker 1975.
Swordbearers (The). Correlli Barnett. Eyre and Spottiswoode 1963.
Testament of Youth. Vera Brittain.
Thirty Fourth Division (The) Shakespear. Witherby 1921.
Two Battles of the Marne (The). Joffre. Thornton Butterworth 1927.
Undertones of War. Blunden. Penguin.
War Letters. Monash. Angus and Robertson, Sydney 1935.
War Memoirs. Lloyd George. Nicholson and Watson 1934.
War Memoirs. Ludendorff. Hutchinson 1920.
Weltkrieg 1914 bis 1918 (Der). Die Militarischen Operationen zu Lande.
    German Official History 1924-29.
West Riding Territorials in the Great War (The). L Magnus p1920.
World Atlas of Military History A. Banks. Seeley Service and Co 1978.
World Crisis (The). W S Churchill. p Odhams 1927.
World War One. Susanne Everett. p Hamlyn.

APPENDIX 1.

Commanders whose Armies were involved in the Marne Battle, the events leading to it, and immediately succeeding it.

France. 1918.
Supreme Commander: Western Front. Marshal Ferdinand Foch.

French Army

Grand Quartier: Marshal Philippe Pétain.
First Army; General Marie Debeney. (Involved in August)

Maistre's Central Army Group.
Fourth Army; General Henri Gouraud.
Fifth Army; General Henri Berthelot.
Ninth Army; General Henri de Mitry replacing Foch.

Fayolle's Army Group of the Reserve.
Sixth Army; General Denis Duchêne, replaced by General Jean Degoutte.
Tenth Army; General Charles Mangin. (Elevated by Foch).

American Army.

Commander in Chief: General John Pershing.
First Army; General Hunter Liggett.
Second Army; Major General Robert Bullard.

British Troops Involved.

XXIInd Corps; Commander, General Sir A. Godley. (51st., 62nd., 15th and 34th Divisions).

British Fourth Army; Sir Henry Rawlinson. (in conjunction with French First Army, 8 August).

Italian Troops Involved.

IInd Italian Army Corps. (Napoli, Salerno, Brescia and Alpi Brigades)

German Army

Commander in Chief. Field Marshal Paul von Beneckendorf and von Hindenburg.

Quartermaster General. Erich Ludendorff.

Crown Prince's Army Group.

First Army; General Fritz von Below.
Third Army; General Karl von Einem.
Seventh Army; General Hans von Böhn.
Ninth Army; General von Eben .
Eighteenth Army; General Oskar von Hutier.

APPENDIX 2.

American Divisions were often known by their Nicknames, and on several occasions reference has been made to their 'Twice as Large' Divisions compared to British or French Units. An American Division was made up as follows:

Squads of 8 men. There were 7 squads in a platoon, plus a platoon sergeant and a lieutenant. (58 men in all).

4 platoons commanded by a captain with a detachment from HQ, formed a company. (250 in all).

4 companies made up a battalion under the command of a major.

3 battalions of Infantry and 1 machine-gun company formed a regiment (under a colonel).

2 regiments of infantry + 1 machine-gun battalion made a brigade, and 2 brigades of infantry + a third machine-gun battalion made the rifles of a division.

Therefore an American Infantry Brigadier General had 250 officers and 8,200 other ranks under his command. A Major General of a division, along with supporting elements, controlled 2 infantry brigades + 1 artillery brigade (each consisting of 2 regiments of French 75s and 1 of 155s, + 1 regiment of engineers and machine-gun battalion). The division also included a field signal battery and sanitary and supply trains.

American Divisions Involved in the Marne Battle.

1st Division (Big Red One) 1st & 2nd Brigades. 16th, 18th, 26th & 28th Infantry Regiments.
  The nickname was given by the Germans who saw the red 1 shoulder flashes. It was the first American division in France, the first into battle and to suffer casualties, the first to take prisoners, the first to take part in a major offensive and the first to enter Germany.

2nd Division (Race Horse Brigade or Indianhead) 3rd & 4th Brigades. 9th, 23rd, 5th & 6th Infantry Regiments.
  A truck driver painted a shield on his cab door, enclosing an Indian's head.

3rd Division (Marne) 5th & 6th Brigades. 4th, 7th, 30th & 38th Infantry Regiments.

Named because of its stand on the Marne. Its insignia's three diagonal stripes represent its involvement in three major 1918 battles.

4th Division (Ivy Leaf) 7th & 8th Brigades. 39th, 47th, 58th & 59th Infantry Regiments.
Nicknamed from its divisional sign. The 'Ivy' is taken from the Roman numeral '1V'.

26th Division (Yankee) 51st & 52nd Brigades. 101st, 102nd, 103rd & 104th Infantry Regiments.
Composed of troops from the New England (Yankee) states.

28th Division (Keystone) 55th & 56th Brigades. 109th, 110th, 111th & 112th Infantry Regiments.
Troops from Pennsylvania (the Keystone state).

32nd Division (Iron Jaws, Gemütlichleit Boys or Red Arrow) 63rd & 64th Brigades. 125th, 126th, 127th & 128th Infantry Regiments.
Enemy lines are marked in red on military maps. The patch represents the fact that the enemy never stopped them.

42nd Division (Rainbows) 83rd & 84th Brigades. 165th, 166th, 167th & 168th Infantry Regiments.
Composed of units from Columbia and 25 other states, comprising all nationalities and religions. A major in the US Army prophesied that the division would stretch over the land 'like a rainbow'.

INDEX